Over 1,100 vessels drop anchor yearly in the world's largest, furthest-inland seaport at Duluth, MN.

Bulk freighters, container & heavy lift ships come from around the world to load iron ore, coal and grain, while cruise ships bring foreign tourists to load up on the atmosphere of this scenic, city-on-a-hill.

canalparkduluth.com

Know Your 2007 SHIPS

Guide to Boats & Boatwatching
Great Lakes & St. Lawrence Seaway

© 2007 – Revised Annually

(No part of this book may be published, broadcast,
rewritten or redistributed by any means, including electronic)

Marine Publishing Co. Inc.

P.O. Box 68, Sault Ste. Marie, MI 49783

(734) 668-4734

www.knowyourships.com

ISBN-13: 978-1891849-10-7
ISBN-10: 1891849-10-7
ISSN: 0190-5562

Founder: Tom Manse, 1915-1994

Editor & Publisher
Roger LeLievre

Researchers: Mac Mackay, Matt Miner,
Gerry Ouderkirk, Wade P. Streeter,
Franz VonRiedel, John Vournakis,
George Wharton and Chris Winters

Crew: Kathryn Lengell,
Nancy Kuharevicz,
Neil Schultheiss
and William Soleau

Front: *Edward L. Ryerson* on the
Detroit River. *(Wade P. Streeter)*

Back: *Canadian Enterprise*
on Lake St. Clair. *(Roger LeLievre)*

This: The *Ryerson* heads
across Lake Superior.
(Roger LeLievre)

CONTENTS '07

Pilot boat *Huron Belle* passes *Herbert C. Jackson* near Port Huron. *(Bob Powers)*

Full ahead: *Edward L. Ryerson* eastbound in the Straits of Mackinac. *(Chris Winters)*

The RYERSON RETURNS

Vessel
of the Year

Defying all the doom-and gloom scenarios floated during eight years of lay-up by virtually everyone in the know, the 1960-built classic *Edward L. Ryerson* raised steam at Sturgeon Bay, Wis., in early June 2006 and returned to service.

Boatwatchers were understandably thrilled and followed her from port to port throughout the shipping season delighted, thanks to Capt. Eric Treece, to hear her powerful twin steam whistles bellowing out salutes to the faithful at every opportunity. The vessel's revival – brought about by a demand for ore – was especially sweet, since it had generally been thought that the only way "Fast Eddie" would ever sail again would be as a barge or on a trip to the scrap heap.

Once written off as hopelessly outmoded for the trade she was built to serve, the *Ryerson* is now the only non-self-unloader engaged in the taconite trade flying the U.S. flag. After a few trips to her Indiana Harbor, Ind., home port, the *Ryerson,* operated by Central Marine Logistics, settled in on the run from Superior, Wis., to Lorain, Ohio, carrying taconite for steel giant Mittal.

No one knows how long the *Ryerson* will continue to sail, so those who enjoy watching the lakes and the ships that sail them took advantage of every chance to spot this Queen of the Lakes in 2006. With its graceful lines and its phoenix-like revival, who could blame them?

Buckets unload the *Ryerson* at Indiana Harbor. *(Roger LeLievre)*

Edward L. Ryerson unloading at Indiana Harbor in July 2006. *(Eric Treece)*

A rainbow greets the *Edward L. Ryerson* as she arrives in Superior for her first cargo.
(Chris Winters)

The *Ryerson* dwarfs the mail boat *J.W. Westcott II* (top). *(Wade P. Streeter)*

Arriving at Escanaba on her first trip in eight years (above) and loading at the Burlington-Northern dock in Superior (right). *(Roger LeLievre)*

Fall on the St. Marys River: The *Ryerson* passes Johnson's Point. *(Chris Winters)*

The *St. Marys Challenger* was all painted up to celebrate its record-setting 100th season as a working Great Lakes steamboat in 2006. *(Chris Winters)*

PASSAGES

Changes in the shipping scene since our last edition

Fleets & Vessels

Oglebay Norton Marine Services wound up the dissolution of its fleet early last summer. When the dust settled, American Steamship Co. owned six more vessels, including two 1,000-footers. New names (old names in parentheses) are *American Century (Columbia Star), American Courage (Fred R. White Jr.), American Fortitude (Courtney Burton), American Integrity (Oglebay Norton), American Valor (Armco)* and *American Victory (Middletown)*. In addition, The Wisconsin & Michigan Steamship Co. took over operation of O-N's three river-class vessels, *David Z. Norton, Earl W. Oglebay* and *Wolverine*. The trio, not yet renamed at press time, is under the management of Grand River Navigation Co.

After 25 years laid up at Superior, Wis., Interlake Steamship Co.'s steamer *John Sherwin* finally left port under tow of the tug *Ohio* last summer. Her ultimate destination was South Chicago, where the hull is now being used as storage for grain products. Interlake considered putting the vessel back into service, but decided the cost of repairs would be too great.

John Sherwin on the move, with the tugs *Ohio* and *Missouri*, above the Soo Locks, Sept. 4, 2006. *(Roger LeLievre)*

(Continued on Page 12)

A LITTLE TO THE LEFT ...
Interlake's steamer *Lee A. Tregurtha* was reborn as a motor vessel during 2006, when her World War II-era steam turbine was replaced with a set of Rolls-Royce Bergen diesels at Bay Shipbuilding Co. Here, the *Tregurtha*'s stack is lowered back into place after the job is done.
(Chris Winters)

Lee A. takes on her first load at Escanaba (inset).
(Rod Burdick)

In with the new *Mackinaw*, out with the old. The 1944-built Big Mac (WAGB-83) was officially retired, with ruffles and flourishes, at Cheboygan, Mich., last June. The same day the new *Mackinaw* (WLBB 30) was placed in service. The original *Mackinaw* is berthed at Mackinaw City, Mich., and open as a museum. The World War II-era buoy tender *Acacia* was also retired in 2006; plans are to open her as a museum at Chicago.

Lewis J. Kuber, the self-unloading vessel created when the steamer *Buckeye* was cut down to a barge, entered service in 2006, pushed by the tug *Olive L. Moore*.

Inland Lakes Management's cement-carrying steamer *J.A.W. Iglehart* laid up at Superior, Wis. late last October and soon took over cement storage duties from the veteran *J.B. Ford*.

Two saltwater vessels traded their overseas flags for the Canadian banner in 2006. One, the *Lady Hamilton*, was built for Great Lakes / Seaway service as *Saskatchewan Pioneer* but sailed mostly on saltwater the past 10 years. She was bought by Canada's Voyageur Pioneer Marine and renamed *Voyageur Pioneer*. The other, the *Menominee*, was bought by the McKeil interests and renamed *Kathryn Spirit*.

Crew members of the *Mackinaw (83)* leave their vessel for the last time after decommissioning ceremonies (left). The new *Mackinaw (30)* (top). *(Dave Wobser)*

Cement carrier *J.A.W. Iglehart* inbound at Duluth in 2006. *(Glenn Blaskiewicz)*

After 25 years of idleness at Escanaba, Mich., the steamer *L.E. Block* was towed to Port Colborne, Ont., by the tug *Shannon* for scrapping in 2006. The small upper laker *D.C. Everest*, which hadn't sailed in years, will meet the same fate at the same yard. *(Paul Beesley)*

Voyageur Pioneer is the former *Lady Hamilton.* (Mike Nicholls)

Old friends, new look

Algonova has left the lakes and now flies the flag of Panama. (Roger LeLievre)

AMERICAN INTEGRITY

American Century (ex-Columbia Star) and *American Integrity* (the former *Oglebay Norton)* pass in the lower St. Marys River in 2006. (Roger LeLievre)

American Fortitude previously sailed as the *Courtney Burton*. (*Wade P. Streeter*)

GREAT LAKES GLOSSARY

AAA CLASS – Vessel design popular on the Great Lakes in the early 1950s. *Arthur M. Anderson* is one example.

AFT – Toward the back, or stern, of a ship.

AHEAD – Forward.

AMIDSHIPS – The middle point of a vessel, referring to either length or width.

ARTICULATED TUG / BARGE (ATB) – Tug-barge combination. The two vessels are mechanically linked in one axis but with the tug free to move, or articulate, on another axis. *Jacklyn M / Integrity* is one example.

BACKHAUL – The practice of carrying a revenue-producing cargo (rather than ballast) on a return trip from hauling a primary cargo.

BARGE – Vessel with no engine, either pushed or pulled by a tug.

BEAM – The width of a vessel measured at the widest point.

BILGE – Lowest part of a hold or compartment, generally where the rounded side of a ship curves from the keel to the vertical sides.

BOW – Front of a vessel.

BOW THRUSTER – Propeller mounted transversely in a vessel's bow under the waterline to assist in moving sideways. A stern thruster may also be installed.

BRIDGE – The platform above the main deck from which a ship is steered / navigated. Also: PILOTHOUSE or WHEELHOUSE.

BULKHEAD – Wall or partition that separates rooms, holds or tanks within a ship's hull.

BULWARK – The part of the ship that extends fore and aft above the main deck to form a rail.

DATUM – Level of water in a given area, determined by an average over time.

DEADWEIGHT TONNAGE – The actual carrying capacity of a vessel, equal to the difference between the light displacement tonnage and the heavy displacement tonnage, expressed in long tons (2,240 pounds or 1,016.1 kilograms).

DISPLACEMENT TONNAGE – The actual weight of the vessel and everything aboard her, measured in long tons. The displacement is equal to the weight of the water displaced by the vessel. Displacement tonnage may be qualified as light, indicating the weight of the vessel without cargo, fuel and stores, or heavy, indicating the weight of the vessel loaded with cargo, fuel and stores.

DRAFT – The depth of water a ship needs to float. Also the distance from keel to waterline.

FIT OUT – The process of preparing a vessel for service after a period of inactivity.

FIVE-YEAR INSPECTION – U.S. Coast Guard survey, conducted in a drydock every five years, of a vessel's hull, machinery and other components.

FLATBACK – Lakes slang for a non-self-unloader.

FOOTER – Lakes slang for 1,000-foot vessel.

FORECASTLE – (FOHK s'l) Area at the forward part of the ship and beneath the main cabins, often used for crew's quarters or storage.

FOREPEAK – The space below the forecastle.

FORWARD – Toward the front, or bow, of a ship.

FREEBOARD – The distance from the waterline to the main deck.

GROSS TONNAGE – The internal space of a vessel, measured in units of 100 cubic feet (2.83 cubic meters) = a gross ton.

HATCH – An opening in the deck through which cargo is lowered or raised. A hatch is closed by securing a hatch cover over it.

HULL – The body of a ship, not including its superstructure, masts or machinery.

INTEGRATED TUG-BARGE (ITB) – Tug-barge combination in which the tug is rigidly mated to the barge. *Presque Isle* is one example.

IRON DECKHAND – Mechanical device that runs on rails on a vessel's main deck and is used to remove and replace hatch covers.

JONES ACT – A U.S. cabotage law that mandates that cargoes moved between American ports be carried by U.S.-flagged, U.S.-built and U.S.-crewed vessels.

KEEL – A ship's steel backbone. It runs along the lowest part of the hull.

LAID UP or **LAY UP** – Out of service.

MARITIME CLASS – Style of lake vessel built during World War II as part of the nation's war effort. *Mississagi* is one example.

NET REGISTERED TONNAGE – The internal capacity of a vessel available for carrying cargo. It does not include the space occupied by boilers, engines, shaft alleys, chain lockers or officers' and crew's quarters. Net registered tonnage is usually referred to as registered tonnage or net tonnage and is used to calculate taxes, tolls and port charges.

RIVER CLASS SELF-UNLOADER – Group of vessels built in the 1970s to service smaller ports and negotiate narrow rivers such as Cleveland's Cuyahoga. *David Z. Norton* is one example.

SELF-UNLOADER – Vessel able to discharge its own cargo using a system of conveyor belts and a movable boom.

SLAG – By-product of the steelmaking process which is later ground up and used for paving roads.

STEM – The extreme forward end of the bow.

STEMWINDER – Vessel with all cabins aft.

STERN – The back of the ship.

STRAIGHT-DECKER – A non-self-unloading vessel. *Edward L. Ryerson* is one example.

TACONITE – Processed, pelletized iron ore. Easy to load and unload, this is the primary type of ore shipped on the Great Lakes and St. Lawrence Seaway. Also known as pellets.

TRACTOR TUG – Highly maneuverable tug propelled by either a Z-drive or cycloidal system rather than the traditional screw propeller.

Vessel Index

Montrealais at Duluth. *(Glenn Blaskiewicz)*

Vessel Name	Fleet #
A	
A-390	A-12
A-397	A-12
A-410	A-12
Aachen	II-2
Abegweit	C-17
Acacia	A-7
Acushnet	M-8
Adamastos	IE-4
Adanac	P-15
Adeevka	IC-14
Agawa Canyon	A-6
Agena	IR-3
Aggie C	I-2
Aird, John B.	A-6
Aivik	T-17
Alabama	G-19
Alam Sejahtera	IP-1
Alam Sempurna	IP-1
Albert C	I-2
Alcona	R-7
Alder	U-3
Aldo H.	M-14
Aleksandrov, Grigoriy	IF-2
Alessia	IE-5
Alexandria Belle	U-1
Alexis-Simard	A-5
Algobay	A-6
Algocape	A-6
Algoeast	A-6
Algoisle	A-6
Algolake	A-6
Algomah	A-14
Algomarine	A-6
Algonorth	A-6
Algontario	A-6
Algoport	A-6
Algorail	A-6
Algosar	A-6
Algoscotia	A-6
Algosea	A-6
Algosoo	A-6
Algosteel	A-6
Algoville	A-6
Algoway	A-6
Algowood	A-6
Alice E	A-8, E-5
Alioth Star	IC-13
Alkyon	II-4
Alouette	T-4
Alouette Spirit	M-14
Alpena	I-3
Altman, Anna Marie	Z-1

Vessel Name	Fleet #
Alton Andrew	M-10
Amalienborg	A-6
Amanda	II-2
Ambassador	IC-19
Amber Jean	G-8
Amber Mae	R-7
AMC 100	A-8
AMC 200	A-8
AMC 300	A-8
American Century	A-9
American Courage	A-9
American Fortitude	A-9
American Girl	S-23
American Integrity	A-9
American Mariner	A-9
American Republic	A-9
American Spirit	A-9
American Valor	A-9
American Victory	A-9
Amundsen	C-3
Anchor Bay	G-21
Anderson, Arthur M.	G-18
Andre H.	L-10
Andrea J.	E-4
Andrea Marie I	D-3
Andrew J.	E-4
Andrie, Barbara	A-12
Andrie, Candace	A-12
Andrie, Clara	A-12
Andrie, Karen	A-12
Andrie, Meredith	A-12
Andromeda	IB-1
Anglian Lady	P-15
Angus, D.J.	G-13
Anja	II-2
Ann Marie	L-16
Annalisa	II-2
Antalina	IT-1
Antikeri	IA-5
Apalachee	T-3
Apollon	IS-4
Appledore IV	B-6
Appledore V	B-6
Arabian Wind	IE-1
Arca	S-6
Arctic	F-3
Arizona	G-19
Arkansas	G-19
Arthur	P-8
Asher, Chas.	R-4
Asher, John R.	R-4
Asher, Stephan M.	R-4
ASL Sanderling	IO-2

Vessel Name	Fleet #
Astron	IC-3
Atigamayg	U-14
Atkinson, Arthur K.	S-2
Atlantic Castle	IK-1
Atlantic Cedar	A-15
Atlantic Eagle	A-15
Atlantic Erie	C-2
Atlantic Fir	A-15
Atlantic Hawk	A-15
Atlantic Hemlock	A-15
Atlantic Huron	C-2
Atlantic Kingfisher	A-15
Atlantic Larch	A-15
Atlantic Oak	A-15
Atlantic Osprey	A-15
Atlantic Pine	A-15
Atlantic Poplar	A-15
Atlantic Spruce	A-15
Atlantic Superior	C-2
Atlantic Swan	IU-1
Atlantic Willow	A-15
Atwell, Idus	M-17
Aurora Borealis	C-16
Aurora Topaz	IA-11
Avantage	L-10
Avenger IV	P-15
B	
B.J. & C.J.	F-5
Badger	L-6
Bagotville	M-17
Baird, Spencer F.	U-6
Balaban I	IE-6
Baldy B.	C-1
Balticland	IE-2
Barbara Rita	A-12
Barge Laviolette	U-15
Barker, James R.	I-6
Barker, Kaye E.	I-6
Barry J	K-7
Basse-Cote	L-10
Bavaria	IB-7
Bayfield	M-4
Bayship	B-5
BBC Asia	IB-7
BBC Atlantic	IB-7
BBC Bornholm	IW-1
BBC California	IW-1
BBC Campana	IW-1
BBC Canada	IB-7
BBC Chile	IW-1
BBC Ems	IB-7
BBC England	IJ-3

Vessel Name	Fleet #	Vessel Name	Fleet #	Vessel Name	Fleet #
BBC Finland	IB-7	Beeghly, Charles M.	I-6	Blue Heron	U-11
BBC France	IB-7	Beluga Elegance	IB-3	Blue Heron V	B-13
BBC Germany	IB-7	Beluga Emotion	IB-3	Bluebill	IN-1
BBC Holland	IB-7	Beluga Endurance	IB-3	Bluewater	U-5
BBC Iceland	IB-7	Beluga Eternity	IB-3	Bluewing	IN-1
BBC India	IB-3	Beluga Federation	IB-3	Boatman No. 3	M-14
BBC Italy	IW-1	Beluga Fusion	IB-3	Boatman No. 6	M-14
BBC Korea	II-3	Beluga Indication	IB-3	Bogdan	IN-2
BBC Northsea	IB-7	Beluga Recognition	IB-3	Boland, John J.	A-9
BBC Ontario	IK-3	Beluga Recommendation	IB-3	Bonnie B. III	M-14
BBC Peru	IW-1	Beluga Resolution	IB-3	Bonnie G.	T-7
BBC Plata	IW-1	Beluga Revolution	IB-3	Borkum	IB-7
BBC Russia	II-3	Berdyansk	IC-14	Bornholm	IH-6
BBC Scotland	IB-7	Betsiamites	L-10	Bowes, Bobby	D-4
BBC Shanghai	IB-7	Bide-A-Wee	S-15	Boyd, David	G-24
BBC Singapore	IB-7	BIG 503	U-15	Boyer, Willis B.	M-27
BBC Spain	IW-1	BIG 543	U-15	Bramble	P-11
BBC Texas	IB-7	BIG 546	U-15	Brandon E.	E-5
BBC Ukraine	IR-4	BIG 548	U-15	Bras d'Or 400	B-9
BBC Venezuela	IB-7	BIG 549	U-15	Bravery	IH-2
Beaupre	S-14	BIG 551	U-15	Breaker	S-31
Beaver	A-14	BIG 9708 B	U-15	Brenda L.	F-6
Beaver D.	M-14	BIG 9917 B	U-15	Bright Laker	ID-2
Beaver Delta II	M-17	Billmaier, D.L.	U-2	Bristol Bay	U-3
Beaver Gamma	M-17	Birchglen	C-2	Brochu	F-2
Beaver Islander	B-8	Black, Martha L.	C-3	Brovig Fjord	IB-8
Beaver Kay	M-17	Block, Joseph L.	C-6	Brovig Ocean	IB-8
Beaver State	M-1	Block, L. E.	I-7	Brutus I	T-13
Bee Jay	G-4	Blough, Roger	G-18	Buckley	K-6

Upper Lakes Group's *Canadian Navigator*. *(John C. Knecht)*

CANADIAN NAVIGATOR
TORONTO

Vessel Name	Fleet #
Buckthorn	U-3
Buffalo	A-9
Bunyan, Paul	U-2
Burns Harbor	A-9
Busch, Gregory J.	B-22
Busse, Fred A.	D-8
Buxton II	K-7

C

Vessel Name	Fleet #
C.T. M. A. Vacancier	G-25
C.T. M. A. Voyageur	G-25
C.T.C. No. 1	S-27
Cabot	IO-2
Cadillac	S-30
California	G-19
Callaway, Cason J.	G-18
Callie M.	M-10
Calumet	L-15
Calypso	IC-5
Cameron O.	S-4
Canadian	M-17
Canadian Argosy	M-17
Canadian Empress	S-24
Canadian Enterprise	U-15
Canadian Jubilee	D-4
Canadian Leader	U-15
Canadian Mariner	U-15
Canadian Miner	U-15
Canadian Navigator	U-15
Canadian Olympic	U-15
Canadian Progress	U-15
Canadian Prospector	U-15
Canadian Provider	U-15
Canadian Ranger	U-15
Canadian Transfer	U-15
Canadian Transport	U-15
Cantankerus	E-11
Cap Streeter	S-12
Cape Crow	E-8
Cape Discovery	C-3
Cape Dundas	C-3
Cape Hurd	C-3
Cape Storm	C-3
Capetan Michalis	IU-2
Capricorn	IB-1
Capt. Shepler	S-8
Carey, Emmet J.	O-6
Caribou Isle	C-3
Carl M.	M-17
Carlee Emily	K-3
Carleton, George N.	G-14
Carol Ann	K-7
Carola	II-2

Vessel Name	Fleet #
Carolina Borealis	C-16
Carrol C. I	M-14
Cartier-Jacques	C-21
Cavalier Des Mers	C-20
Cavalier Maxim	C-20
Cavalier Royal	C-20
CEC Fantasy	IC-10
CEC Fighter	IC-10
CEC Future	IC-10
CEC Oceanic	IC-10
CEC Polaris	IC-10
CEC Spring	IC-10
Cedarglen	C-2
Celebrezze, Anthony J.	C-15
Celine	IE-5
Cemba	C-5
CGB-12000	U-3
CGB-12001	U-3
Challenge	G-23
Champion	C-7
Champion	D-14
Channel Cat	M-20
Charles XX	M-18
Charlevoix	C-8
Charlie E.	I-7
Chem Bothnia	IC-7
Chem Oceania	IC-7
Chemical Trader	IE-7
Cheraw	U-2
Chicago's First Lady	M-19
Chicago's Little Lady	M-19
Chi-Cheemaun	O-7
Chief Shingwauk	L-13
Chief Wawatam	P-15
Chinook	M-20
Chios Charity	IH-3
Chios Pride	IH-3
Chios Sailor	IH-3
Chippewa	A-14
Chippewa III	S-19
Chris Ann	H-11
Cicero	IO-2
Cinnamon	IN-1
City of Algonac	D-2
City of Milwaukee	S-20
Clarke, Philip R.	G-18
Claudia	IE-5
Cleveland	L-8
Cleveland Rocks	L-8
Clipper Eagle	IC-9
Clipper Falcon	IC-9
Clipper Golfito	IC-11
Clipper Kristin	IC-11

Vessel Name	Fleet #
Clipper Leader	IC-11
Clipper Legacy	IC-11
Clipper Legend	IC-11
Clipper Tobago	IC-11
Clipper Trinidad	IC-11
Clipper Trojan	IC-11
Clyde	G-8
Coastal Cruiser	T-5
Cobia	W-5
Cod	G-20
Cohen, Wilfred M.	P-15
Cojak	S-16
Coleman	B-11
Colombe, J.E.	Y-1
Colorado	G-19
Columbia	S-33
Columbus, C.	IH-2
Commodore Straits	U-15
Condarrell	I-7
Cooper, J.W.	C-18
Cooper, Wyn	F-5
Coriolis II	U-9
Cormorant	F-1
Cornelius, Adam E.	A-9
Corsair	A-14
Cort, Stewart J.	I-7
Cotter, Edward M.	B-20
Coucoucache	L-10
Covadonga	IA-4
Cove Isle	C-3
Crapo, S.T.	I-3
Cresswell, Peter R.	A-6
Croaker	B-17
CSL Asia	IC-19
CSL Assiniboine	C-2
CSL Atlas	IC-19
CSL Cabo	IC-19
CSL Laurentien	C-2
CSL Niagara	C-2
CSL Pacific	IC-19
CSL Spirit	IC-19
CSL Tadoussac	C-2
CSL Trailblazer	IC-19
Cuyahoga	L-14

D

Vessel Name	Fleet #
Dagna	IW-2
Dahlke, Ronald J.	A-12
Daldean	B-15
Dalhousie Princess	P-10
Dalmig	H-9
Danicia	B-2
Daniel E.	E-5

Lake Superior's spray flies high above the *American Mariner's* bow. *(Terry W.F. Heyns)*

Vessel Name	Fleet #
Daniele M.	M-14
Daniella	IJ-4
Dapper Dan	M-17
Darrell, William	H-13
Dauntless	M-16
David Allen	N-9
David E.	E-5, H-4
Daviken	IV-2
Dawn Light	T-8
de Champlain, Samuel	L-2
Dean, Annie M.	D-4
Dean, Elmer	G-1
Debbie Lyn	M-3
Defiance	A-8
Delaware	G-19
Demolen	U-2
Denis M	S-14
Denise E.	E-5
Derek E.	E-5
Des Groseilliers	C-3
Des Plaines	C-1
Deschenes, Jos	S-13
Desgagnés, Amelia	T-16
Desgagnés, Anna	T-16
Desgagnés, Camilla	T-16

Vessel Name	Fleet #
Desgagnés, Catherine	T-16
Desgagnés, Cecelia	T-16
Desgagnés, Maria	T-16
Desgagnés, Mathilda	T-16
Desgagnés, Melissa	T-16
Desgagnés, Petrolia	T-16
Desgagnés, Thalassa	T-16
Desgagnés, Vega	T-16
Desjardins, Alphonse	S-13
Detroit Princess	D-6
Devine, Barney	W-4
Diamond Belle	D-7
Diamond Jack	D-7
Diamond Queen	D-7
Diamond Star	R-2
Diezeborg	IW-2
Dilly, William B.	M-17
Ditte Theresa	IH-7
Dobrush	IC-14
Doc Morin	U-15
Dona	D-13
Donald Bert	M-3
Donald Mac	G-14
Donner, William H.	K-9
Dora	IT-2

Vessel Name	Fleet #
Dorothea	IL-5
Dorothy Ann	I-6
Dover	M-3
Dover Light	E-1
Doxa D	IB-2
Dr. Bob	T-1
Drechtborg	IW-2
Drummond Islander II	M-1
Drummond Islander III	E-2
Drummond Islander IV	E-2
Duc d' Orleans II	D-11
Duga	L-10
Duluth	G-16
Durocher, Ray	D-14

E

Vessel Name	Fleet #
Eagle	S-11
Ecosse	N-1
Edelweiss I	E-3
Edelweiss II	E-3
Edith J.	E-4
Edna G.	L-4
Eider	IP-2
Eileen C	I-2
Elikon	IH-5

The downbound *Reserve* meets *CSL Tadoussac* above Lake St. Clair. *(Scott Tomlinson)*

Joseph L. Block and American Spirit at the DMIR dock in Duluth. (Eric Treece)

Canadian Provider in the St. Clair River, headed for Lake Superior. *(John C. Meyland)*

Vessel Name	Fleet #
Laud, Sam	A-9
Laurentian	U-10
Lauzier, Louis M.	C-3
LCU 1680	N-5
Le Bateau-Mouche	B-3
Le Draveur	C-21
Le Phil D	L-10
Le Survenant III	C-22
Le Taureau	M-17
Le Voyageur	S-15
Lebasee	IT-6
Lee, Nancy A.	L-12
Legardeur, Catherine	S-13
Leitch, Gordon C.	U-15
Leitch, John D.	U-15
Leona B.	M-23
Lime Island	V-3
Limnos	C-3
Linda Jean	N-9
Linnhurst	F-1
Lisa E.	E-5
Lisbon Express	IH-2
Liski	IL-4
Little Rock	B-17
Lodestar Grace	IY-1
Louie S.	R-4
Louisbourg	C-3

Vessel Name	Fleet #
Louisiana	G-19
Love, Roy R.	U-8
LST-393	G-22
LT-5	H-1
Lucien L.	S-13
Ludington	C-13
Luedtke, Alan K.	L-16
Luedtke, Chris E.	L-16
Luedtke, Erich R.	L-16
Luedtke, Karl E.	L-16
Luedtke, Kurt R.	L-16

M

Macassa Bay	M-2
MacKay, Tony	M-14
Mackenzie, Wm. Lyon	T-10
Mackinac Express	A-14
Mackinac Islander	A-14
Mackinaw (WAGB-83)	I-1
Mackinaw (WLBB-30)	U-3
Mackinaw City	M-1
Madeline	M-4
Magdalena Green	IB-3
Magnetic	F-4
Maid of the Mist IV	M-5
Maid of the Mist V	M-5
Maid of the Mist VI	M-5

Vessel Name	Fleet #
Maid of the Mist VII	M-5
Maine	G-19
Maineborg	IW-2
Maisonneuve	S-14
Makeevka	IC-14
Makiri Green	IB-3
Malden	P-15
Malyovitza	IN-2
Manatra	U-8
Mandarin	IN-1
Manistee	L-15
Manistique	M-17
Manitou	M-6, M-13, T-19
Manitou Isle	M-7
Manitowoc	K-9, U-2
Manora Naree	IM-2
Maple	U-17
Maple City	T-13
Maple Grove	O-1
Marcoux, Camille	S-13
Margaret Ann	H-11
Margaret M.	H-4
Margaretha Green	IB-3
Margot	N-6
Marie-Jeanne	IE-5
Marin	B-2
Marine Star	E-6

Vessel Name	Fleet #
Marine Trader	L-17
Marinus Green	IB-3
Marion Green	IB-3
Mariposa Belle	M-11
Maritime Trader	V-6
Mariupol	IC-14
Market, Wm.	M-24
Marquette	C-11
Marquette II	S-30
Martin, Rt. Hon. Paul J.	C-2
Mary Ann	H-11
Marysville	G-2
Massachusetts	G-19
Matador IV	C-1
Matfen	IF-8
Mather, William G.	H-5
Matt Allen	K-7
Maumee	L-15
MBT 10	M-25
MBT 20	M-25
MBT 33	M-25
McAllister 132	A-1
McAllister, Daniel	B-9
McAsphalt 401	M-12
McBride, Sam	T-12
McCarthy, Walter J.	A-9
McCauley	S-25
McCleary's Spirit	K-1
McGrath, James E.	M-14
McKee Sons	L-15
McKeil, Evans	M-14
McKeil, Jarrett	M-14
McKeil, Wyatt	H-9
McLane	G-22
McLeod, Norman	M-12
Medemborg	IW-2
Medill, Joseph	B-2
Menasha	G-4, M-18
Menier Consol	T-9
Menominee	L-7
Mermaid	A-11
Merwedelta	IS-8
Mesabi Miner	I-6
Meta	IO-7
Meteor	S-21
Metis	E-15
Michigan	K-5, U-2
Michiganborg	IW-2
Michipicoten	L-14
Middle Channel	C-7
Mighty Jake	G-8
Mighty Jessie	G-8
Mighty Jimmy	G-8

Vessel Name	Fleet #
Mighty John III	G-8
Miles, Paddy	H-14
Milin Kamak	IN-2
Milo	IS-4
Milroy, Phil	F-6
Milwaukee	G-19
Milwaukee Clipper	G-15
Miners Castle	P-5
Minnesota	G-19
Miseford	T-6
Mishe-Mokwa	M-7
Misner, H. H.	B-12
Miss Buffalo II	B-18
Miss Edna	K-7
Miss Laura	M-10
Miss Libby	T-1
Miss Midland	M-22
Miss Munising	S-9
Miss Olympia	N-4
Miss Superior	P-5
Mississagi	L-14
Mississauga Express	IH-2
Mississippi	G-19
Missouri	G-19
Mister Joe	M-17
Mljet	IA-10
Mobile Bay	U-3
Moby Dick	G-8
Moezelborg	IW-2
Mohawk	M-1
Molly M. 1	M-14
Montana	G-19
Montreal Express	IH-2
Montrealais	U-15
Moore, Olive L.	K-9
Moore, William J.	K-1
Morgan	K-6
Morpeth	IF-8
Mount Ace	IT-4
Mount McKay	N-8
Mountain Blossom	IL-2
Mrs. C	C-18
Munson, John G.	G-18
Murray R.	F-6
Musky II	U-4

N

Vessel Name	Fleet #
Nadro Clipper	N-1
Namaycush	U-14
Nancy Anne	D-14
Nanticoke	C-2
Nantucket Clipper	IC-18
Nassauborg	IW-2

Vessel Name	Fleet #
Nathan S.	C-1
National Honor	IM-1
Nautica Queen	N-2
Navcomar No. 1	L-10
Neah Bay	U-3
Nebraska	G-19
Neebish Islander IV	E-2
Neeskay	U-12
Neptune III	D-4
New Beginnings	T-15
New Jersey	G-19
New York	G-19
Newberry, Jerry	M-14
Niagara	E-12
Niagara Prince	IA-6
Niagara Queen II	O-5
Nichevo II	M-4
Nicola	II-2
Nicole M.	M-14
Nicole S.	N-8
Nicolet	U-2
Nida	IP-3
Nils B.	IW-1
Nina	II-2
Nindawayma	V-2
Nipigon Osprey	U-14
No. 55	M-1
No. 56	M-1
Nobility	IA-1
Noble, Robert	W-1
Nogat	IP-3
Nokomis	S-15
Nordic Blossom	IL-2
Nordik Express	T-16
Nordik Passeur	T-16
Norgoma	S-28
Norisle	S-22
Norma B.	F-4
Norris, James	U-15
North Carolina	G-19
North Channel	C-7
North Dakota	G-19
Northern Spirit I	S-17
Northwestern	G-21
Norton, David Z.	L-15
Noyes, Hack	W-4

O

Vessel Name	Fleet #
Oatka	A-4
Ocean Abys	L-10
Ocean Bravo	L-10
Ocean Charlie	L-10
Ocean Delta	L-10

Vessel Name	Fleet #	Vessel Name	Fleet #	Vessel Name	Fleet #
Ocean Echo II	L-10	Palawan	IH-4	Power	IH-2
Ocean Foxtrot	L-10	Palessa	IH-4	Prairieland	G-8
Ocean Golf	L-10	Pan Voyager	IS-12	Presque Isle	G-18
Ocean Hauler	M-14	Panam Atlantico	IC-20	Pride of Michigan	U-8
Ocean Hercule	L-10	Panam Felice	IC-20	Primary 1	B-22
Ocean Intrepide	L-10	Panam Flota	IC-20	Princess Wenonah	B-4
Ocean Jupiter	L-10	Panam Linda	IC-17	Prinsenborg	IW-2
Ocean K. Rusby	L-10	Panam Oceanica	IC-20	Provmar Terminal	U-15
Oceanex Avalon	IO-2	Panam Sol	IC-17	Provmar Terminal II	U-15
Oconto	P-12	Panam Trinity	IC-20	Puffin	IH-4
Odra	IP-3	Panama	B-11	Purcell, Robert	A-12
Oglebay, Earl W.	L-15	Pancaldo	IH-4	Purha	IF-6
Ohio	G-19	Panos G.	IG-1	Purves, John	D-9
Oil Queen	S-23	Papoose III	K-8	Purvis, W.I. Scott	P-15
Ojibway	M-1	Park State	Z-1	Purvis, W.J. Ivan	P-15
Okapi	IF-4	Pathfinder	I-6	Put-In-Bay	M-24
Oklahoma	G-19	Patronicola, Calliroe	IO-4	Pyrgos	IF-4
Okoltchitza	IN-2	Paul E. No. 1	M-14		
Old Mission	K-6	Paula M.	M-17		
Oldendorff, Elise	IO-3	Peach State	M-1	**Q**	
Olympic Melody	IO-4	Pearkes, George R.	C-3	Quebecois	U-15
Olympic Mentor	IO-4	Pelee Islander	O-4	Queen Trader	IA-2
Olympic Merit	IO-4	Peninsula	G-14	Quinte Loyalist	O-4
Olympic Miracle	IO-4	Pennsylvania	G-19		
Omni-Atlas	L-10	Pere Marquette 10	E-14	**R**	
Omni-Richelieu	L-10	Pere Marquette 41	P-3	R.C.L. No. II	M-17
Omni-St-Laurent	L-10	Perelik	IN-2	Racine	U-2
Onego Merchant	IO-6	Performance	S-25	Radisson	S-13, S-30
Onego Trader	IO-6	Perry, John M.	C-1	Radisson, Pierre	C-3
Onego Traveller	IO-6	Persenk	IN-2	Radium Yellowknife	N-7
Ongiara	T-12	Pete, C. West	B-1	Randolph, Curtis	D-5
Ontamich	B-15	Petite Forte	S-27	Ranger III	U-7
Opeongo	G-7	Pictured Rocks	P-5	Rebecca	II-2
Oriole	S-17	Pilica	IP-3	Rebecca Lynn	A-12
Orla	IP-3	Pilot 1	M-14	Redhead	IP-2
Orna	IS-4	Pineglen	C-2	Rega	IP-3
Orsula	IA-10	Pintail	IN-1	Reliance	P-15
Osborne, F.M.	O-6	Pioneer	IC-19	Rennie, Thomas	T-12
Oshawa	M-17	Pioneer II	S-29	Reserve	K-9
Oshkosh # 15	Y-1	Pioneer Princess	T-11	Rest, William	T-13
Ostrander, G.L.	L-2	Pioneer Queen	T-11	Rhode Island	G-19
Ottawa	A-14	Pioneerland	G-8	Richter, Arni J.	W-1
Ottawa Express	IH-2	Pochard	IH-4	Richter, C.G.	W-1
Ours Polaire	N-7	Point Valour	T-6	Rio Glory	IG-2
Outer Island	E-10	Point Viking	A-2	Risley, Samuel	C-3
		Polaris	I-8	Robert John	G-14
		Polydefkis P	IC-16	Robert W.	T-5
P		Pomorze Zachodnie	IP-3	Robin E.	E-5
P. & P. No. 1	T-12	Pontokratis	IO-1	Robin Lynn	S-7
P.M.L. 2501	P-15	Pontoporos	IO-1	Robinson Bay	S-25
P.M.L. 357	P-15	Port City Princess	P-9	Rochelle Kaye	R-7
P.M.L. 9000	P-15	Port Mechins	D-10	Rocket	P-15
P.M.L. Alton	P-15	Powell, C.S.	C-23	Roman, Stephen B.	E-15
Pacific Standard	M-14			Rosaire	D-10

Anna Desgagnés in the St. Lawrence Seaway. *(Kent Malo)*

Vessel Name	Fleet #	Vessel Name	Fleet #	Vessel Name	Fleet #
Rosalee D.	T-5	Shark	C-3	Spruceglen	C-2
Rosemary	M-11	Shark 1	B-21	Spuds	R-4
Rouble, J.R.	T-1	Sheila Ann	IC-19	St. Clair	A-9, M-14
Royal Pescadores	IS-5	Shelter Bay	U-7	St. John, J.S.	E-13
Ryerson, Edward L.	C-6	Shenehon	G-17	St. Marys Cement	S-27
		Sherwin, John	I-6	St. Marys Cement II	S-27
S		Shipka	IN-2	St. Marys Cement III	S-27
S Pacific	IJ-3	Shipsands	T-15	St. Marys Challenger	S-27
S.M.T.B. No. 7	E-1	Shirley Irene	K-3	St. Marys Conquest	S-27
Sabina	IE-5	Shoreline II	S-12	Stacey Dawn	C-18
Sacre Bleu	S-8	Showboat Royal Grace	M-11	Star of Chicago	S-12
Saginaw	L-14	Siam Star	IE-3	Staris	IL-3
Sagittarius	II-1	Sichem Maya	IB-5	Starlight	IO-5
Salvage Monarch	N-7	Sichem Padua	IC-1	State of Michigan	G-21
Salvor	M-14	Sichem Palace	IC-1	Statesboro	B-22
Sandpiper	H-6	Sichem Peace	IC-1	STC 2004	B-22
Sandra Mary	M-17	Sichem Princess		Ste. Claire	S-32
Sandviken	IV-2	Marie-Chantal	IC-1	Steelhead	M-20
Santiago	IB-7	Sichem Singapore	IC-1	Stefania I	IF-7
Sarah B	G-16	Silversides	G-22	Stella Borealis	C-16
Sarah No. 1	T-1	Simcoe	C-3	Stellanova	IJ-4
Sault au Cochon	M-14	Simcoe Islander	C-19	Stellaprima	IJ-4
Sauniere	A-6	Simmonds	M-26	Stolt Aspiration	IS-11
Savard, Felix Antoine	S-13	Simonsen	U-2	Stolt Kite	IS-11
Savard, Joseph	S-13	Simpson, Miss Kim	T-15	Stormont	M-14
Scan Arctic	IS-2	Sioux	M-1, Z-1	Straits Express	A-14
Scandrett, Fred	T-13	Sir Walter	IA-3	Straits of Mackinac II	A-14
Schlaeger, Victor L.	C-10	Siscowet	B-2	Strekalovskiy, Mikhail	IM-4
Schwartz, H.J.	U-2	Skaftafell	IB-7	Sturgeon	U-4
SCL Bern	IE-5	Skyline Princess	M-19	Sugar Islander II	E-2
Scoter	IN-1	Skyline Queen	M-19	Sullivan, Denis	P-6
Sea Chief	B-2	Smith Jr., L.L.	U-13	Sundew	D-12
Sea Colt	S-3	Smith, Dean R.	M-10	Sundstraum	IA-8
Sea Eagle II	S-27	Smith, F.C.G.	C-3	Sunliner	W-2
Sea Fox II	T-4	Snohomish	S-1	Superior	G-19
Sea Prince II	R-3	Sofia	II-2	Susan L.	S-4
Sea Veteran	IV-1	Songa Aneline	IB-5	Susan Michelle	D-3
Seaguardian II	IT-3	Songa Defiance	IB-5	Suvorov, Aleksandr	IM-4
Seahound	N-1	Soo River Belle	N-9	Swan Lake	IL-2
Sealink	IT-3	Sora	C-3	Sykes, Wilfred	C-6
Segwun	M-28	Soulanges	E-8		
Selvick, Carla Anne	S-4	South Bass	M-24	**T**	
Selvick, John M.	C-1	South Carolina	G-19	Tandem I	N-4
Selvick, Kimberly	C-1	South Channel	C-7	Tatjana	II-2
Selvick, Sharon M.	S-4	Spar Garnet	IS-10	Taxideftis	IS-1
Selvick, William C.	S-4	Spar Jade	IS-10	TCAA 1	T-13
Seneca	IA-5, Z-1	Spar Opal	IS-10	Techno-Venture	M-14
Serendipity Princess	M-22	Spar Ruby	IS-10	Tecumseh II	P-15
Sevilla Wave	IT-1	Spartan	L-6	Tenacious	R-7
Seymour, Wilf	M-14	Speer, Edgar B.	G-18	Tennessee	G-19
Shamrock	J-2	Spence, John	M-14	Texas	G-19
Shamrock Moon	ID-1	Spencer, Sarah	T-2	The Columbia V	A-10
Shannon	G-2	Spirit of Chicago	S-18	The Hope	S-8

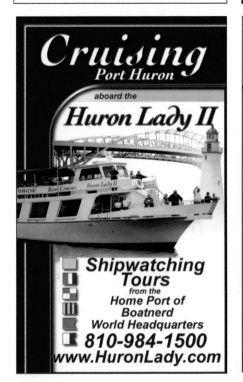
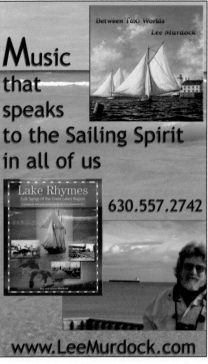

Fleet
Listings

Herbert C. Jackson passes the *Buffalo* in the Rouge River. *(Wade P. Streeter)*

GREAT LAKES / SEAWAY FLEETS

Listed after each vessel in order are: Type of Vessel, Year Built, Type of Engine, Maximum Cargo Capacity (at midsummer draft in long tons) or Gross Tonnage*, Overall Length, Breadth and Depth (from the top of the keel to the top of the upper deck beam) or Draft*. Only vessels over 30 feet long are included. The figures given are as accurate as possible and are given for informational purposes only. Vessels and owners are listed alphabetically as per American Bureau of Shipping and Lloyd's Register of Shipping format. Builder yard and location, as well as other pertinent information, are listed for major vessels; former names of vessels and years of operation under the former names appear in parentheses. A number in brackets following a vessel's name indicates how many vessels, including the one listed, have carried that name.

KEY TO TYPE OF VESSEL

2B ....Brigantine	**DS**..............................Spud Barge	**PA** ....Passenger Vessel
2S ....2-Masted Schooner	**DV**...............................Drilling Vessel	**PB** .... Pilot Boat
3S ....3-Masted Schooner	**DW** .... Scow	**PF** ....Passenger Ferry
4S ....4-Masted Schooner	**ES** .... Excursion Ship	**PK**.........................Package Freighter
AC.............................. Auto Carrier	**EV**...................Env. Response Ship	**PO**.................................Police Boat
AT ....Articulated Tug	**FB** .... Fire Boat	**RR**.........................Roll On/Roll Off
ATB...........Articulated Tug/Barge	**FD**....................Floating Dry Dock	**RT** ....Refueling Tanker
BB ....Bum Boat	**FT** ....Fishing Tug	**RV** ....Research Vessel
BC.................................Bulk Carrier	**GA** .... Gambling Casino	**SB** ....Supply Boat
BK................. Bulk Carrier/Tanker	**GC** ....General Cargo	**SC** .... Sand Carrier
BT..............................Buoy Tender	**GL**................................Gate Lifter	**SR** ....Search & Rescue
CA...............................Catamaran	**GR** .... Grocery Launch	**SU** ....Self-Unloader
CC .... Cement Carrier	**GU** ....Grain Self-Unloader	**SV** ....Survey Vessel
CF...................................Car Ferry	**HL**...................... Heavy Lift Vessel	**TB** ....Tug Boat
CO ....Container Vessel	**IB** ....Ice Breaker	**TF** ....Train Ferry
CS.................................Crane Ship	**IT** ....Integrated Tug	**TK** ....Tanker
DB ....Deck Barge	**ITB**..................Integrated Tug/Barge	**TW** ....Towboat
DH ....Hopper Barge	**MB** ....Mailboat	**TT** ....Tractor Tug Boat
DR ....Dredge	**MU** ....Museum Vessel	**TV** .... Training Vessel

KEY TO PROPULSION

B..Barge	**R**.....................Steam - Triple Exp. Compound Engine
D ....Diesel	**S**.............................Steam - Skinner "Uniflow" Engine
DE..................................... Diesel Electric	**T**... Steam - Turbine Engine
Q.....................Steam - Quad Exp. Compound Engine	**W** ....Sailing Vessel (Wind)

Fleet #. Vessel Name	Fleet Name 	Type of Vessel	Year Built	Type of Engine	Cargo Cap. or Gross*	Overall Length	Breadth	Depth or Draft*
A-1	**A. B. M. MARINE, THUNDER BAY, ON**							
	McAllister 132	DB	1954	B	7,000	343' 00"	63' 00"	19' 00"
	(Powell No. 1 '54-'61, Alberni Carrier '61-'77, Genmar 132 '77-'79)							
	W. N. Twolan	TB	1962	D	299*	106' 00"	29' 05"	15' 00"
A-2	**ABITIBI-CONSOLIDATED INC., MONTREAL, QC**							
	Point Viking	TB	1962	D	207*	98' 05"	27' 10"	13' 05"
	(Foundation Viking '62-'75)							
A-3	**ACHESON VENTURES LLC, PORT HURON, MI**							
	Highlander Sea	ES/2S	1927	W/D	140*	154' 00"	25' 06"	14' 00"
	(Pilot '27-'76, Star Pilot '76-'98, Caledonia '98-'98)							
A-4	**ACME MARINE SERVICE, DULUTH, MN**							
	Oatka	TB	1935	D	10*	40' 00"	10' 00"	4' 06"
A-5	**ALCAN INC., MONTREAL, QC**							
	Alexis-Simard	TT	1980	D	286*	92' 00"	34' 00"	13' 07"
	Grande Baie	TT	1972	D	194*	86' 06"	30' 00"	12' 00"

A-6   ALGOMA CENTRAL CORP., SAULT STE. MARIE, ON

* VESSELS OPERATED & MANAGED BY SEAWAY MARINE TRANSPORT, ST. CATHARINES, ON, A PARTNERSHIP BETWEEN ALGOMA CENTRAL AND UPPER LAKES GROUP INC.

Vessel Name	Type of Vessel	Year Built	Type of Engine	Cargo Cap. or Gross*	Overall Length	Breadth	Depth or Draft*
Agawa Canyon*	SU	1970	D	23,400	647' 00"	72' 00"	40' 00"
Built: Collingwood Shipyards, Collingwood, ON							
Algobay*	SU	1978	D	34,900	730' 00"	75' 10"	46' 06"
Built: Collingwood Shipyards, Collingwood, ON; last operated in 2002; laid up at Toronto, ON (Algobay '78-'94, Atlantic Trader '94-'97)							
Algocape* {2}	BC	1967	D	29,950	729' 09"	75' 04"	39' 08"
Built: Davie Shipbuilding Ltd., Lauzon, QC (Richelieu {3} '67-'94)							
Algoisle*	BC	1963	D	26,700	730' 00"	75' 05"	39' 03"
Built: Verolme Cork Shipyard, Ltd., Cork, Ireland (Silver Isle '63-'94)							
Algolake*	SU	1977	D	32,150	730' 00"	75' 06"	46' 06"
Built: Collingwood Shipyards, Collingwood, ON							
Algomarine*	SU	1968	D	27,000	729' 10"	75' 04"	39' 08"
Built: Davie Shipbuilding Ltd., Lauzon, QC; converted to a self-unloader in '89 (Lake Manitoba '68-'87)							
Algonorth*	BC	1971	D	28,000	729' 11"	75' 02"	42' 11"
Built: Upper Clyde Shipbuilders, Govan, Scotland (Temple Bar '71-'76, Lake Nipigon '76-'84, Laketon {2} '84-'86, Lake Nipigon '86-'87)							
Algontario*	BC	1960	D	29,100	730' 00"	75' 09"	40' 02"
Built: Schlieker-Werft, Hamburg, West Germany ([**Fore Section**] Cartiercliffe Hall '76-'88, Winnipeg {2} '88-'94 [**Stern Section**] Ruhr Ore '60-'76)							
Algoport*	SU	1979	D	32,000	658' 00"	75' 10"	46' 06"
Built: Collingwood Shipyards, Collingwood, ON							
Algorail* {2}	SU	1968	D	23,750	640' 05"	72' 03"	40' 00"
Built: Collingwood Shipyards, Collingwood, ON							
Algosoo* {2}	SU	1974	D	31,300	730' 00"	75' 05"	44' 06"
Built: Collingwood Shipyards, Collingwood, ON							
Algosteel* {2}	SU	1966	D	27,000	729' 11"	75' 04"	39' 08"
Built: Davie Shipbuilding, Lauzon, QC (A. S. Glossbrenner '66-'87, Algogulf {1} '87-'90)							
Algoville*	BC	1967	D	31,250	730' 00"	77' 11"	39' 08"
Built: St. John Shipbuilding & Drydock Co., St. John, NB; widened by 3' in '96 (Senneville '67-'94)							
Algoway* {2}	SU	1972	D	24,000	650' 00"	72' 00"	40' 00"
Built: Collingwood Shipyards, Collingwood, ON							
Algowood*	SU	1981	D	31,750	740' 00"	76' 01"	46' 06"
Built: Collingwood Shipyards, Collingwood, ON							
Capt. Henry Jackman*	SU	1981	D	30,550	730' 00"	76' 01"	42' 00"
Built: Collingwood Shipyards, Collingwood, ON; converted to a self-unloader in '96 (Lake Wabush '81-'87)							
John B. Aird*	SU	1983	D	31,300	730' 00"	76' 01"	46' 06"
Built: Collingwood Shipyards, Collingwood, ON							
Peter R. Cresswell*	SU	1982	D	31,700	730' 00"	76' 01"	42' 00"
Built: Collingwood Shipyards, Collingwood, ON; converted to a self-unloader '98 (Algowest '82-'01)							

ALGOMA TANKERS LTD., DARTMOUTH, NS – DIVISION OF ALGOMA CENTRAL CORP.

Vessel Name	Type of Vessel	Year Built	Type of Engine	Cargo Cap. or Gross*	Overall Length	Breadth	Depth or Draft*
Algoeast	TK	1977	D	9,750	431' 05"	65' 07"	35' 05"
Built: Mitsubishi Heavy Industries Ltd., Shimonoseki, Japan; converted from single to double hull in '00 (Texaco Brave {2} '77-'86, Le Brave '86-'97, Imperial St. Lawrence {2} '97-'97)							
Algosar {2}	TK	1978	D	10,099	432' 06"	65' 00"	29' 04"
Built: Levingston Shipbuilding Co., Orange, Texas (Gemini '78-'05)							
Algoscotia	TK	2004	D	18,010	488' 01"	78' 00"	42' 00"
Built: Jiangnan Shipyard (Group) Co., Ltd., Shangahi, People's 'Republic of China							
Algosea	TK	1998	D	16,775	472' 04"	75' 04"	41'09"
Built: Alabama Shipyard Inc., Mobile, Ala. (Aggersborg '98-'05)							
Amalienborg	TK	1998	D	16,775	472' 04"	75' 04"	41'09"
Built: Alabama Shipyard Inc., Mobile, Ala. (Currently engaged in saltwater service)							

SOCIETE QUEBECOISE D' EXPLORATION MINIERE, SAINTE-FOY, QC – CHARTERER

	Sauniere	SU	1970	D	23,900	642' 10"	74' 10"	42' 00"

Built: Lithgows Ltd., East Yard, Glasgow, Scotland; converted to a self-unloader, lengthened 122' in '76
(Bulknes '70-'70, Brooknes '70-'76, Algosea {1} '76-'82)

VESSEL IS JOINTLY OWNED BY ALGOMA CENTRAL MARINE & UPPER LAKES SHIPPING LTD.

	Windoc {2}	BC	1959	B	29,100	730' 00"	75' 09"	40' 02"

Built: Schlicting-Werlt Willy H. Schlieker, East Germany; damaged by fire in 2001; laid up and awaiting a
decision on its future at Port Colborne, ON (Rhine Ore '59-'76, Steelcliffe Hall '76-'88)

A-7   AMERICAN ACADEMY OF INDUSTRY, CHICAGO, IL

	Acacia	MU	1944	DE	1,025*	180' 00"	37' 00"	17' 04"

Former U.S. Coast Guard buoy tender/icebreaker; decommissioned in '06; scheduled to become a museum
at Chicago, IL (Launched as USCGC Thistle [WAGL-406])

A-8   AMERICAN MARINE CONSTRUCTION, BENTON HARBOR, MI

	Alice E	TB	1944	T	146*	81' 01"	24' 00"	9' 10"
	AMC 100	DB	1979	B	2,273	200' 00"	52' 00"	14' 00"
	AMC 200	DB	1979	B	2,273	200' 00"	36' 00"	11' 08"
	AMC 300	DB	1977	B	1,048	180' 00"	54' 00"	12' 00"
	Defiance	TW	1966	D	26*	44' 08"	18' 00"	6' 00"

A-9   AMERICAN STEAMSHIP CO., WILLIAMSVILLE, NY

	Adam E. Cornelius {4}	SU	1973	D	28,200	680' 00"	78' 00"	42' 00"

Built: American Shipbuilding Co., Toledo, OH (Roger M. Kyes '73-'89)

	American Century	SU	1981	D	78,850	1,000' 00"	105' 00"	56' 00"

Built: Bay Shipbuilding Co., Sturgeon Bay, WI (Columbia Star '81-'06)

	American Courage	SU	1979	D	23,800	636' 00"	68' 00"	40' 00"

Built: Bay Shipbuilding Co., Sturgeon Bay, WI (Fred R. White Jr. '79-'06)

	American Fortitude	SU	1953	T	22,300	690' 00"	70' 00"	37' 00"

Built: American Shipbuilding Co., Lorain, OH; converted to a self-unloader in '81
(Ernest T. Weir {2} '53-'78, Courtney Burton '78-'06)

	American Integrity	SU	1978	D	78,850	1,000' 00"	105' 00"	56' 00"

Built: Bay Shipbuilding Co., Sturgeon Bay, WI (Lewis Wilson Foy '78-'91, Oglebay Norton '91-'06)

	American Mariner	SU	1980	D	37,200	730' 00"	78' 00"	45' 00"

Built: Bay Shipbuilding Co., Sturgeon Bay, WI (Laid down as Chicago {3})

	American Republic	SU	1981	D	24,800	634' 10"	68' 00"	40' 00"

Built: Bay Shipbuilding Co., Sturgeon Bay, WI

	American Spirit	SU	1978	D	59,700	1,004' 00"	105' 00"	50' 00"

Built: American Shipbuilding Co., Lorain, OH (George A. Stinson '78-'04)

	American Valor	SU	1953	T	25,500	767' 00"	70' 00"	36' 00"

Built: American Shipbuilding Co., Lorain, OH; lengthened by 120' in '74, converted to a self-unloader in '82
(Armco '53-'06)

	American Victory	SU	1942	T	26,300	730' 00"	75' 00"	39' 03"

Built: Bethlehem Shipbuilding and Drydock Co., Sparrows Point, MD; converted from saltwater tanker to
a Great Lakes bulk carrier in '61; converted to a self-unloader in '82; laid down as Marquette
(USS Neshanic [AO-71] '42-'47, Gulfoil '47-'61, Pioneer Challenger '61-'62, Middletown '62-'06)

	Buffalo {3}	SU	1978	D	23,800	634' 10"	68' 00"	40' 00"

Built: Bay Shipbuilding Co., Sturgeon Bay, WI

	Burns Harbor {2}	SU	1980	D	78,850	1,000' 00"	105' 00"	56' 00"

Built: Bay Shipbuilding Co., Sturgeon Bay, WI

	H. Lee White {2}	SU	1974	D	35,200	704' 00"	78' 00"	45' 00"

Built: Bay Shipbuilding Co., Sturgeon Bay, WI

	Indiana Harbor	SU	1979	D	78,850	1,000' 00"	105' 00"	56' 00"

Built: Bay Shipbuilding Co., Sturgeon Bay, WI

	John J. Boland {4}	SU	1973	D	33,800	680' 00"	78' 00"	45' 00"

Built: Bay Shipbuilding Co., Sturgeon Bay, WI (Charles E. Wilson '73-'00)

	Sam Laud	SU	1975	D	23,800	634' 10"	68' 00"	40' 00"

Built: Bay Shipbuilding Co., Sturgeon Bay, WI

	St. Clair {3}	SU	1976	D	44,000	770' 00"	92' 00"	52' 00"
	Built: Bay Shipbuilding Co., Sturgeon Bay, WI							
	Walter J. McCarthy Jr.	SU	1977	D	78,850	1,000' 00"	105' 00"	56' 00"
	Built: Bay Shipbuilding Co., Sturgeon Bay, WI (Belle River '77-'90)							
A-10	**AMHERSTBURG FERRY CO., AMHERSTBURG, ON**							
	The Columbia V	PA/CF	1946	D	65*	65' 00"	28' 10"	8' 06"
	(Crystal O, St. Clair Flats)							
	The Ste. Claire V	PA/CF	1997	D	82*	86' 06"	32' 00"	6' 00"
	(Courtney O., M. Bourbonnais)							
A-11	**ANDREW G. MUELLER, MILWAUKEE, WI**							
	Mermaid	TB	1936	D	11*	41'00"	10'00"	4' 9"
	(Calship I, James Kenneth, Quitin, Jake M. Kadinger)							
A-12	**ANDRIE INC., MUSKEGON, MI**							
	A-390	TK	1982	B	2,346*	310' 00"	60' 00"	19' 03"
	(Canonie 40 '82-'92)							
	A-397	TK	1962	B	2,928*	270' 00"	60' 00"	25' 00"
	(Auntie Mame '62-'91, Iron Mike '91-'93)							
	A-410	TK	1955	B	3,793*	335' 00"	54' 00"	26' 06"
	(Methane '55-'63, B-6400 '63-'71, Kelly '71-'86, Canonie 50 '86-'93)							
	Barbara Andrie	TB	1940	D	298*	121' 10"	29' 06"	16' 00"
	(Edmond J. Moran '40-'76)							
	Barbara Rita	TO	1981	D	15*	36' 00"	14' 00"	6' 00"
	Candace Andrie	CS	1958	B	1,000	150' 00"	52' 00"	10' 00"
	(MCD '58-'73, Minnesota '73-'88)							
	Clara Andrie	DR	1930	B	1,000	110' 00"	30' 00"	6' 10"
	John Joseph	TB	1993	D	15*	40' 00"	14' 00"	5' 00"
	Karen Andrie {2}	TB	1965	D	433*	120' 00"	31' 06"	16' 00"
	(Sarah Hays '65-'93)							
	Meredith Andrie	DS	1971	B	521*	140' 00"	50' 00"	9' 00"
	(Illinois '71-'02)							
	Rebecca Lynn	TB	1964	D	433*	120' 00"	31' 08"	18' 09"
	(Kathrine Clewis '64-'96)							
	Robert Purcell	TB	1943	D	29*	45' 02"	12' 08"	7' 09"
	Ronald J. Dahlke	TB	1903	D	58*	63' 03"	17' 05"	9' 03"
	(Bonita '03-'14, Chicago Harbor No. 4 '14-'60, Eddie B. '60-'69, Seneca Queen '69-'70, Ludington '70-'96, Seneca Queen '96-'04)							
A-13	**APOSTLE ISLANDS CRUISE SERVICE, BAYFIELD, WI**							
	Island Princess {2}	ES	1973	D	63*	65' 07"	20' 05"	7' 03"
A-14	**ARNOLD TRANSIT CO., MACKINAC ISLAND, MI**							
	Algomah	PF/PK	1961	D	125	93' 00"	31' 00"	8' 00"
	Beaver	CF	1952	D	87*	64' 09"	30' 02"	8' 00"
	Chippewa {6}	PF/PK	1962	D	125	93' 00"	31' 00"	8' 00"
	Corsair	CF	1955	D	98*	94' 06"	33' 00"	8' 06"
	Huron {5}	PF/PK	1955	D	80	91' 06"	25' 00"	10' 01"
	Island Express	PF/CA	1988	D	90*	82' 07"	28' 06"	8' 05"
	Mackinac Express	PF/CA	1987	D	90*	82' 07"	28' 06"	8' 05"
	Mackinac Islander	CF	1947	D	99*	84' 00"	30' 00"	8' 03"
	(Drummond Islander '47-'02)							
	Ottawa {2}	PF/PK	1959	D	125	93' 00"	31' 00"	8' 00"
	Straits Express	PF/CA	1995	D	99*	101' 00"	29' 11"	6' 08"
	Straits of Mackinac II	PF/PK	1969	D	89*	89' 11"	27' 00"	8' 08"
A-15	**ATLANTIC TOWING LTD., SAINT JOHN, NB**							
	Atlantic Cedar	TB	2005	D	402*	94' 04"	36' 05"	17' 09"
	Atlantic Eagle	TB	1999	D	3,080*	247' 06"	59' 05"	19' 10"

Fleet #.	Fleet Name Vessel Name	Type of Vessel	Year Built	Type of Engine	Cargo Cap. or Gross*	Overall Length	Breadth	Depth or Draft*
	Atlantic Fir	TB	2005	D	402*	94' 04"	36' 05"	17' 09"
	Atlantic Hawk	TB	2000	D	3,080*	247' 06"	59' 05"	19' 10"
	Atlantic Hemlock	TT	1996	D	290*	101' 00"	36' 06"	12' 06"
	Atlantic Kingfisher	TB	2002	D	3,453*	239' 08"	59' 00"	26' 02"
	Atlantic Larch	TT	1999	D	392*	101' 01"	36' 07"	17' 01"
	Atlantic Oak	TB	2004	D	402*	94' 04"	36' 05"	17' 09"
	Atlantic Osprey	TB	2003	D	3,453*	239' 08"	59' 00"	26' 02"
	Atlantic Pine	TB	1976	D	159*	70' 00"	24' 00"	7' 08"
	(Grampa Shorty '76-'76, Irving Pine '76-'98)							
	Atlantic Poplar	TB	1965	D	195*	96' 06"	30' 00"	14' 00"
	(Amherstburg '65-'75, Irving Poplar '75-'96)							
	Atlantic Spruce {2}	TT	1998	D	290*	101' 00"	36' 06"	17' 00"
	Atlantic Willow	TT	1998	D	360*	101' 00"	36' 06"	17' 00"
	Irving Dolphin	TK	1964	B	1,441	200' 00"	50' 00"	13' 00"
B-1	**B & L TUG SERVICE, THESSALON, ON**							
	C. West Pete	TB	1958	D	29*	65' 00"	17' 05"	6' 00"
B-2	**BASIC TOWING INC., ESCANABA, MI**							
	Danicia	TB	1944	DE	382*	110' 02"	27' 03"	15' 07"
	(USCGC Chinook [WYT / WYTM-96] '44-'86, Tracie B '86-'98)							
	Erika Kobasic	TB	1939	DE	226*	110' 00"	26' 05"	15' 01"
	(USCGC Arundel [WYT / WYTM-90] '39-'84, Karen Andrie {1} '84-'90)							
	Escort	TB	1969	D	26*	50' 00"	13' 00"	7' 00"
	Greenstone	TK	1977	B	30*	81' 00"	24' 00"	6' 01"
	Former Isle Royale fuel barge; inactive at Escanaba, MI							
	Jenny L.	TB	1909	D	49*	75'00	16' 08"	7'00
	Inactive at Escanaba, MI (Lorain '09-'56, Harry S. Price '56-'73)							
	Joseph Medill	FB	1949	D	351*	92' 00	23' 00	7' 06"
	Former Chicago fire boat; stripped and inactive at Escanaba, MI							
	Krystal	TB	1954	D	23*	45' 02"	12' 08"	6' 00"
	(ST-2168 '54-'62, Thunder Bay '62-'02)							
	Lake Explorer	RV	1962	D	69*	82' 10"	17' 07"	5' 11"
	Former EPA research vessel; inactive at Escanaba, MI (USCGC Point Roberts [WPB-82332] '62-'92)							
	Marin	TB	1960	D	282*	109' 00	31' 00	14' 00
	Under reconstruction at Escanaba, MI (Marin YTB-753 '60-'94)							
	Sea Chief	TB	1952	D	390*	107' 00"	26' 06"	14' 10"
	Inactive at Escanaba, MI (U. S. Army LT-1944 '52-'62, USCOE Washington '62-'00)							
	Siscowet	RV	1946	D	54*	57' 00"	14' 06"	7' 00"
	Former U.S. Department of the Interior research vessel; inactive at Escanaba, MI							
B-3	**BATEAU-MOUCHE AU VIEUX-PORT INC., MONTREAL, QC**							
	Le Bateau-Mouche	ES	1992	D	190*	108' 00"	22' 00"	3' 00"
B-4	**BAY CITY BOAT LINE LLC, BAY CITY, MI**							
	Islander {1}	ES	1946	D	39*	53' 04"	21' 00"	5' 05"
	Princess Wenonah	ES	1954	D	96*	64' 09"	32' 09"	9' 09"
	(William M. Miller '54-'98)							
	West Shore {2}	ES	1947	D	94*	64' 10"	30' 00"	9' 03"
B-5	**BAY SHIPBUILDING CO., STURGEON BAY, WI**							
	Bayship	TB	1943	D	19*	45' 00"	12' 06"	6' 00"
	(Sturshipco)							
B-6	**BAYSAIL, BAY CITY, MI**							
	Appledore IV	2S/ES	1989	W/D	72*	85' 00"	19' 00"	9' 06"
	Appledore V	2S/ES	1992	W/D	34*	65' 00"	16' 00"	8' 06"
B-7	**BEAUSOLEIL FIRST NATION, CHRISTIAN ISLAND, ON**							
	Indian Maiden	PA/CF	1987	D	91.5*	73' 06"	23' 00"	8' 00"
	Sandy Graham	PA/CF	1957	D	212*	125' 07"	39' 09"	8' 00"

PAUL H. TOWNSEND

Vessel Spotlight

A product of World War II shipbuilding, the *Paul H. Townsend* was built as a type C1-M-AV1 small cargo ship designed by the U.S. Maritime Commission for short coastal runs not requiring fast ships. Launched as *Hickory Coll*, the vessel began trading in September 1945 renamed *Coastal Delegate*, operating under charter to the Southern Steamship Co. of Philadelphia, Pa. However she entered service too late to see war service.

Coastal Delegate was acquired by the Huron Transportation Co. of Detroit on Nov. 7, 1951 and was converted in 1952-53 to a self-unloading cement carrier. The conversion was started at the Bethlehem Steel Co. Shipbuilding Div. of Hoboken, N.J., with the vessel eventually brought to the Great Lakes via the Mississippi River system for the conversion to be completed at the Calumet Shipyard, Chicago. On April 30, 1953, the new carrier was christened *Paul H. Townsend* at Detroit in honor of Mr. Paul Henson Townsend, who was elected president of Huron Portland Cement in 1953. With the conversion, her capacity dropped to 5,200 tons. Her self-unloading system moved the cement by screw conveyors discharging at a rate of only 536 tons per hour.

During the winter lay-up of 1957-58, the *Paul H. Townsend* was rebuilt and lengthened 108 feet, moving the wheelhouse forward and giving the vessel a distinct, if not top-heavy, appearance. The rebuild was completed by Great Lakes Engineering Works, Ashtabula, Ohio, and increased the small laker's cargo capacity to her current 7,850 tons.

The *Townsend* has remained with the same fleet since entering service on the Great Lakes, a fleet that has survived ownership changes at various levels over the years. She currently sails under the banner of Inland Lakes Management Inc., Alpena, Mich., (an affiliate of Andrie Inc.). Inland Lakes operates and manages the vessels under a contract with Lafarge North America.

Even though the *Townsend* is the only diesel-powered vessel in the fleet, her smaller capacity has left her laid up at various times while her larger fleetmates *Alpena* and, until recently, *J.A.W. Iglehart,* have remained active. With the recent introduction of efficient articulated tug/barge operations carrying Lafarge products, the *Townsend* did not see service in 2006. Even though she received a fresh coat of paint, her future as an active carrier on the Great Lakes is in question. With her larger fleetmate *J.A.W. Iglehart* entering long term lay-up at Superior on Oct. 31, 2006, any return to active service by the *Townsend* in the near future is unlikely.

– George Wharton

Paul H. Townsend in 1954 (top) and laid up in 2006 at Muskegon. *(Mike Nicholls)*

B-8   **BEAVER ISLAND BOAT CO., CHARLEVOIX, MI**

	Beaver Islander	PF/CF	1963	D	95*	96' 03"	27' 05"	9' 09"
	Emerald Isle {2}	PF/CF	1997	D	95*	130' 00"	38' 08"	12' 00"

B-9   **BERNIER MARITIME MUSEUM (MUSEE MARITIME DU QUEBEC), L' ISLET, QC**

	Bras d'Or 400	MU	1967	D		151' 00"	21' 05"	
	Former Fast Hydrofoil Escort open to the public at L'Islet, QC (FHE 400)							
	Daniel McAllister	MU	1907	D	268*	115' 00"	23' 02"	12' 00"
	Former McAllister Towing & Salvage Inc. tug; laid up at Montreal, QC (Helena '07-'57, Helen M.B. '57-'66)							
	Ernest Lapointe	MU	1941	R	1,179*	185' 00"	36' 00"	22' 06"
	Former Canadian Coast Guard icebreaker; open to the public at L'Islet, QC							

B-10   **BEST OF ALL TOURS, ERIE, PA**

	Lady Kate {2}	ES	1952	D	11*	59' 03"	15' 00"	4' 00"
	(G. A. Boeckling II '52-?, Cedar Point III ?-'89, Island Trader '89-'97)							

B-11   **BILLINGTON CONTRACTING INC., DULUTH, MN**

	Col. D.D. Gaillard	DB	1916	B		116' 00"	40' 00"	11' 06"
	Long-inactive former U.S. Army Corps of Engineers dipper dredge is for sale at Duluth							
	Coleman	CS	1923	B	502*	153' 06"	40' 06"	10' 06"
	Panama	DS	1942	B		210' 01"	44' 01"	10' 01"

B-12   **BLACK CREEK CONSTRUCTION CO., NANTICOKE, ON**

	H. H. Misner	TB	1946	D	28*	66' 09"	16' 04"	4' 05"

B-13   **BLUE HERON CO., TOBERMORY, ON**

	Blue Heron V	ES	1983	D	24*	54' 06"	17' 05"	7' 02"
	Great Blue Heron	ES	1994	D	112*	79' 00"	22' 00"	6' 05"

B-14   **BLUE WATER EXCURSIONS INC., FORT GRATIOT, MI**

	Huron Lady II	ES	1993	D	82*	65' 00"	19' 00"	10' 00"
	(Lady Lumina '93-'99)							

B-15   **BLUE WATER FERRY LTD., SOMBRA, ON**

	Daldean	CF	1951	D	145*	75' 00"	35' 00"	7' 00"
	Ontamich	CF	1939	D	55*	65' 00"	28' 10"	8' 06"
	(Harsens Island '39-'73)							

B-16   **BOATWORX, MANITOWOC, WI**

	Forney	TB	1944	D	142*	86' 00"	23' 00"	10' 04"
	(ST-707 '44-'60)							

B-17   **BUFFALO AND ERIE COUNTY NAVAL AND MILITARY PARK, BUFFALO, NY**

	Croaker	MU	1944	D	1,526*	311' 07"	27' 02"	33' 09"
	Former U. S. Navy "Gato" class submarine IXSS-246; open to the public at Buffalo, NY							
	Little Rock	MU	1945	T	10,670*	610' 01"	66' 04"	25' 00"
	Former U. S. Navy "Cleveland / Little Rock" class guided missile cruiser; open to the public at Buffalo, NY							
	The Sullivans	MU	1943	T	2,500*	376' 06"	39' 08"	22' 08"
	Former U. S. Navy "Fletcher" class destroyer; open to the public at Buffalo, NY (Launched as USS Putnam)							

B-18   **BUFFALO CHARTERS INC. , BUFFALO, NY**

	Miss Buffalo II	ES	1972	D	88*	81' 09"	24' 00"	6' 00"

B-19   **BUFFALO INDUSTRIAL DIVING (BIDCO), BUFFALO, NY**

	West Wind	TB	1941	D	54*	60' 04"	17' 01"	7' 07"
	(West Wind '41-'46, Russell 2 '61-'97)							
	Joanne	TB	1935	D	18*	42' 06"	11' 09"	6' 09"
	(Paul L. Luedtke '94-'98)							

B-20   **BUFFALO PUBLIC WORKS DEPARTMENT, BUFFALO, NY**

	Edward M. Cotter	FB	1900	D	208*	118' 00"	24' 00"	11' 06"
	(W. S. Grattan 1900-'53, Firefighter '53-'54)							

Fleet #.	Fleet Name / Vessel Name	Type of Vessel	Year Built	Type of Engine	Cargo Cap. or Gross*	Overall Length	Breadth	Depth or Draft*
B-21	**BUS AND BOAT COMPANY INC., TORONTO, ON**							
	Harbour Star	ES	1978	D	45*	63' 06"	15' 09"	3' 09"
	(K. Wayne Simpson '78-'95)							
	Shark 1	ES	2003	Gas	10*	39' 06"	14' 01"	6' 00"
B-22	**BUSCH MARINE INC., CARROLLTON, MI**							
	Gregory J. Busch	TB	1919	D	299*	151' 00"	28' 00"	16' 09"
	(Humaconna '19-'77)							
	Primary 1	DB	1982	B	2,262*	240' 00"	72' 00"	17' 00"
	Statesboro	TB	1938	DE	158*	89' 04"	25' 02"	10 00"
	(Thomas E. Moran 38-'40, USS Namontack YTB 738 '40-'47, Thomas E. Moran '47-'47, Harriet Moran '47-'75, Viking '75-'93, Georgetown '93-'99, Sharon Elizabeth '99-'05)							
	STC 2004	TK	1986	B	2,364	240' 00"	50' 00"	9' 05"
C-1	**CALUMET RIVER FLEETING INC., CHICAGO, IL**							
	Baldy B.	TB	1932	D	36*	62' 00"	16' 01"	8' 00"
	(G. F. Becker)							
	Des Plaines	TW	1956	D	175*	98' 00"	28' 00"	8' 04"
	John M. Perry	TB	1954	D	76*	66' 00"	19' 00"	9' 00"
	(Sanita '54-'77, Soo Chief '77-'81, Susan M. Selvick '81-'96, Nathan S. '96-'02)							
	John M. Selvick	TB	1898	D	256*	118' 00"	24' 00"	12' 07"
	(Illinois {1} 1898-'41, John Roen III '41-'74)							
	Jimmy Wray	TB	1954	D	95*	72' 00"	22' 00"	8' 00"
	(Sea Wolf '54-'01)							
	Matador VI	TW	1971	D	39*	42' 00"	18' 00"	6' 00"
	(Miss Josie '71-'79)							
	Nathan S.	TB	1951	D	144*	90' 00"	24' 00"	12'00"
	(Huntington '51-'05, Spartacus '05-'06, Huntington '06-'07)							
	Kimberly Selvick	TW	1975	D	93*	51' 10"	28' 00"	10' 00"
	(Scout '75-'02)							
C-2	**CANADA STEAMSHIP LINES INC., MONTREAL, QC** ***(VESSELS MANAGED BY V.SHIPS CANADA INC., MONTREAL, QC)***							
	Atlantic Erie	SU	1985	D	37,411	736' 07"	75' 10"	50' 00"
	Built: Collingwood Shipyards, Collingwood, ON (Hon. Paul Martin '85-'88)							
	Atlantic Huron {2}	SU	1984	D	34,800	736' 07"	78' 01"	46' 06"
	Built: Collingwood Shipyards, Collingwood, ON; converted to a self-unloader in '89; widened by 3' in '03)							
	(Prairie Harvest '84-'89, Atlantic Huron {2} '89-'94, Melvin H. Baker II {2} '94-'97)							
	Atlantic Superior	SU	1982	D	36,219	730' 00"	75' 10"	50' 00"
	Built: Collingwood Shipyards, Collingwood, ON (Atlantic Superior '82-'97, M. H. Baker III '97-'03)							
	Birchglen {2}	BC	1983	D	33,824	730' 01"	75' 09"	48' 00"
	Built: Govan Shipyards, Glasgow, Scotland							
	(Canada Marquis '83-'91, Federal Richelieu '91-'91, Federal MacKenzie '91-'01, MacKenzie '01-'02)							
	Cedarglen {2}	BC	1959	D	29,510	730' 00"	75' 09"	40' 02"
	Built: Schlieker-Werft, Hamburg, West Germany (Ems Ore '59-'76, Montcliffe Hall '76-'88, Cartierdoc '88-'02)							
	CSL Assiniboine	SU	1977	D	36,768	739' 10"	78' 01"	48' 05"
	Built: Davie Shipbuilding Co., Lauzon, QC; rebuilt with a new forebody in '05 at Port Weller Drydocks							
	(Jean Parisien '77-'05)							
	CSL Laurentien	SU	1977	D	37,795	739' 10"	78' 01"	48' 05"
	Built: Collingwood Shipyards, Collingwood; ON, rebuilt with new forebody in '01 at Port Weller Drydocks							
	(Stern section: Louis R. Desmarais '77-'01)							
	CSL Niagara	SU	1972	D	37,694	739' 10"	78' 01"	48' 05"
	Built: Collingwood Shipyards, Collingwood, ON; rebuilt with a new forebody in '99 at Port Weller Drydocks							
	(Stern section: J. W. McGiffin '72-'99)							
	CSL Tadoussac	SU	1969	D	30,051	730' 00"	78' 00"	42' 00"
	Built: Collingwood Shipyards, Collingwood, ON; rebuilt with new midbody, widened by 3' in '01							
	(Tadoussac {2} '69-'01)							
	Frontenac {5}	SU	1968	D	26,822	729' 07"	75' 03"	39' 08"
	Built: Davie Shipbuilding Co., Lauzon, QC; converted to a self-unloader in '73							

from the tug *William Hoey* in the Detroit River. *(Mike Nicholls)*

Fleet #.	Fleet Name Vessel Name	Type of Vessel	Year Built	Type of Engine	Cargo Cap. or Gross*	Overall Length	Breadth	Depth or Draft*
	Halifax	SU	1963	T	29,283	730' 02"	75' 00"	39' 03"
	Built: Davie Shipbuilding Co., Lauzon, QC; converted to a self-unloader, deepened 6' in '80							
	(Frankcliffe Hall {2} '63-'88)							
	Nanticoke	SU	1980	D	35,123	729' 10"	75' 08"	46' 06"
	Built: Collingwood Shipyards, Collingwood, ON							
	Pineglen {2}	BC	1985	D	33,197	736' 07"	75' 10"	42' 00"
	Built: Collingwood Shipyards, Collingwood, ON (Paterson '85-'02)							
	Rt. Hon. Paul J. Martin	SU	1973	D	37,694	739' 10"	78' 01"	48' 05"
	Built: Collingwood Shipyards, Collingwood, ON; rebuilt with a new forebody in '00 at Port Weller Drydocks							
	(Stern section: H. M. Griffith '73-'00)							
	Spruceglen {2}	BC	1983	D	33,824	730' 01"	75' 09"	48' 00"
	Built: Govan Shipyards, Glasgow, Scotland							
	(Selkirk Settler '83-'91, Federal St. Louis '91-'91, Federal Fraser {2} '91-2001, Fraser '01-'02)							

C-3   CANADIAN COAST GUARD (MINISTER OF FISHERIES AND OCEANS), OTTAWA, ON

CENTRAL AND ARCTIC REGION, SARNIA, ON

	Cape Discovery	SR	2004	D	34*	47' 09"	14' 00"	4' 05"
	Cape Hurd	SR	1982	D	55*	70' 10"	18' 00"	8' 09"
	(CG 126 '82-'85)							
	Cape Dundas	SR	2004	D	39*	47' 09"	14' 00"	4' 05"
	Cape Storm	SR	1999	D	34*	47' 09"	14' 00"	4' 05"
	Caribou Isle	BT	1985	D	92*	75' 06"	19' 08"	7' 04"
	Cove Isle	BT	1980	D	92*	65' 07"	19' 08"	7' 04"
	Griffon	IB	1970	D	2,212*	234' 00"	49' 00"	21' 06"
	Built: Davie Shipbuilding Co., Lauzon, QC							
	Gull Isle	BT	1980	D	80*	65' 07"	19' 08"	7' 04"
	Limnos	RV	1968	D	460*	147' 00"	32' 00"	12' 00"
	Samuel Risley	IB	1985	D	1,988*	228' 09"	47' 01"	21' 09"
	Built: Vito Steel Boat & Barge Construction Ltd., Delta, BC							
	Shark	RV	1971	D	30*	52' 06"	14' 09"	7' 03"
	Simcoe	BT	1962	D	961*	179' 01"	38' 00"	15' 06"
	Built: Canadian Vickers, Montreal, QC							
	Thunder Cape	SR	2000	D	34*	47' 09"	14' 00"	4' 05"

LAURENTIAN REGION, QUEBEC, QC (Vessels over 100' only have been listed)

	Amundsen	RV	1978	D	5,910*	295' 09"	63' 09"	31' 04"
	(Sir John Franklin '78-'03)							
	Des Groseilliers	IB	1983	D	5,910*	322' 07"	64' 00"	35' 06"
	F. C. G. Smith	SV	1985	D	439*	114' 02"	45' 11"	11' 02"
	George R. Pearkes	IB	1986	D	3,809*	272' 04"	53' 02"	25' 02"
	Louisbourg	RV	1977	D	295*	124' 00"	26' 11"	11' 06"
	Martha L. Black	IB	1986	D	3,818*	272' 04"	53' 02"	25' 02"
	Pierre Radisson	IB	1978	D	5,910*	322' 00"	62' 10"	35' 06"
	Tracy	BT	1968	D	963*	181' 01"	38' 00"	16' 00"

C-4   CELEST BAY TIMBER & MARINE, DULUTH, MN

	Barbara Wing	TW	1942	D	11*	36' 00"	9' 08"	3' 05"
	(Blake '42-'62, John V. II '62-'06)							
	Essayons	TB	1908	R	117*	85' 06"	21' 02"	11' 09"

C-5   CEMBA MOTORSHIPS LTD., PELEE ISLAND, ON

	Cemba	TK	1960	D	17*	50' 00"	15' 06"	7' 06"

C-6   CENTRAL MARINE LOGISTICS INC., GRIFFITH, IN

	Edward L. Ryerson	BC	1960	T	27,500	730' 00"	75' 00"	39' 00"
	Built: Manitowoc Shipbuilding Inc., Manitowoc, WI							
	Joseph L. Block	SU	1976	D	37,200	728' 00"	78' 00"	45' 00"
	Built: Bay Shipbuilding Co., Sturgeon Bay, WI							
	Wilfred Sykes	SU	1949	T	21,500	678' 00"	70' 00"	37' 00"
	Built: American Shipbuilding Co., Lorain, OH; converted to a self-unloader in '75							

Fleet #.	Fleet Name Vessel Name	Type of Vessel	Year Built	Type of Engine	Cargo Cap. or Gross*	Overall Length	Breadth	Depth or Draft*
C-7	**CHAMPION'S AUTO FERRY INC., ALGONAC, MI**							
	Champion {1}	CF	1941	D	65*	65' 00"	29' 00"	8' 06"
	Middle Channel	CF	1997	D	97*	79' 00"	31' 00"	8' 03"
	North Channel	CF	1967	D	67*	75' 00"	30' 00"	8' 00"
	South Channel	CF	1973	D	94*	79' 00"	31' 00"	8' 03"
C-8	**CHARLEVOIX COUNTY TRANSPORTATION AUTHORITY, CHARLEVOIX, MI**							
	Charlevoix {1}	CF	1926	D	43*	50' 00"	32' 00"	3' 09"
C-9	**CHERYL STONE, PICTON, ON**							
	Halton	TB	1942	D	15*	42' 07"	14' 09"	5' 08"
C-10	**CHICAGO FIRE DEPARTMENT, CHICAGO, IL**							
	Victor L. Schlaeger	FB	1949	D	350*	92' 06"	24' 00"	11' 00"
C-11	**CHICAGO FROM THE LAKE LTD., CHICAGO, IL**							
	Fort Dearborn	ES	1985	D	72*	64' 10"	22' 00"	7' 04"
	Marquette {6}	ES	1957	D	29*	50' 07"	15' 00"	4' 00"
C-12	**CHICAGO WATER PUMPING STATION, CHICAGO, IL**							
	James J. Versluis	TB	1957	D	126*	83' 00"	22' 00"	11' 02"
C-13	**CITY OF KEWAUNEE, KEWAUNEE, WI**							
	Ludington	MU	1943	D	249*	115' 00"	26' 00"	13' 08"
	Former U.S. Army Corps of Engineers tug is open to the public as a marine museum at Kewaunee, WI *(Major Wilbur F. Browder [LT-4] '43-'47)*							
C-14	**CLAYTON FIRE DEPARTMENT, CLAYTON, NY**							
	Last Chance	FB	2003	D		36' 00"	13' 00"	2' 04"
C-15	**CLEVELAND FIRE DEPARTMENT, CLEVELAND, OH**							
	Anthony J. Celebrezze	FB	1961	D	42*	66' 00"	17' 00"	5' 00"
C-16	**CLUB CANAMAC CRUISES, TORONTO, ON**							
	Aurora Borealis	ES	1983	D	277*	101' 00"	24' 00"	6' 00"
	Carolina Borealis	ES	1943	D	182*	84' 06"	20' 00"	10' 04"
	Rebuilt from a tug in '02 (HMCS Glenmont [W-27] '43-'45, Glenmont '43-'02)							
	Jaguar II	ES	1968	D	142*	95' 03"	20' 00"	9' 00"
	(Jaguar '68-'86)							
	Stella Borealis	ES	1989	D	356*	118' 00"	26' 00"	7' 00"
C-17	**COLUMBIA YACHT CLUB, CHICAGO, IL**							
	Abegweit	CF	1947	D	6,694*	372' 06"	61' 00"	24' 09"
	Former CN Marine Inc. vessel last operated in 1981; in use as a private, floating clubhouse in Chicago, IL *(Abegweit '47- 81, Abby '81-'97)*							
C-18	**COOPER MARINE LTD., SELKIRK, ON**							
	J. W. Cooper	PB	1984	D	25*	48' 00"	14' 07"	5' 00"
	Juleen I	PB	1972	D	23*	46' 00"	14' 01"	4' 05"
	Lady Kim	PB	1974	D	20*	44' 00"	13' 00"	4' 00"
	Mrs. C.	PB	2006	D	26*	50' 00"	14' 05"	4' 05"
	Stacey Dawn	TB	1993	D	14*	35' 09"	17' 04"	3' 05"
C-19	**CORPORATION OF THE TOWNSHIP OF FRONTENAC ISLANDS, WOLFE ISLAND, ON**							
	Howe Islander	CF	1946	D	13*	53' 00"	12' 00"	3' 00"
	Simcoe Islander	PF	1964	D	24*	47' 09"	18' 00"	3' 06"
C-20	**CROISIERES AML INC., QUEBEC, QC**							
	Cavalier des Mers	ES	1974	D	161*	91' 08"	21' 03"	8' 05"
	(Marine Sprinter '74-'84)							
	Cavalier Maxim	ES	1962	D	752*	191' 02"	42' 00"	11' 07"
	(Osborne Castle '62-'78, Le Gobelet D' Argent '78-'88, Gobelet D' Argent '88-'89, Le Maxim '89-'93)							
	Cavalier Royal	ES	1971	D	283*	125' 00"	24' 00"	5' 00"

Fleet #.	Fleet Name Vessel Name	Type of Vessel	Year Built	Type of Engine	Cargo Cap. or Gross*	Overall Length	Breadth	Depth or Draft*
	Grand Fleuve	ES	1987	D	499*	145′ 00″	30′ 00″	5′ 06″
	Louis Jolliet	ES	1938	R	2,436*	170′ 01″	70′ 00″	17′ 00″
	Transit	ES	1992	D	102*	66′ 00″	22′ 00″	2′ 08″
C-21	**CROISIERES M/S JACQUES-CARTIER, TROIS-RIVIERES, QC**							
	Jacques-Cartier	ES	1924	D	457*	135′ 00″	35′ 00″	10′ 00″
	Le Draveur	ES	1992	D	79*	58′ 07″	22′ 00″	5′ 24″
C-22	**CROISIERES RICHELIEU INC., SAINT-JEAN-SUR-RICHELIEU, QC**							
	Fort Saint Jean II	ES	1967	D	109*	62′ 09″	19′ 10″	7′ 08″
	(Miss Gananoque '67-'77)							
	Le Survenant III	ES	1974	D	105*	65′ 00″	13′ 00″	5′ 00″
C-23	**C.S. POWELL CHARTERS LTD., SIMCOE, ON**							
	C.S. Powell	PA	1928	D	20*	50′ 06″	18′ 08″	3′ 04″
D-1	**D. K. CONSTRUCTION INC., HOLLAND, MI**							
	Haskell	TB	1936	D	19*	40′ 00″	10′ 00″	4′ 06″
D-2	**DALE T. DEAN – WALPOLE-ALGONAC FERRY LINE, PORT LAMBTON, ON**							
	City of Algonac	CF	1990	D	82*	62′ 06″	27′ 09″	5′ 09″
	Walpole Islander	CF	1986	D	72*	54′ 05″	27′ 09″	6′ 03″
D-3	**DAN MINOR & SONS INC., PORT COLBORNE, ON**							
	Andrea Marie I	TB	1963	D	87*	75′ 02″	24′ 07″	7′ 03″
	Susan Michelle	TB	1995	D	89*	79′ 10″	20′ 11″	6′ 02″
	Welland	TB	1954	D	94*	86′ 00″	20′ 00″	8′ 00″
D-4	**DEAN CONSTRUCTION CO. LTD., BELLE RIVER, ON**							
	Annie M. Dean	TB	1981	D	58*	50′ 00″	19′ 00″	5′ 00″
	Bobby Bowes	TB	1944	D	11*	37′ 04″	10′ 02″	3′ 06″
	Canadian Jubilee	DR	1978	D	896*	149′ 09″	56′ 01″	11′ 01″
	Neptune III	TB	1939	D	23*	53′ 10″	15′ 06″	5′ 00″
D-5	**DETROIT CITY FIRE DEPARTMENT, DETROIT, MI**							
	Curtis Randolph	FB	1979	D	85*	77′ 10″	21′ 06″	9′ 03″
D-6	**DETROIT PRINCESS LLC, DETROIT, MI**							
	Detroit Princess	PA	1993	D	1,430*	190′ 09″	60′ 00″	11′ 01″
	(Players Riverboat Casino II '93-'04)							
D-7	**DIAMOND JACK'S RIVER TOURS, DETROIT, MI**							
	Diamond Belle	ES	1958	D	93*	93′ 06″	25′ 10″	10′ 01″
	(Mackinac Islander {2} '58-'90, Sir Richard '90-'91)							
	Diamond Jack	ES	1955	D	82*	72′ 00″	25′ 00″	8′ 00″
	(Emerald Isle {1} '55-'91)							
	Diamond Queen	ES	1956	D	94*	92′ 00″	25′ 00″	10′ 00″
	(Mohawk '56-'96)							
D-8	**DOOR COUNTY CRUISES LLC, STURGEON BAY, WI**							
	Fred A. Busse	ES	1937	D	99*	92′ 00″	22′ 04″	11′ 00″
D-9	**DOOR COUNTY MARITIME MUSEUM & LIGHTHOUSE PRESERVATION SOCIETY INC., STURGEON BAY, WI**							
	John Purves	MU	1919	D	436*	150′ 00″	27′ 06″	16′ 08″
	Former Roen/Andrie Inc. tug is being refurbished as a museum display (Butterfield '19-'42, LT-145 '42-'57)							
D-10	**DRAGAGE VERREAULT INC., LES MECHINS, QC**							
	I.V. No. 8	DR	1967	B	348*	96′ 03″	36′ 00″	8′ 05″
	I.V. No. 9	GC	1936	D	148*	106′ 08″	23′ 10″	8′ 05″
	(A.C.D. '36-'69)							
	I.V. No. 10	GC	1936	D	320*	110′ 00″	23′ 10″	8′ 05″
	(G.T.D. '36-'69)							

Fleet #.	Fleet Name / Vessel Name	Type of Vessel	Year Built	Type of Engine	Cargo Cap. or Gross*	Overall Length	Breadth	Depth or Draft*
	I.V. No. 11	GC	1935	D	144*	106' 08"	24' 00"	8' 00"
	(Donpaco '35-'72)							
	I.V. No. 13	GC	1936	D	148*	106' 08"	24' 00"	8' 00"
	(Newscarrier '36-'72)							
	I.V. No. 14	GC	1937	D	229*	113' 00"	22' 05"	8' 06"
	(Kermic '37-'74)							
	Port Mechins	DR	1949	R	1,321*	200' 00"	40' 02"	18' 00"
	(Haffar '49-'88, Lockeport '88-'92)							
	Rosaire	DR	1952	B	714*	137' 07"	44' 06"	9' 01"
D-11	**DUC D' ORLEANS CRUISE BOAT, CORUNNA, ON**							
	Duc d' Orleans II	ES	1987	D	120*	71' 03		7' 07"
	(Spirit of Newport '87-'06)							
D-12	**DULUTH ENTERTAINMENT AND CONVENTION CENTER, DULUTH, MN**							
	Lake Superior	MU	1943	D	248*	114' 00"	26' 00"	13' 08"
	Former U.S. Army Corps of Engineers tug last operated in 1995; open to the public at Duluth, MN							
	(Major Emil H. Block '43-'47, U. S. Army LT-18 '47-'50)							
	Sundew	MU	1944	DE	1,025*	180' 00"	37' 00"	17' 04"
	Built: Marine Ironworks and Shipbuilding Corp., Duluth, MN; former U.S. Coast Guard cutter WLB-404 was decommissioned in 2004; open to the public at Duluth, MN							
	William A. Irvin	MU	1938	T	14,050	610' 09"	60' 00"	32' 06"
	Built: American Shipbuilding Co., Lorain, OH; former United States Steel Corp. bulk carrier last operated Dec. 16, 1978; open to the public at Duluth, MN							
D-13	**DULUTH TIMBER CO., DULUTH, MN**							
	Faith	CS	1906	B	705*	120' 00"	38' 00"	10' 03"
	Dona	GR	1929	Gas		38' 00	10' 00"	4' 00"
D-14	**DUROCHER MARINE, DIVISION OF KOKOSING CONSTRUCTION CO., CHEBOYGAN, MI**							
	Champion {3}	TB	1974	D	125*	75' 00"	24' 00"	9' 06"
	General {2}	TB	1954	D	119*	71' 00"	19' 06"	9' 06"
	(U. S. Army ST-1999 '54-'61, USCOE Au Sable '61-'84, Challenger {3} '84-'87)							
	Joe Van	TB	1955	D	32*	57' 09"	16' 06"	9' 00"
	Valerie B.	TB	1981	D	101*	65' 00"	24' 06"	10' 00"
	(Mr. Joshua '81-?, Michael Van ?-'03)							
	Nancy Anne	TB	1969	D	73*	60' 00"	20' 00"	6' 00"
	Ray Durocher	TB	1943	D	20*	45' 06"	12' 05"	7' 06"
E-1	**EASTERN CANADA RESPONSE CORP. LTD., OTTAWA, ON**							
	Dover Light	EV	1968	B	7,870	146' 05"	50' 00"	13' 07"
	(Jackson Purchase '68-'83, Eliza S-1877 '83-'86)							
	S.M.T.B. No. 7	EV	1969	B	7,502	150' 00"	33' 00"	14' 00"
E-2	**EASTERN UPPER PENINSULA TRANSIT AUTHORITY, SAULT STE. MARIE, MI**							
	Drummond Islander III	CF	1989	D	96*	108' 00"	37' 00"	12' 03"
	Drummond Islander IV	CF	2000	D	377*	148' 00"	40' 00"	12' 00"
	Neebish Islander II	CF	1946	D	90*	89' 00"	29' 06"	6' 09"
	(Sugar Islander '46-'95)							
	Sugar Islander II	CF	1995	D	223*	114' 00"	40' 00"	10' 00"
E-3	**EDELWEISS CRUISE DINING, MILWAUKEE, WI**							
	Edelweiss I	ES	1988	D	87*	64' 08"	18' 00"	6' 00"
	Edelweiss II	ES	1989	D	89*	73' 08"	20' 00"	7' 00"
E-4	**EDWARD E. GILLEN CO., MILWAUKEE, WI**							
	Andrea J.	PA	1958	D	24*	39' 00"	11' 00"	6' 05"
	(Kayla D. Kadinger '58-'06)							
	Andrew J.	TB	1950	D	25*	47' 00"	15' 07"	8' 00"
	Edith J.	TB	1962	D	19*	45' 03"	13' 00"	8' 00"
	Edward E. Gillen III	TB	1988	D	95*	75' 00"	26' 00"	9' 06"

KEEWATIN LOGS 100

Vessel Spotlight

Before the *Titanic*, before World War I, before any of us were born, there was the *Keewatin*. That she survives today to celebrate the 100th anniversary of her launch is a tribute to Douglas, Mich.-area businessman R.J. Peterson, who stepped in in 1967 to save her from the scrapyard, and his wife, Diane, who presides over the Edwardian-era vessel and keeps her shipshape.

The majestic, 350-foot *Keewatin* (her name means "Blizzard of the North" in the language of the Cree Indians) was built in Scotland for the Canadian Pacific Railway. Delivered to the Great Lakes in 1907, this lovely steamer was destined to make history. For over 50 years, she served as a railway link, connecting Georgian Bay and upper Lake Superior railheads. She is the last of the classic Great Lakes passenger steamships still afloat.

A tour of the *Kee* transports one back in time to the bygone era of elegant passenger steamship travel. It's easy to imagine passengers enjoying the luxurious first-class staterooms, the Flower Well Lounge and the dining room, with its fine china and gracious service.

An on-board marine museum also explores the history of the *Keewatin*, her passengers and the crews who sailed her over the years.

For details about the *Keewatin's* anniversary season, visit www.keewatinmaritimemuseum.com.

Keewatin in the 1960s.
(Tom Manse)

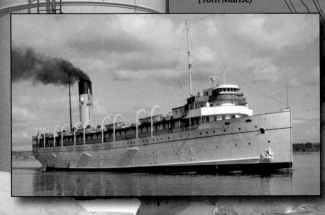

Fleet #.	Fleet Name / Vessel Name	Type of Vessel	Year Built	Type of Engine	Cargo Cap. or Gross*	Overall Length	Breadth	Depth or Draft*
	Jullane J.	TB	1969	D	98*	65' 06"	22' 00"	8' 06
	(N. F. Candies ?-?, Connie Guidry ?-'89, David J. Kadinger '89-'06)							
	Kristin J.	TB	1963	D	60*	52' 06"	19' 01"	7' 04"
	(Jason A. Kadinger '63-'06)							
E-5	**EGAN MARINE CORP., LEMONT, IL**							
	Alice E.	TB	1950	D	183*	100' 00"	26' 00"	9' 00"
	(L. L. Wright '50-'55, Martin '55-'74, Mary Ann '74-'77, Judi C. '77-'94)							
	Brandon E.	TB	1945	D	21*	45' 00"	12' 08"	6' 00"
	(ST-929 '45-'45, Heron '46-'62, Heidi '62-'64, James Edward '64-?, David E. ?-'96)							
	Daniel E.	TW	1967	D	70*	70' 00"	18' 06"	6' 08"
	(Foster M. Ford '67-'84)							
	David E.	TW	1952	D	236*	95' 00"	30' 00"	8' 06"
	(Irving Crown '52-'01)							
	Denise E.	TB	1912	D	138*	80' 07"	21' 06"	10' 03"
	(Caspian '12-'48, Trojan '48-'81, Cherokee {1} '81-'93)							
	Derek E.	TB	1907	D	85*	72' 06"	20' 01"	10' 06"
	(John Kelderhouse '07-'13, Sachem '13-'90)							
	Lisa E.	TB	1963	D	75*	65' 06"	20' 00"	8' 06"
	(Dixie Scout '63-'90)							
	Robin E.	TB	1889	D	123*	84' 09"	19' 00"	9' 00"
	(Asa W. Hughes 1889-'13, Triton {1} '13-'81, Navajo {2} '81-'92)							
E-6	**EMPIRE CRUISE LINES U. S. A., ST. THOMAS, ON**							
	Marine Star	PA	1945	T	12,773*	520' 00"	71' 06"	43' 06"
	Last operated in 1962; laid up at Lackawanna, NY (USNS Marine Star '45-'55, Aquarama '55-'94)							
E-7	**EMPRESS OF CANADA ENTERPRISES LTD., TORONTO, ON**							
	Empress of Canada	ES	1980	D	399*	116' 00"	28' 00"	6' 06"
	(Island Queen V {2} '80-'89)							
E-8	**ENTREPRISE MARISSA INC., BEAUPORT, QC**							
	Cape Crow	TB	1951	D	14*	37' 08"	10' 04"	4' 09"
	Soulanges	TB	1905	D	72*	77' 00"	17' 00"	8' 00"
	(Dandy '05-'39)							
E-9	**EQUIPMENTS VERREAULT INC., LES MECHINS, QC**							
	Epinette II	TB	1965	D	75*	61' 03"	20' 01"	8' 05"
E-10	**ERICKSON MARINE FREIGHT INC., BAYFIELD, WI**							
	Outer Island	PK	1942	D	136*	103' 05"	32' 00"	5' 00"
	(LCT 203 '42-'46, Pluswood '46-'53)							
E-11	**ERIE ISLANDS PETROLEUM INC., PUT-IN-BAY, OH**							
	Cantankerus	TK	1955	D	43*	53' 02"	14' 00"	7' 00"
E-12	**ERIE MARITIME MUSEUM, ERIE, PA**							
	Niagara	MU/2B	1988	W	295*	198' 00"	32' 00"	10' 06"
	Reconstruction of Oliver Hazard Perry's U. S. Navy brigantine from the War of 1812							
E-13	**ERIE SAND AND GRAVEL CO., ERIE, PA**							
	J. S. St. John	SC	1945	D	680	174' 00"	32' 02"	15' 00"
	(USS YO-178 '45-'51, Lake Edward '51-'67)							
E-14	**ESCANABA & LAKE SUPERIOR RAILROAD CO., WELLS, MI**							
	Pere Marquette 10	TF	1945	B	27 rail cars	400' 00"	53' 00"	22' 00"
	Last operated Oct. 7, 1994; laid up at Toledo, OH							
E-15	**ESSROC CANADA INC., NORTH YORK, ON**							
	(VESSELS MANAGED BY UPPER LAKES GROUP INC.)							
	Metis	CC	1956	B	5,800	331' 00"	43' 09"	26' 00"
	Built: Davie Shipbuilding Ltd., Lauzon, QC; converted to a self-unloading cement barge in '91							

Fleet #.	Fleet Name / Vessel Name	Type of Vessel	Year Built	Type of Engine	Cargo Cap. or Gross*	Overall Length	Breadth	Depth or Draft*
	Stephen B. Roman	CC	1965	D	7,600	488' 09"	56' 00"	35' 06"

Built: Davie Shipbuilding Ltd., Lauzon, QC; converted to a self-unloading cement carrier in '83 (Fort William '65-'83)

Fleet #.	Fleet Name / Vessel Name	Type of Vessel	Year Built	Type of Engine	Cargo Cap. or Gross*	Overall Length	Breadth	Depth or Draft*
F-1	**FAUST CORPORATION, GROSSE POINTE FARMS, MI**							
	Cormorant	TB	1991	D	10*	25' 02"	14' 00"	4' 06"
	Linnhurst	TB	1930	D	11*	37' 06"	10' 06"	4' 08"
F-2	**FEDERAL TERMINALS LTD., PORT CARTIER, QC**							
	Brochu	TT	1973	D	390*	100' 00"	36' 00"	14' 06"
	Vachon	TT	1973	D	390*	100' 00"	36' 00"	14' 06"
F-3	**FEDNAV LTD., MONTREAL, QUEBEC, CANADA**							
	CANARCTIC SHIPPING CO. LTD. - DIVISION OF FEDNAV LTD. (SEE ALSO SALTWATER FLEET IF-3)							
	Arctic	GC	1978	D	26,440	692' 04"	75' 05"	49' 05"

Built: Port Weller Drydocks, Port Weller, ON

Fleet #.	Fleet Name / Vessel Name	Type of Vessel	Year Built	Type of Engine	Cargo Cap. or Gross*	Overall Length	Breadth	Depth or Draft*
F-4	**FERRISS MARINE CONTRACTING CORP., DETROIT, MI**							
	Magnetic	TB	1925	D	30*	55' 00"	14' 00"	6' 06"

(Col. J.D. Graham '24-'65, Nicholson '65-'83)

	Norma B.	TB	1940	D	14*	43' 00"	15' 00"	4' 00"
F-5	**FITZ SUSTAINABLE FORESTRY MANAGEMENT LTD., MANITOWANING, ON**							
	B.J. & C.J.	TB	1952	G	12*	42' 04"	12' 00"	3' 05"
	Wyn Cooper	TB	1973	D	25*	48' 00"	13' 00"	4' 00"
F-6	**FRASER SHIPYARDS INC., SUPERIOR, WI**							
	Brenda L.	TO	1941	D	11*	36' 00"	10' 00"	3' 08"

(Harbour I '41-'58, Su-Joy III '58 -'78)

	Maxine Thompson	TB	1959	D	30*	47' 04"	13' 00"	6' 06"

(Susan A. Fraser '59-'78)

	Murray R.	TB	1946	D	17*	42' 10"	12' 00"	4' 07"
	Phil Milroy	TB	1957	D	41*	47' 11"	16' 08"	8' 04"

(Merchant of St. Marys '57-'60, Barney B. Barstow '57-'78)

Algoma Central's *Algocape* enters Lock 1 on the Welland Canal. *(Bill Bird)*

Fleet #.	Fleet Name / Vessel Name	Type of Vessel	Year Built	Type of Engine	Cargo Cap. or Gross*	Overall Length	Breadth	Depth or Draft*
	Reuben Johnson	TB	1912	D	71*	78' 00"	17' 00"	11' 00"
	(Buffalo {1} '12-'28, USCOE Churchill '28-'48, Buffalo {1} '48-'74, Todd Fraser '74-'78)							
	Todd L.	TB	1965	D	22*	42' 10"	12' 00"	5' 06"
	(Robert W. Fraser '65-'78)							
	Troy L. Johnson	TB	1959	D	24*	42' 08"	12' 00"	5' 05"
	Wally Kendzora	TB	1956	D	24*	43' 00"	12' 00"	5' 06"
G-1	**GABRIEL MARINE, ALGONAC, MI**							
	Elmer Dean	TB	1998	D	45*	68' 00"	16' 08"	6' 00"
G-2	**GAELIC TUG BOAT CO., DETROIT, MI**							
	Carolyn Hoey	TB	1951	D	146*	88' 06"	25' 06"	11' 00"
	(Atlas '51-'84, Susan Hoey {1} '84-'85, Atlas '85-'87)							
	Marysville	TK	1973	B	1,136*	200' 00"	50' 00"	12' 06"
	(N.M.S. No. 102 '73-'81)							
	Patricia Hoey {2}	TB	1949	D	146*	88' 06"	25' 06"	11' 00"
	(Propeller '49-'82, Bantry Bay '82-'91)							
	Shannon	TB	1944	D	145*	101' 00"	28' 00"	13' 00"
	(USS Connewango [YT / YTB / YTM-388] '44-'77)							
	William Hoey {2}	TB	1924	D	99*	85' 00"	21' 06"	10' 09"
	(Martha C. '24-'52, Langdon C. Hardwicke '52-'82, Wabash {2} '82-'93, Katie Ann {1} '93-'99)							
G-3	**GALCON MARINE LTD., TORONTO, ON**							
	Kenteau	TB	1937	D	15*	54' 07"	16' 04"	4' 02"
G-4	**GALLAGHER MARINE CONSTRUCTION CO. INC., ESCANABA, MI**							
	Bee Jay	TB	1939	D	19*	45' 00"	13' 00"	7' 00"
	Menasha	CS	1926	B	168*	94' 04"	20' 00"	5' 00"
G-5	**GANANOQUE BOAT LINE LTD., GANANOQUE, ON**							
	Thousand Islander	ES	1972	D	200*	96' 11"	22' 01"	5' 05"
	Thousand Islander II	ES	1973	D	200*	99' 00"	22' 01"	5' 00"
	Thousand Islander III	ES	1975	D	376*	118' 00"	28' 00"	6' 00"
	Thousand Islander IV	ES	1976	D	347*	110' 09"	28' 04"	10' 08"
	Thousand Islander V	ES	1979	D	246*	88' 00"	24' 00"	5' 00"
G-6	**GANNON UNIVERSITY, ERIE, PA**							
	Environaut	RV	1950	D	13*	36' 05"	12' 00"	5' 00"
G-7	**GARDINER MARINE, RICHARD'S LANDING, ON**							
	Joyce B. Gardiner	TB	1962	D	71*	72' 00"	19' 00"	12' 00"
	(Angus M. '62-'92, Omni Sorel '92-'02)							
	Opeongo	TB	1947	D	20*	50' 00"	13' 00"	6' 00"
G-8	**GEO. GRADEL CO., TOLEDO, OH**							
	Amber Jean	TB	1942	D	59*	61' 00"	18' 02"	8' 02"
	Clyde	DB	1922	B	704*	134' 00"	41' 00"	12' 00"
	John Francis	TB	1965	D	99*	75' 00"	22' 00"	9' 00"
	(Dad '65-'98, Creole Eagle '98-'03)							
	Josephine	TB	1957	D	103*	86' 09"	20' 06"	7' 09"
	(Wambrau '57-'87, Sea Diver II '87-'03)							
	Mighty Jake	TB	1969	D	15*	36' 00"	12' 03"	7' 03"
	Mighty Jessie	TB	1954	D	57*	61' 02"	18' 00"	7' 03"
	Mighty Jimmy	TB	1945	D	27*	56' 00"	15' 10"	7' 00"
	Mighty John III	TB	1962	D	24*	45' 00"	15' 00"	5' 10"
	(Niagara Queen '62-'99)							
	Moby Dick	DB	1952	B	835	121' 00"	33' 02"	10' 06"
	Pioneerland	TB	1943	D	53*	58' 00"	16' 08"	8' 00"
	Prairieland	TB	1955	D	35*	49' 02"	15' 02"	6' 00"
	Timberland	TB	1946	D	20*	41' 03"	13' 01"	7' 00"

Cement-carrying barge *Innovation*, pushed by *Samuel de Champlain*, seen from the Fort Gratiot lighthouse in Port Huron. *(Dick Wicklund)*

Fleet #.	Fleet Name / Vessel Name	Type of Vessel	Year Built	Type of Engine	Cargo Cap. or Gross*	Overall Length	Breadth	Depth or Draft*
G-9	**GOODTIME ISLAND CRUISES INC., SANDUSKY, OH**							
	Goodtime I	ES	1960	D	81*	111' 00"	29' 08"	9' 05"
G-10	**GOODTIME TRANSIT BOATS INC., CLEVELAND, OH**							
	Goodtime III	ES	1990	D	95*	161' 00"	40' 00"	11' 00"
G-11	**GRAMPA WOO EXCURSIONS, BEAVER BAY, MN**							
	Grampa Woo III	ES	1978	D	99*	95' 09"	21' 05"	7' 00"
	(Melissa Briley '78-'98)							
G-12	**GRAND PORTAGE – ISLE ROYALE TRANSPORTATION LINES, SUPERIOR, WI**							
	Voyageur II	ES	1970	D	40*	63' 00"	18' 00"	5' 00"
	Wenonah	ES	1960	D	91*	70' 07"	19' 04"	9' 07"
	(Jamaica '60-'64)							
G-13	**GRAND VALLEY STATE UNIVERSITY, ALLENDALE, MI – ANNIS WATER RESOURCES INSTITUTE**							
	D. J. Angus	RV	1986	D	16*	45' 00"	14' 00"	4' 00"
	W. G. Jackson	RV	1996	D	80*	64' 10"	20' 00"	5' 00"
G-14	**GRAVEL & LAKE SERVICES LTD., THUNDER BAY, ON**							
	Donald Mac	TB	1914	D	69*	71' 00"	17' 00"	10' 00"
	George N. Carleton	TB	1943	D	97*	82' 00"	21' 00"	11' 00"
	(HMCS Glenlea [W-25] '43-'45, Bansaga '45-'64)							
	Peninsula	TB	1944	D	261*	111' 00"	27' 00"	13' 00"
	(HMCS Norton [W-31] '44-'45, W.A.C. 1 '45-'46)							
	Robert John	TB	1945	D	98*	82' 00"	20' 01"	11' 00"
	(HMCS Gleneagle [W-40] '45-'46, Bansturdy '46-'65)							
	Wolf River	BC	1956	D	5,880	349' 02"	43' 07"	25' 04"
	Built: Port Weller Drydocks, Port Weller, ON; last operated in 998; laid up at Thunder Bay, ON							
	(Tecumseh {2} '56-'67, New York News {3} '67-'86, Stella Desgagnes '86-'93, Beam Beginner '94-'95)							
G-15	**GREAT LAKES CLIPPER PRESERVATION ASSOCIATION, MUSKEGON, MI**							
	Milwaukee Clipper	MU	1904	Q	4,272	361' 00"	45' 00"	28' 00"
	Built: American Ship Building Co., Cleveland, OH; rebuilt '40 Manitowoc Shipbuilding Co., Manitowoc, WI							
	Former Wisconsin & Michigan Steamship Co. passenger/auto carrier last operated in 1970; undergoing							
	restoration and open to the public at Muskegon, MI (Juniata '04-'41)							
G-16	**GREAT LAKES DOCK & MATERIALS LLC, MUSKEGON, MI**							
	Fischer Hayden	TB	1967	D	64*	54' 00"	22' 1"	7' 1"
	(Gloria G. Cheramie, Joyce P. Crosby)							
	Duluth	TB	1954	D	87*	70' 01"	19' 05"	9' 08"
	(U. S. Army ST-2015 '54-'62)							
	Sarah B	TB	1953	D	23*	45' 00"	13' 00"	7' 00"
	(ST-2161 '53-'63, Tawas Bay '63-'03)							
G-17	**GREAT LAKES ENVIRONMENTAL RESEARCH LABORATORY, MUSKEGON, MI**							
	Shenehon	SV	1952	D	90*	65' 00"	17' 00"	6' 00"
G-18	**GREAT LAKES FLEET INC. / KEY LAKES INC., DULUTH, MN (MANAGER)**							
	CANADIAN NATIONAL RAILWAY, MONTREAL, QC – OWNER							
	Arthur M. Anderson	SU	1952	T	25,300	767' 00"	70' 00"	36' 00"
	Built: American Shipbuilding Co., Lorain, OH; lengthened 120' in '75; converted to a self-unloader in '82							
	Cason J. Callaway	SU	1952	T	25,300	767' 00"	70' 00"	36' 00"
	Built: Great Lakes Engineering Works, River Rouge, MI; lengthened 120' in '74; converted to a self-unloader in '82							
	Edgar B. Speer	SU	1980	D	73,700	1,004' 00"	105' 00"	56' 00"
	Built: American Shipbuilding Co., Lorain, OH							
	Edwin H. Gott	SU	1979	D	74,100	1,004' 00"	105' 00"	56' 00"
	Built: Bay Shipbuilding Co., Sturgeon Bay, WI; converted from shuttle self-unloader to deck-mounted self-unloader in '96							
	John G. Munson {2}	SU	1952	T	25,550	768' 03"	72' 00"	36' 00"
	Built: Manitowoc Shipbuilding Inc., Manitowoc, WI; lengthened 102' in '76							

	Philip R. Clarke	SU	1952	T	25,300	767' 00"	70' 00"	36' 00"
	Built: American Shipbuilding Co., Lorain, OH; lengthened 120' in '74; converted to a self-unloader in '82							
	Presque Isle {2}	IT	1973	D	1,578*	153' 03"	54' 00"	31' 03"
	Built: Halter Marine Services, New Orleans, LA							
	Presque Isle {2}	SU	1973	B	57,500	974' 06"	104' 07"	46' 06"
	Built: Erie Marine Inc., Erie, PA							
	[ITB Presque Isle OA dimensions together]					1,000' 00"	104' 07"	46' 06"
	Roger Blough	SU	1972	D	43,900	858' 00"	105' 00"	41' 06"
	Built: American Shipbuilding Co., Lorain, OH							
G-19	**THE GREAT LAKES GROUP, CLEVELAND, OH**							
	THE GREAT LAKES TOWING CO., CLEVELAND, OH – DIVISION OF THE GREAT LAKES GROUP							
	Alabama {2}	TB	1916	DE	98*	81' 00"	21' 03"	12' 05"
	Arizona	TB	1931	D	98*	84' 04"	20' 00"	12' 06"
	Arkansas {2}	TB	1909	D	98*	81' 00"	21' 03"	12' 05"
	(Yale '09-'48)							
	California	TB	1926	DE	98*	81' 00"	20' 00"	12' 06"
	Colorado	TB	1928	D	98*	84' 04"	20' 00"	12' 06"
	Delaware {4}	TB	1924	DE	98*	81' 00"	20' 00"	12' 06"
	Florida	TB	1926	D	99*	81' 00"	20' 00"	12' 06"
	(Florida '26-'83, Pinellas '83-'84)							
	Idaho	TB	1931	DE	98*	84' 00"	20' 00"	12' 06"
	Illinois {2}	TB	1914	D	99*	81' 00"	20' 00"	12' 06"
	Indiana	TB	1911	DE	97*	81' 00"	20' 00"	12' 06"
	Iowa	TB	1915	D	98*	81' 00"	20' 00"	12' 06"
	Kansas	TB	1927	D	98*	81' 00"	20' 00"	12' 06"
	Kentucky {2}	TB	1929	D	98*	84' 04"	20' 00"	12' 06"
	Louisiana	TB	1917	D	98*	81' 00"	20' 00"	12' 06"
	Maine {1}	TB	1921	D	96*	81' 00"	20' 00"	12' 06"
	(Maine {1} '21-'82, Saipan '82-'83, Hillsboro '83-'84)							
	Massachusetts	TB	1928	D	98*	84' 04"	20' 00"	12' 06"
	Milwaukee	DB	1924	B	1,095	172' 00"	40' 00"	11' 06"
	Minnesota {1}	TB	1911	D	98*	81' 00"	20' 00"	12' 06"
	Mississippi	TB	1916	DE	98*	81' 00"	20' 00"	12' 06"
	Missouri {2}	TB	1927	D	149*	88' 04"	24' 06"	12' 03"
	(Rogers City {1} '27-'56, Dolomite {1} '56-'81, Chippewa {7} '81-'90)							
	Montana	TB	1929	DE	98*	84' 04"	20' 00"	12' 06"
	Nebraska	TB	1929	D	98*	84' 04"	20' 00"	12' 06"
	New Jersey	TB	1924	D	98*	81' 00"	20' 00"	12' 06"
	(New Jersey '24-'52, Petco-21 '52-'53)							
	New York	TB	1913	D	98*	81' 00"	20' 00"	12' 06"
	North Carolina {2}	TB	1952	DE	145*	87' 09"	24' 01"	10' 07"
	(Limestone '52-'83, Wicklow '83-'90)							
	North Dakota	TB	1910	D	97*	81' 00"	20' 00"	12' 06"
	(John M. Truby '10-'38)							
	Ohio {3}	TB	1903	D	194*	118' 00"	24' 00"	13' 06"
	(M.F.D. No. 15 '03-'52, Laurence C. Turner '52-'73)							
	Oklahoma	TB	1913	DE	97*	81' 00"	20' 00"	12' 06"
	(T. C. Lutz {2} '13-'34)							
	Pennsylvania {3}	TB	1911	D	98*	81' 00"	20' 00"	12' 06"
	Rhode Island	TB	1930	D	98*	84' 04"	20' 00"	12' 06"
	South Carolina	TB	1925	D	102*	86' 00"	21' 00"	11' 00"
	(Welcome {2} '25-'53, Joseph H. Callan '53-'72, South Carolina '72-'82, Tulagi '82-'83)							
	Superior {3}	TB	1912	D	147*	97' 00"	22' 00"	12' 00"
	(Richard Fitzgerald '12-'46)							
	Tennessee	TB	1917	D	98*	81' 00"	20' 00"	12' 06"
	Texas	TB	1916	DE	97*	81' 00"	20' 00"	12' 06"
	Vermont	TB	1914	D	98*	81' 00"	20' 00"	12' 06"

Fleet #.	Fleet Name Vessel Name	Type of Vessel	Year Built	Type of Engine	Cargo Cap. or Gross*	Overall Length	Breadth	Depth or Draft*
	Virginia {2}	TB	1914	DE	97*	81' 00"	20' 00"	12' 06"
	Washington {1}	TB	1925	DE	97*	81' 00"	20' 00"	12' 06"
	Wisconsin {4}	TB	1897	D	105*	90' 03"	21' 00"	12' 03"
	(America {3} 1897-1882, Midway '82-'83)							
	Wyoming	TB	1929	D	104*	84' 04"	20' 00"	12' 06"

G-20 GREAT LAKES HISTORICAL SOCIETY, CLEVELAND, OH

	Fleet Name Vessel Name	Type of Vessel	Year Built	Type of Engine	Cargo Cap. or Gross*	Overall Length	Breadth	Depth or Draft*
	Cod	MU	1943	D/V	1,525*	311' 08"	27' 02"	33' 09"
	Built: Electric Boat Co., Groton, CT; former U.S. Navy "Albacore (Gato)" class submarine IXSS-224 open to the public at Cleveland, OH							

G-21 GREAT LAKES MARITIME ACADEMY – NORTHWESTERN MICHIGAN COLLEGE, TRAVERSE CITY, MI

	Anchor Bay	TV	1953	D	23*	45' 00"	13' 00"	7' 00"
	Northwestern {2}	TV	1969	D	12*	55' 00"	15' 00"	6' 06"
	(USCOE North Central '69-'98)							
	State of Michigan	TV	1986	D	1,914*	224' 00"	43' 00"	20' 00"
	(USS Persistent '86-'98, USCG Persistent '98-'02)							

G-22 GREAT LAKES NAVAL MEMORIAL AND MUSEUM, MUSKEGON, MI

	LST-393	MU	1942	D	2,100	328' 00"	50' 00"	25' 00"
	Built: Newport News Shipbuilding and Dry Dock Co., at Newport News, VA; former U.S. Navy / Wisconsin & Michigan Steamship Co. vessel last operated July 31, 1973; on display at Muskegon, MI							
	(USS LST-393 '42-'47, Highway 16 '47-'99)							
	McLane	MU	1927	D	289*	125' 00"	24' 00"	12' 06"
	Built: American Brown Boveri Electric Co., Camden, NJ; former U.S. Coast Guard "Buck & A Quarter" class medium endurance cutter; on display at Muskegon, MI							
	(USCGC McLane [WSC / WMEC-146] '27-'70, Manatra II '70-'93)							
	Silversides	MU	1941	D/V	1,526*	311' 08"	27' 03"	33' 09"
	Built: Mare Island Naval Yard, Vallejo, CA; former U.S. Navy "Albacore (Gato)" class submarine AGSS-236; open to the public at Muskegon, MI							

G-23 GREAT LAKES SCHOONER CO., TORONTO, ON

	Challenge	ES	1980	W/D	76*	96' 00"	16' 06"	8' 00"
	Kajama	ES	1930	W/D	263*	128' 09"	22' 09"	11' 08"

G-24 GREAT LAKES SHIPWRECK HISTORICAL SOCIETY, SAULT STE. MARIE, MI

	David Boyd	RV	1982	D	26*	47' 00"	17' 00"	3' 00"*

G-25 GROUPE C.T.M.A. (NAVIGATION MADELEINE INC.), CAP-AUX-MEULES, QC

	C.T.M.A. Vacancier	PA/RR	1973	D	11,481*	388' 04"	70' 02"	43' 06"
	(Aurella '80-'82, Saint Patrick II '82-'98, Egnatia II '98-'00, Ville de Sete '00-'01, City of Cork '01-'02)							
	C.T.M.A. Voyageur	PA/RR	1972	D	4,526*	327' 09"	52' 06"	31' 07"
	(Anderida)							

H-1 H. LEE WHITE MARINE MUSEUM, OSWEGO, NY

	LT-5	MU	1943	D	305*	115' 00"	28' 00"	14' 00"
	Former U.S. Army Corps of Engineers tug last operated in 1989; open to the public at Oswego, NY							
	(Major Elisha K. Henson '43-'47, U.S. Army LT-5 '47-'47, Nash '47-'95)							

H-2 HAMILTON HARBOUR QUEEN CRUISES, HAMILTON, ON

	Hamilton Harbour Queen	ES	1956	D	252*	100' 00"	22' 00"	4' 05"
	(Johnny B. '56-'89, Garden City '89-'00, Harbour Princess '00-'05)							

H-3 HAMILTON PORT AUTHORITY, HAMILTON, ON

	Judge McCombs	TB	1948	D	10*	36' 00"	10' 03"	4' 00"
	(Bronte Sue '48-'50)							

H-4 HANNAH MARINE CORP., LEMONT, IL

	Daryl C. Hannah {2}	TW	1956	D	268*	102' 00"	28' 00"	8' 00"
	(Cindy Jo '56-'66, Katherine L. '66-'93)							
	David E.	TB	1944	D	602*	149' 00"	33' 00"	16' 00"
	(LT 815 '44-'64, Henry Foss '64-'84, Kristin Lee '84-'93, Kristin Lee Hannah '93-'00)							
	Donald C. Hannah	TB	1962	D	191*	91' 00"	29' 00"	11' 06"

PORT HURON AT 150

Historic Spotlight

A lot of water has gone under the bridge since Port Huron was founded 150 years ago. Throughout its history, the St. Clair River and the marine traffic that passing Port Huron's shores have been an integral part of the community.

Although sesquicentennial celebrations this year commemorate the past, Port Huron's waterfront is looking toward the future. The retired U.S. Coast Guard lightship *Huron* is open for tours, as is the former cutter *Bramble* and the Fort Gratiot Lighthouse. Parks and a riverwalk occupy one-time industrial property. Desmond Landing, a mile-long waterfront redevelopment project by Acheson Ventures, is reclaiming land for public use on the Port Huron waterfront from the Black River south. Acheson has also renovated the Seaway Terminal "Bean Dock" building, brought the tall ship *Highlander Sea* to town and built the 6,000 square-foot, non-profit Great Lakes Maritime Center at Vantage Point, near the mouth of the Black River. The current building is a temporary facility; ground is expected to be broken in 2007 on a larger, permanent structure.

Construction continues on the Blue Water Bridge around 1938.
(Erhardt Peters photo / Steve Elve Coll.)

The location also includes a separate building that serves as the real-world home for the popular Web site www.boatnerd.com – Great Lakes and Seaway Shipping On-line Inc.

Paying attention to its waterfront is just one of the reasons Port Huron is living up to its claim as Maritime Capital of the Great Lakes.

For details about this year's citywide celebration, visit www.ph150.org

The modern U.S. Coast Guard cutter *Hollyhock* is based at Port Huron. Inset: the historic Fort Gratiot Lighthouse. *(both, Roger LeLievre)*

Boatwatching Paradise: *Frontenac upbound under the Blue Water Bridge in 2006.* *(Roger LeLievre)*

Fleet #.	Fleet Name Vessel Name	Type of Vessel	Year Built	Type of Engine	Cargo Cap. or Gross*	Overall Length	Breadth	Depth or Draft*
	Hannah 1801	TK	1967	B	1,560*	240' 00"	50' 00"	12' 00"
	Hannah 1802	TK	1967	B	1,560*	240' 00"	50' 00"	12' 00"
	Hannah 2901	TK	1962	B	1,702*	264' 00"	52' 06"	12' 06"
	Hannah 2902	TK	1962	B	1,702*	264' 00"	52' 06"	12' 06"
	Hannah 2903	TK	1962	B	1,702*	264' 00"	52' 06"	12' 06"
	Hannah 3601	TK	1972	B	2,369*	290' 00"	60' 00"	18' 03"
	Hannah 5101	TK	1978	B	3,356*	360' 00"	60' 00"	22' 06"
	Hannah D. Hannah	TB	1955	D	134*	86' 00"	24' 00"	10' 00"
	(Harbor Ace '55-'61, Gopher State '61-'71, Betty Gale '71-'93)							
	James A. Hannah	TB	1945	D	593*	149' 00"	33' 00"	16' 00"
	(U. S. Army LT-820 '45-'65, Muskegon {1} '65-'71)							
	Kristin Lee Hannah	TW	1953	D	397*	111' 10"	35' 00"	8' 04"
	(Inwaco '53-'61, Carrie S. '61-'68, Clark Frame '68-'96, Cheri Conway '96-'96, David E '96-'00)							
	Margaret M.	TB	1956	D	167*	89' 06"	24' 00"	10' 00"
	(Shuttler '56-'60, Margaret M. Hannah '60-'84)							
	Mark Hannah	ATB	1969	D	191*	127' 05"	32' 01"	14' 03"
	(Lead Horse '69-'73, Gulf Challenger '73-'80, Challenger {2} '80-'93)							
	Mary E. Hannah	TB	1945	D	612*	149' 00"	33' 00"	16' 00"
	(U. S. Army LT-821 '45-'47, Brooklyn '47-'66, Lee Reuben '66-'75)							
	Peggy D. Hannah	TB	1920	D	145*	108' 00"	25' 00"	14' 00"
	(William A. Whitney '20-'92)							
	Susan W. Hannah	ATB	1977	D	174*	121' 06"	34' 06"	18' 02"
	(Lady Elda '77-'78, Kings Challenger '78-'78, ITM No. 1 '78-'81, Kings Challenger '81-'86)							
	HMC SHIP MANAGEMENT LTD., LEMONT, IL – AFFILIATE OF HANNAH MARINE CORP.							
	William L. Warner	RT	1973	D	492*	120' 00"	40' 00"	14' 00"
	(Jos. F. Bigane '73-'04)							
H-5	**HARBOR HERITAGE SOCIETY / GREAT LAKES SCIENCE CENTER, CLEVELAND, OH**							
	William G. Mather {2}	MU	1925	T	13,950	618' 00"	62' 00"	32' 00"
	Built: Great Lakes Engineering Works, Ecorse, MI; former Cleveland-Cliffs Steamship Co. bulk carrier last operatedDec. 21, 1980; open to the public at Cleveland, OH							
H-6	**HARBOR LIGHT CRUISE LINES INC., TOLEDO, OH**							
	Sandpiper	ES	1984	D	19*	65' 00"	16' 00"	4' 00"
H-7	**HARRY GAMBLE SHIPYARDS, PORT DOVER, ON**							
	Hamilton Trader	TB	1951	D	10*	39' 05"	12' 05"	2' 09"
	John D.	TB	1954	D	36*	55' 05"	19' 08"	4' 09"
H-8	**HCMS HAIDA NATIONAL HISTORICAL SITE, HAMILTON, ON**							
	Haida	MU	1943	T	2,744*	377' 00"	37' 06"	15' 02"
	Former Royal Canadian Navy "Tribal" class destroyer [G-63 / DDE-215; open to the public at Hamilton, ON							
H-9	**HEDDLE MARINE SERVICE INC., HAMILTON, ON**							
	Dalmig	CF	1957	D	538*	175' 10"	40' 01"	11' 10"
	Vessel laid up at Hamilton, ON (Pierre de Saurel '57-'87)							
	Wyatt McKeil	TB	1950	D	237*	102' 06"	26' 00"	13' 06"
	(Otis Wack '50-'97)							
H-10	**HERITAGE CRUISE LINES, ST. CATHARINES, ON**							
	Georgian Clipper	PA	1967	D	170*	78' 08"	12' 06"	6' 00"
H-11	**HOLLY MARINE TOWING, CHICAGO, IL**							
	Chris Ann	TB	1981	D	45*	51' 09"	17' 00"	6' 01"
	(Captain Robbie '81-'90, Philip M. Pearse '90-'97)							
	Holly Ann	TB	1926	D	220*	108' 00"	26' 06"	15' 00"
	(Wm. A. Lydon '26-'92)							
	Katie Ann {3}	TW	1962	D	84*	60' 04"	24' 00"	8' 06"
	Margaret Ann	TB	1954	D	131*	82' 00"	24' 06"	11' 06"
	(John A. McGuire '54-'87, William Hoey {1} '87-'94)							
	Mary Ann	TW	1946	D	46*	52' 02"	18' 00"	5' 00"

H-12	**HORNBECK OFFSHORE SERVICES, COVINGTON, LA**							
	Tradewind Service	TB	1975	D	183*	104' 07"	30' 00"	12' 08"
	Energy 5501	TK	1969	B	2,878*	341' 00"	54' 00"	17' 09"
H-13	**HORNE TRANSPORTATION LTD., WOLFE ISLAND, ON**							
	William Darrell	CF	1952	D	66*	66' 00"	28' 00"	6' 00"
H-14	**HUFFMAN EQUIPMENT RENTAL INC., EASTLAKE, OH**							
	Hamp Thomas	TB	1968	D	22*	43' 00"	13' 00"	4' 00"
	Paddy Miles	TB	1934	D	16*	45' 04"	12' 04"	4' 07"
I-1	**ICEBREAKER MACKINAW MARITIME MUSEUM INC., MACKINAW CITY, MI**							
	Mackinaw **[WAGB-83]**	MU	1944	D	5,252*	290' 00"	74' 00"	29' 00"

Built: Toledo Shipbuilding Co., Toledo, OH; launched as USCGC Manitowoc [WAG-83]
Former U.S. Coast Guard icebreaker decommissioned 2006; open to the public at Mackinaw City, MI

I-2	**ILLINOIS MARINE TOWING INC., LEMONT, IL**							
	Aggie C	TW	1977	D	134*	81' 00"	26' 00"	9' 00"
	Albert C	TW	1971	D	65*	61' 02"	18' 00"	6' 00"
	Eileen C	TW	1982	D	145*	75' 00"	26' 00"	9' 00"
	William C	TW	1968	D	143*	76' 06"	24' 00"	8' 00"
I-3	**INLAND LAKES MANAGEMENT INC., ALPENA, MI**							
	Alpena {2}	CC	1942	T	15,550	519' 06"	67' 00"	35' 00"

Built: Great Lakes Engineering Works, River Rouge, MI; shortened by 120' and converted to a self-unloading
cement carrier in '91 (Leon Fraser '42-'91)

| | E. M. Ford | CC | 1898 | Q | 7,100 | 428' 00" | 50' 00" | 28' 00" |

Built: Cleveland Shipbuilding Co., Cleveland, OH; converted to a self-unloading cement carrier in '56; last
operated Sept. 16, 1996; in use as a cement storage and transfer vessel at Saginaw, MI
(Presque Isle {1} 1898-'56)

| | J. A. W. Iglehart | CC | 1936 | T | 12,500 | 501' 06" | 68' 03" | 37' 00" |

Built: Sun Shipbuilding and Drydock Co., Chester, PA; converted from a saltwater tanker to a self-unloading
cement carrier in '65; in use as a cement storage/transfer vessel at Superior, WI
(Pan Amoco '36-'55, Amoco '55-'60, H. R. Schemn '60-'65)

| | Paul H. Townsend | CC | 1945 | D | 7,850 | 447' 00" | 50' 00" | 29' 00" |

Built: Consolidated Steel Corp., Wilmington, CA; converted from a saltwater cargo vessel to a self-unloading
cement carrier in '52; lengthened in '58; laid up at Muskegon, MI since Dec. 5, 2005
(USNS Hickory Coll '45-'46, USNS Coastal Delegate '46-'52)

| | S. T. Crapo | CC | 1927 | B | 8,900 | 402' 06" | 60' 03" | 29' 00" |

Built: Great Lakes Engineering Works, River Rouge, MI; last operated Sept. 4, 1996; in use as a cement storage
and transfer vessel in Green Bay, WI

I-4	**INLAND SEAS EDUCATION ASSOCIATION, SUTTONS BAY, MI**							
	Inland Seas	RV	1994	W	41*	61' 06"	17' 00"	7' 00"
I-5	**INLAND TUG & BARGE CO., BROCKVILLE, ON**							
	Katanni	TB	1991	D	19*	34' 08"	14' 05"	5' 05"
I-6	**INTERLAKE STEAMSHIP CO., RICHFIELD, OH**							
	Charles M. Beeghly	SU	1959	T	31,000	806' 00"	75' 00"	37' 06"

Built: American Shipbuilding Co., Lorain, OH; lengthened 96' in '72; converted to a self-unloader in '81
(Shenango II '59-'67)

| | Herbert C. Jackson | SU | 1959 | T | 24,800 | 690' 00" | 75' 00" | 37' 06" |

Built: Great Lakes Engineering Works, River Rouge, MI; converted to a self-unloader in '75

| | James R. Barker | SU | 1976 | D | 63,300 | 1,004' 00" | 105' 00" | 50' 00" |

Built: American Shipbuilding Co., Lorain, OH

| | Mesabi Miner | SU | 1977 | D | 63,300 | 1,004' 00" | 105' 00" | 50' 00" |

Built: American Shipbuilding Co., Lorain, OH

| | Paul R. Tregurtha | SU | 1981 | D | 68,000 | 1,013' 06" | 105' 00" | 56' 00" |

Built: American Shipbuilding Co., Lorain, OH (William J. DeLancey '81-'90)

| | Stewart J. Cort | SU | 1972 | D | 58,000 | 1,000' 00" | 105' 00" | 49' 00" |

Built: Erie Marine Inc., Erie, PA; the Cort was the first 1,000-footer to enter Great Lakes service

INTERLAKE TRANSPORTATION INC., RICHFIELD, OH – DIVISION OF INTERLAKE STEAMSHIP CO.

	Dorothy Ann	AT/TT	1999	D	1,600*	124' 03"	44' 00"	24' 00"
	Built: Bay Shipbuilding Co., Sturgeon Bay, WI							
	Pathfinder {3}	SU	1953	B	26,700	606' 02"	70' 00"	36' 00"
	Built: Great Lakes Engineering Works, River Rouge, MI; converted from a powered vessel to a self-unloading barge in '98 (J. L. Mauthe '53-'98)							
	[ATB Dorothy Ann / Pathfinder {3} OA dimensions together]					700' 00"	70' 00"	36' 00"

LAKES SHIPPING CO. INC., RICHFIELD, OH – DIVISION OF INTERLAKE STEAMSHIP CO.

	John Sherwin {2}	BC	1958	T	31,500	806' 00"	75' 00"	37' 06"
	Built: American Steamship Co., Lorain, OH; lengthened 96' in '73; last operated Nov. 16, 1981; in use as a grain storage hull at South Chicago, IL							
	Kaye E. Barker	SU	1952	T	25,900	767' 00"	70' 00"	36' 00"
	Built: American Shipbuilding Co., Toledo, OH; lengthened 120' in '76; converted to a self-unloader in '81 (Edward B. Greene '52-'85, Benson Ford {3} '85-'89)							
	Lee A. Tregurtha	SU	1942	D	29,360	826' 00"	75' 00"	39' 00"
	Built: Bethlehem Shipbuilding and Drydock Co., Sparrows Point, MD; converted from a saltwater tanker to a Great Lakes bulk carrier in '61; lengthened 96' in '76; converted to a self-unloader in '78; converted from steam to diesel power in '06 (Laid down as Mobiloil; launched as Samoset. USS Chiwawa [AO-68] '42-'46, Chiwawa '46-'61, Walter A. Sterling '61-'85, William Clay Ford {2} '85-'89)							

I-7   INTERNATIONAL MARINE SALVAGE CO. LTD., PORT COLBORNE, ON

	Charlie E.	TB	1943	D	32*	63' 00"	16' 06"	7' 06"
	(Kolbe '43-'86, Lois T. '86-'02)							
	Condarrell	DH	1953	D	3,017	259' 00"	43' 06"	21' 00"
	Awaiting scrapping at Port Colborne, ON (D. C. Everest '53-'81)							
	L. E. Block	BC	1927	T	15,900	621' 00"	64' 00"	33' 00"
	Former Inland Steel Co. vessel last operated Oct. 31, 1981; scrapping underway at Port Colborne, ON							

I-8   ISLAND FERRY SERVICES CORP., CHEBOYGAN, MI

	Polaris	PF	1952	D	99*	60' 02"	36' 00"	8' 06"

I-9   ISLE ROYALE LINE INC., COPPER HARBOR, MI

	Isle Royale Queen IV	PA/PK	1980	D	93*	98 09"	22' 01"	7' 00"
	(American Freedom, John Jay, Shuttle V, Danielle G, Harbor Commuter V)							

J-1   J. W. WESTCOTT CO., DETROIT, MI

	J. W. Westcott II	MB	1949	D	11*	46' 01"	13' 04"	4' 06"
	Floating post office is the only such service to have its own U.S. zip code, 48222							
	Joseph J. Hogan	MB	1957	D	16*	40' 00"	12' 06"	5' 00"
	Backup mail boat and water taxi for vessels docked at Great Lakes Steel / Zug Island (USCOE Ottawa '57-'95)							

J-2   JOSEPH B. MARTIN, BEAVER ISLAND, MI

	Shamrock {1}	TB	1933	D	60*	64' 00"	18' 00"	7' 04"

J-3   JUBILEE QUEEN CRUISES, TORONTO, ON

	Jubilee Queen	ES	1986	D	269*	122' 00"	23' 09"	5' 05"
	(Pioneer Princess III '86-'89)							

J-4   JULIO CONTRACTING CO., HANCOCK, MI

	Winnebago	TW	1945	D	14*	40' 00"	10' 02"	4' 06"

K-1   K-SEA CANADA CORP., HALIFAX, NS

	McCleary's Spirit	TK	1969	B	6,888*	379' 09"	63' 03"	33' 08"
	Built: Boelwerf, Belgium (LeVent '69-'02)							
	William J. Moore	TB	1970	D	564*	135' 00"	34' 09"	19' 04"
	Built: Adelaide Ship Construction Pty Ltd., Port Adelaide, SA (Warrawee '70-'76, Seaspan Raider '76-'87, Raider '87-'87, Raider IV '87-'88, Alice A. '88-'02)							

K-2   KEHOE MARINE CONSTRUCTION CO., ROCKPORT, ON

	Houghton	TB	1944	D	15*	45' 00"	13' 00"	6' 00"

|---|---|---|---|---|---|---|---|---|
K-3	**KELLEYS ISLAND BOAT LINES, MARBLEHEAD, OH**							
	Carlee Emily	PA/CF	1987	D	98*	101' 00"	34' 06"	10' 00"
	(Endeavor '87-'02)							
	Kayla Marie	PA/CF	1975	D	93*	122' 00"	40' 00"	8' 00"
	(R. Bruce Etherige '75-'97)							
	Shirley Irene	PA/CF	1991	D	68*	160' 00"	46' 00"	9' 00"
K-4	**KEWEENAW EXCURSIONS INC., HOUGHTON, MI**							
	Keweenaw Star	ES	1981	D	97*	110' 00"	23' 04"	6' 03"
	(Atlantic Star, Privateer, De De Bruce)							
K-5	**KEYSTONE GREAT LAKES INC., BALA CYNWYD, PA**							
	Great Lakes {2}	TK	1982	B	5,024*	414' 00"	60' 00"	30' 00"
	Built: Bay Shipbuilding Co., Sturgeon Bay, WI (Amoco Great Lakes '82-'85)							
	Michigan {10}	AT	1982	D	293*	107' 08"	34' 00"	16' 00"
	Built: Bay Shipbuilding Co., Sturgeon Bay, WI (Amoco Michigan '82-'85)							
	[ATB Michigan / Great Lakes {2} OA dimensions together]					454' 00"	60' 00"	30' 00"
K-6	**KINDRA LAKE TOWING LP, DOWNERS GROVE, IL**							
	Buckley	TW	1958	D	94*	95' 00"	26' 00"	11' 00"
	(Linda Brooks '58-'67, Eddie B. {2} '67-'95)							
	Morgan	TB	1974	D	134*	90' 00"	30' 00"	10' 06"
	(Donald O' Toole '74-'86, Bonesey B. '86-'95)							
	Old Mission	TB	1945	D	94*	85' 00"	23' 00"	10' 04"
	(U. S. Army ST-880 '45-'47, USCOE Avondale '47-'64, Adrienne B. '64-'95)							
K-7	**KING COMPANY INC., HOLLAND, MI**							
	Barry J	TB	1943	D	42*	46' 00"	13' 00"	7' 00"
	Buxton II	DR	1976	B	147*	130' 02"	28' 01"	7' 00"
	Carol Ann	TB	1981	D	115*	68' 00"	24' 00"	8' 08"
	Julie Dee	TB	1903	D	64*	68' 08"	18' 01"	8' 00"
	(Bonita {1} '03-'16, Chicago Harbor No. 4 '16-'60, Eddie B. {1} '60-'69, Seneca Queen '69-'70, Ludington '70 -?)							
	John Henry	TB	1954	D	66*	70' 00"	20' 06"	9' 07"
	(U. S. Army ST-2013 '54-'80)							
	Matt Allen	TB	1961	D	147*	87' 00"	24' 00"	11' 06"
	(Gladys Bea '61-'73, American Viking '73-'83, Maribeth Andrie '83-'05)							
	Miss Edna	TB	1935	D	29*	36' 08"	11' 02"	4' 08"
K-8	**KINGSTON & THE ISLANDS BOAT LINES LTD., KINGSTON, ON**							
	Island Belle I	ES	1988	D	150*	65' 00"	22' 00"	8' 00"
	(Spirit of Brockville '88-'91)							
	Island Queen	ES	1975	D	300*	96' 00"	26' 00"	11' 00"
	Island Star	ES	1994	D	220*	97' 00"	30' 00"	10' 00"
	(Le Bateau-Mouche II '94-'98)							
	Papoose III	ES	1968	D	110*	64' 08"	23' 03"	7' 03"
	(Peche Island II)							
K-9	**KK INTEGRATED LOGISTICS LLC, MENOMINEE, MI**							
	William H. Donner	CS	1914	B	9,400	524' 00"	54' 00"	30' 00"
	Last operated in 1969; in use as a cargo transfer vessel at Marinette, WI							
	KK INTEGRATED SHIPPING LLC, MENOMINEE, MI							
	Lewis J. Kuber	SU	1952	B	22,300	698' 00"	70' 00"	37' 00"
	Built: Bethlehem Steel Corp., Sparrows Point, MD; lengthened by 72' in '58; converted to a self-unloader in '80; converted to a barge in '06; operated by VanEnkevort Tug & Barge (Sparrows Point '52-'90, Buckeye {3} '90-'06)							
	Manitowoc	DB	1926	B	3,080*	371' 03"	67' 03"	22' 06"
	Laid up at Marinette, WI							
	Olive L. Moore	AT	1928	D	301*	125' 00"	27' 01"	13' 09"
	Built: Manitowoc Shipbuilding Inc., Manitowoc, WI (John F. Cushing '28-'66, James E. Skelly '66-'66)							

| | Reserve | SU | 1953 | T | 25,500 | 767' 00" | 70' 00" | 36' 00" |

Built: Great Lakes Engineering Works, River Rouge, MI; lengthened 120' in '75; converted to a self-unloader in '83; managed by Central Marine Logistics Inc.

| | Victory | TB | 1980 | D | 194* | 129' 00" | 43' 01" | 18' 00" |

Built: McDermott Shipyard Inc., Amelia, LA

| | Viking I | CF | 1925 | D | 2,713* | 360' 00" | 56' 03" | 21' 06" |

Laid up at Marinette, WI (Ann Arbor No. 7 '25-'64, Viking {2} '64-'96)

L-1   LAFARGE CANADA INC., MONTREAL, QC (MANAGED BY CANADA STEAMSHIP LINES INC.)

| | English River | CC | 1961 | D | 7,450 | 404' 03" | 60' 00" | 36' 06" |

Built: Canadian Shipbuilding and Engineering Ltd., Collingwood, ON; converted to a self-unloading cement carrier in '74

L-2   LAFARGE NORTH AMERICA INC., SOUTHFIELD, MI

| | J. B. Ford | CC | 1904 | R | 8,000 | 440' 00" | 50' 00" | 28' 00" |

Built: American Ship Building Co., Lorain, OH; converted to a self-unloading cement carrier in '59; last operated Nov. 15, 1985; most recently used as a cement storage and transfer vessel at Superior, WI (Edwin F. Holmes '04-'16, E. C. Collins '16-'59)

THE FOLLOWING VESSELS MANAGED BY ANDRIE INC., MUSKEGON, MI

| | G. L. Ostrander | AT | 1976 | D | 198* | 140' 02" | 40' 01" | 22' 03" |

Built: Halter Marine, New Orleans, LA (Andrew Martin '76-'90, Robert L. Torres '90-'94, Jacklyn M '94-'04)

| | Integrity | CC | 1996 | B | 14,000 | 460' 00" | 70' 00" | 37' 00" |

Built: Bay Shipbuilding Corp., Sturgeon Bay, WI

| | [ATB G.L. Ostrander/Integrity OA dimensions together] | | | | | 543' 00" | 70' 00" | 37' 00" |
| | Innovation | CC | 2006 | B | 7,320* | 460' 00" | 70' 00" | 37' 00" |

Built: Bay Shipbuilding Co., Sturgeon Bay, WI

| | Samuel de Champlain | AT | 1975 | D | 299* | 140' 02" | 39' 02" | 20' 00" |

Built: Mangone Shipbuilding, Houston, TX (Musketeer Fury '75-'78, Tender Panther '78-'79, Margarita '79-'83, Vortice '83-'99, Norfolk '99-'06)

L-3   LA GOELETTE MARIE-CLARISSE INC., BEAUPRE, QC

| | Famille DuFour | ES | 1992 | D | 451* | 132' 00" | 29' 00" | 11' 00" |

L-4   LAKE COUNTY HISTORICAL SOCIETY, TWO HARBORS, MN

| | Edna G. | MU | 1896 | R | 154* | 102' 00" | 23' 00" | 14' 06" |

Former Duluth, Missabe & Iron Range Railroad tug last operated in 1981; open to the public at Two Harbors, MN

L-5   LAKE EXPRESS LLC , MILWAUKEE, WI

| | Lake Express | PA/CF | 2004 | D | 96* | 179' 02" | 57' 07" | 16' 00" |

Built: Austal USA, Mobile, AL; high-speed ferry in service from Milwaukee, WI, to Muskegon, MI

L-6   LAKE MICHIGAN CARFERRY SERVICE INC., LUDINGTON, MI

| | Badger | PA/CF | 1953 | S | 4,244* | 410' 06" | 59' 06" | 24' 00" |

Built: Christy Corp, Sturgeon Bay, WI; traditional ferry in service from Ludington, MI to Manitowoc, MI

| | Spartan | PA/CF | 1952 | S | 4,244* | 410' 06" | 59' 06" | 24' 00" |

Built: Christy Corp, Sturgeon Bay, WI; last operated Jan. 20, 1979; in long-term layup at Ludington, MI

L-7   LAKE TOWING INC., CLEVELAND, OH

| | Menominee | TB | 1967 | D | 235* | 108' 00" | 29' 00" | 14' 00" |
| | Upper Canada | PA/CF | 1949 | D | 165* | 143' 00" | 36' 00" | 11' 00" |

Vessel laid up in Lorain, OH (Romeo and Annette '49-'66)

L-8   LAKEN SHIPPING CORP., CLEVELAND, OH

VESSELS CHARTERED AND COMMERCIALLY MANAGED BY SMT (US) INC.

| | Cleveland | TB | 1999 | D | 149* | 105' 02" | 34' 01" | 15' 00" |

Built: C & G Boat Works, Bayou La Batre, AL (James Palladino '99-'04)

| | Cleveland Rocks | SU | 1957 | B | 6,280* | 390' 00" | 71' 00" | 27' 00" |

Built: Todd Shipyards Corp., Houston, TX (M-211 '57-'81, Virginia '81-'88, C-11 '88-'93, Kellstone 1 '93-'04)

L-9   LAKES PILOTS ASSOCIATION, PORT HURON, MI

	Huron Belle	PB	1979	D	21*	50' 00"	16' 00"	7' 09"
	Vessel offers pilot service at Port Huron, MI.							
	Huron Maid	PB	1976	D	26*	46' 00"	16' 00"	3' 05"
	Vessel offers pilot service at Detroit, MI.							

L-10   LE GROUPÉ OCEAN INC., QUEBEC, QC

	Basse-Cote	DB	1932	B	400	201' 00"	40' 00"	12' 00"
	Betsiamites	SU	1969	B	11,600	402' 00"	75' 00"	24' 00"
	Coucoucache	TB	1934	D	95*	34' 01"	9' 05"	4' 02"
	Jerry G.	TB	1960	D	202*	91' 06"	27' 03"	12' 06"
	Kim R. D.	TB	1954	D	30*	48' 07"	14' 01"	5' 08"
	La Prairie	TB	1975	D	110*	73' 09"	25' 09"	11' 08"
	Lac St-Francois	BC	1979	B	1,200	195' 00"	35' 00"	12' 00"
	Le Phil D.	TB	1961	D	38*	56' 01"	16' 00"	5' 08"
	Navcomar No. 1	DB	1955	B	500	135' 00"	35' 00"	9' 00"
	Ocean Abys	DB	1948	B	1,000	140' 00"	40' 00"	9' 00"
	Ocean Bravo	TB	1970	D	320*	110' 00"	28' 06"	17' 00"
	(Takis V. '70-'80, Donald P '80-'80, Nimue '80-'83, Donald P. '83-'98)							
	Ocean Delta	TB	1973	D	722*	136' 08"	35' 08"	22' 00"
	(Sistella '73-'78, Sandy Cape '78-'80, Captain Ioannis S. '80-'99)							
	Ocean Golf	TB	1959	D	159*	103' 00"	25' 10"	11' 09"
	(Launched as Stranton. Helen M. McAllister '59-'97)							
	Ocean Hercule	TB	1976	D	448*	120' 00"	32' 00"	19' 00"
	(Stril Pilot '76-'81, Spirit Sky '81-'86, Ierland '86-'89, Ierlandia '89-'95, Charles Antoine '95-'97)							
	Ocean Intrepide	TT	1998	D	302*	80' 00"	30' 01"	14' 09"
	Ocean Jupiter {2}	TT	1999	D	302*	80' 00"	30' 00"	13' 04"
	Ocean K. Rusby	TB	2005	D	401*	94' 05"	36' 05"	17' 01"
	Omni-Atlas	CS	1913	B	479*	133' 00"	42' 00"	10' 00"
	Omni-Richelieu	TB	1969	D	144*	83' 00"	24' 06"	13' 06"
	(Port Alfred II '69-'82)							
	Omni St-Laurent	TB	1957	D	161*	99' 02"	24' 09"	12' 06"
	(Diligent '57-'89)							

OCEAN REMORQUAGE TROIS-RIVIERES INC. – SUBSIDIARY OF LE GROUPE OCEAN INC.

	Andre H.	TB	1963	D	317*	126' 00"	28' 06"	15' 06"
	(Foundation Valiant '63-'73, Point Valiant {1} '73-'95)							
	Avantage	TB	1969	D	367*	116' 10"	32' 09"	16' 03"
	(Sea Lion '69-'97)							
	Duga	TB	1977	D	403*	111' 00"	33' 00"	16' 01"
	Escorte	TT	1964	D	120*	85' 00"	23' 08"	11' 00"
	(USS Menasha [YTB / YTM-773, YTM-761] '64-'92, Menasha {1} '92-'95)							
	Josee H.	PB	1961	D	66*	63' 50"	16' 02"	9' 50"
	Ocean Charlie	TB	1973	D	448*	123' 02"	31' 06"	18' 09"
	(Leonard W. '73-'98)							
	Ocean Echo II	AT	1969	D	438*	104' 08"	35' 05"	18' 00"
	(Atlantic '69-'75, Laval '75-'96)							
	Ocean Foxtrot	TB	1971	D	700*	184' 05"	38' 05"	16' 07"
	(Polor Shore '71-'77, Canmar Supplier VII '77-'95)							
	R. F. Grant	TB	1969	D	78*	71' 00"	17' 00"	8' 00"

L-11   LE SAULT DE SAINTE MARIE HISTORIC SITES INC., SAULT STE. MARIE, MI

	Valley Camp {2}	MU	1917	R	12,000	550' 00"	58' 00"	31' 00"
	Built: American Shipbuilding Co., Lorain, OH; former Hanna Mining Co./Wilson Marine Transit Co./Republic Steel Corp. bulk carrier last operated in 1966; open to the public at Sault Ste. Marie, MI (Louis W. Hill '17-'55)							

L-12   LEE MARINE LTD., SOMBRA, ON

	Hammond Bay	ES	1992	D	43*	54' 00"	16' 00"	3' 00"
	(Scrimp & Scrounge '92-'95)							
	Nancy A. Lee	TB	1939	D	9*	40' 00"	12' 00"	3' 00"

Fleet #.	Fleet Name Vessel Name	Type of Vessel	Year Built	Type of Engine	Cargo Cap. or Gross*	Overall Length	Breadth	Depth or Draft*
L-13	**LOCK TOURS CANADA BOAT CRUISES, SAULT STE. MARIE, ON**							
	Chief Shingwauk	ES	1965	D	109*	70' 00"	24' 00"	4' 06"
L-14	**LOWER LAKES TOWING LTD., PORT DOVER, ON**							
	Cuyahoga	SU	1943	D	15,675	620' 00"	60' 00"	35' 00"

Built: American Shipbuilding Co., Lorain, OH; converted to a self-unloader in 74; repowered in '01 (J. Burton Ayers '43-'95)

	Michipicoten {2}	SU	1952	T	22,300	698' 00"	70' 00"	37' 00"

Built: Bethlehem Shipbuilding & Drydock Co., Sparrows Point, MD; lengthened 72' in '57; converted to a self-unloader in '80 (Elton Hoyt 2nd '52-'03)

	Mississagi	SU	1943	D	15,800	620' 06"	60' 00"	35' 00"

Built: Great Lakes Engineering Works, River Rouge, MI; converted to a self-unloader in '67; repowered in '85 (Hill Annex '43-'43, George A. Sloan '43-'01)

	Saginaw {3}	SU	1953	T	20,200	639' 03"	72' 00"	36' 00"

Built: Manitowoc Shipbuilding Inc., Manitowoc, WI (John J. Boland {3} '53-'99)

L-15	**LOWER LAKES TRANSPORTATION CO., WILLIAMSVILLE, NY, A DIVISION OF LOWER LAKES TOWING LTD.**							

GRAND RIVER NAVIGATION CO., CLEVELAND, OH – OWNER – AFFILIATE OF LOWER LAKES TOWING LTD.

	Calumet	SU	1929	D	12,450	603' 09"	60' 00"	32' 00"

Built: Great Lakes Engineering Works, River Rouge, MI; converted to a self-unloader in 56; repowered in '68 (Myron C. Taylor '29-'01)

	Invincible	ATB	1979	D	180*	100' 00"	35' 00"	22' 06"

Built: Atlantic Marine Inc., Fort George Island, FL (R. W. Sesler '79-'91)

	Maumee	SU	1929	D	12,650	604' 09"	60' 00"	32' 00"

Built: American Shipbuilding Co., Lorain, OH; converted to a self-unloader in '61; repowered in '64 (William G. Clyde '29-'61, Calcite II '61-'01)

Canadian-flagged *Maritime Trader* at speed on the St. Clair River. *(Wade P. Streeter)*

LAKE SERVICE SHIPPING CO., GROSSE POINTE FARMS, MI – OWNER

	Manistee	SU	1943	D	14,900	620' 06"	60' 03"	35' 00"

Built: Great Lakes Engineering Works, River Rouge, MI; converted to a self-unloader in '64; repowered in '76 (Launched as Adirondack. Richard J. Reiss {2} '43-'86, Richard Reiss '86-'05)

	McKee Sons	SU	1945	B	19,900	579' 02"	71' 06"	38' 06"

Built: Sun Shipbuilding and Drydock Co., Chester, PA; converted from saltwater vessel to a self-unloading Great Lakes bulk carrier in '53; engine removed and converted to a self-unloading barge in '91 USNS Marine Angel '45-'52)

	[ATB McKee Sons / Invincible OA dimensions together]					615' 00"	71' 06"	38' 06"

WISCONSIN & MICHIGAN STEAMSHIP CO., LAKEWOOD, OH – OWNER

	David Z. Norton {3}	SU	1973	D	19,650	630' 00"	68' 00"	36' 11"

Built: American Shipbuilding Co., Lorain, OH (William R. Roesch '73-'95)

	Earl W. Oglebay	SU	1973	D	19,650	630' 00"	68' 00"	36' 11"

Built: American Shipbuilding Co., Lorain, OH (Paul Thayer '73-'95)

	Wolverine {4}	SU	1974	D	19,650	630' 00"	68' 00"	36' 11"

Built: American Shipbuilding Co., Lorain, OH

L-16 LUEDTKE ENGINEERING CO., FRANKFORT, MI

	Alan K. Luedtke	TB	1944	D	149*	86' 04"	23' 00"	10' 03"

(U. S. Army ST-527 '44-'55, USCOE Two Rivers '55-'90)

	Ann Marie	TB	1954	D	119*	71' 00"	19' 06"	9' 06"

(ST-9684 '54-'80, Lewis Castle '80-'97, Apache '97-'01)

	Chris E. Luedtke	TB	1936	D	18*	42' 05"	11' 09"	5' 00"
	Erich R. Luedtke	TB	1939	D	18*	42' 05"	11' 09"	5' 00"
	Gretchen B.	TB	1943	D	18*	41' 09"	12' 05"	6' 00"
	Karl E. Luedtke	TB	1928	D	32*	55' 02"	14' 09"	6' 00"
	Kurt R. Luedtke	TB	1956	D	96*	72' 00"	22' 06"	7' 06"

(Jere C. '56-'90)

L-17 LUHTA CHANDLERY, DETROIT, MI

	Marine Trader	BB	1939	D	67*	65' 00"	15' 00"	7' 06

M-1 M. C. M. MARINE INC., SAULT STE. MARIE, MI

	Beaver State	TB	1935	D	18*	43' 07"	12' 00"	5' 02"
	Drummond Islander II	CF	1961	D	97*	65' 00"	36' 00"	9' 00"
	Mackinaw City	TB	1943	D	23*	38' 00"	11' 05"	4' 07"
	Mohawk	TB	1945	D	46*	65' 00"	19' 00"	10' 06"
	No. 55	DR	1927	DE	721*	165' 00"	42' 08"	12' 00"
	No. 56	DR	1927	DE	721*	165' 00"	42' 08"	12' 00"
	Peach State	TB	1961	D	19*	42' 01"	12' 04"	5' 03"
	Sioux	DS	1954	B	504*	120' 00"	50' 00"	10' 00"
	William C. Gaynor	TB	1956	D	146*	94' 00"	27' 00"	11' 09"

(William C. Gaynor '56-'88, Captain Barnaby '88-'02)

SOO MARINE SUPPLY, SAULT STE. MARIE, MI – A DIVISION OF M.C.M. MARINE

	Ojibway	SB	1945	D	65*	53' 00"	28' 00"	7' 00"

M-2 MACASSA BAY LIMITED, CORUNNA, ON

	Macassa Bay	ES	1986	D	200*	93' 07"	29' 07"	10' 04"

M-3 MacDONALD MARINE LTD., GODERICH, ON

	Debbie Lyn	TB	1950	D	10*	45' 00"	14' 00"	10' 00"

(Skipper '50-'60)

	Donald Bert	TB	1953	D	11*	45' 00"	14' 00"	10' 00"
	Dover	TB	1931	D	70*	84' 00"	17' 00"	6' 00"

(Earleejune, Iveyrose)

	Ian Mac	TB	1955	D	12*	45' 00"	14' 00"	10' 00"

M-4 MADELINE ISLAND FERRY LINE INC., LaPOINTE, WI

	Bayfield {2}	PA/CF	1952	D	83*	120' 00"	43' 00"	10' 00"

(Charlotte '52-'99)

Russian-flagged *Khudozhnik Kraynev* at Sault Ste. Marie. *(Roger LeLievre)*

Fleet #.	Fleet Name Vessel Name	Type of Vessel	Year Built	Type of Engine	Cargo Cap. or Gross*	Overall Length	Breadth	Depth or Draft*
	Island Queen {2}	PA/CF	1966	D	90*	75' 00"	34' 09"	10' 00"
	Madeline	PA/CF	1984	D	97*	90' 00"	35' 00"	8' 00"
	Nichevo II	PA/CF	1962	D	89*	65' 00"	32' 00"	8' 09"
M-5	**MAID OF THE MIST STEAMBOAT CO. LTD., NIAGARA FALLS, ON**							
	Maid of the Mist IV	ES	1976	D	74*	72' 00"	16' 00"	7' 00"
	Maid of the Mist V	ES	1983	D	74*	72' 00"	16' 00"	7' 00"
	Maid of the Mist VI	ES	1990	D	155*	78' 09"	29' 06"	7' 00"
	Maid of the Mist VII	ES	1997	D	160*	80' 00"	30' 00"	7' 00"
M-6	**MALCOLM MARINE, ST. CLAIR, MI**							
	Manitou {2}	TB	1943	D	491*	110' 00"	26' 05"	11' 06"
	(USCGC Manitou [WYT-60] '43-'84)							
M-7	**MANITOU ISLAND TRANSIT, LELAND, MI**							
	Manitou Isle	PA/PK	1946	D	39*	52' 00"	14' 00"	8' 00"
	(Namaycush '46-'59)							
	Mishe-Mokwa	PA/CF	1966	D	49*	65' 00"	17' 06"	8' 00"
M-8	**MARINE ONE TOWING & SALVAGE LTD., DETROIT, MI**							
	Acushnet	TB	1943	D	58*	65' 00"	18' 00"	7' 03"
	(LaSalle '66-'80)							
M-9	**MARINE MUSEUM OF THE GREAT LAKES AT KINGSTON, KINGSTON, ON**							
	Alexander Henry	MU	1959	D	1,674*	210' 00"	44' 00"	17' 09"
	Built: Port Arthur Shipbuilding Co., Port Arthur, ON; former Canadian Coast Guard icebreaker was retired in 1985; open to the public at Kingston, ON							
M-10	**MARINE TECH LLC, DULUTH, MN**							
	Alton Andrew	CS	1958	B		70' 00"	50' 00	6' 00"
	(No. 1 '58-'01)							
	Callie M.	TB	1910	D	51*	64' 03"	16' 09"	8' 06"
	(Chattanooga '10-'79, Howard T. Hagen '79-'94, Nancy Ann '94-'01)							
	Dean R. Smith	DR	1985	B	338*	120' 00"	48' 00"	7' 00"
	(No. 2 '85-'94, B. Yetter '94-'01)							
	Miss Laura	TB	1943	D	146*	81' 01"	24' 00"	9' 10"
	(DPC-3 '43-'46, DS-43 '46-'50, Fresh Kills '50-'69, Richard K. '69-'93, Leopard '93-'03)							
M-11	**MARIPOSA CRUISE LINE LTD., TORONTO, ON**							
	Captain Matthew Flinders	ES	1982	D	696*	144' 00"	40' 00"	8' 06"
	Mariposa Belle	ES	1970	D	195*	93' 00"	23' 00"	8' 00"
	(Niagara Belle '70-'73)							
	Rosemary	ES	1960	D	52*	68' 00"	15' 06"	6' 08"
	Showboat Royal Grace	ES	1988	D	135*	58' 00"	18' 00"	4' 00"
	Torontonian	ES	1962	D	68*	68' 00"	18' 06"	6' 08"
	(Shiawassie '62-'82)							
M-12	**McASPHALT MARINE TRANSPORTATION LTD., SCARBOROUGH, ON**							
	Everlast	ATB	1976	D	1,361*	143' 04"	44' 04"	21' 04"
	Built: Hakodate Dock Co., Hakodate, Japan (Bilibino '77-'96)							
	McAsphalt 401	TK	1966	B	3,642*	300' 00"	60' 00"	23' 00"
	Built: Todd Shipyards Corp., Houston, TX (Pittson 200 '66-'73, Pointe Levy '73-'87)							
	Norman McLeod	TK	2001	B	6,809*	379' 02"	71' 06"	30' 02"
	Built: Jinling Shipyard, Nanjing, China							
	[ATB Everlast / Norman McLeod OA dimensions together]					500' 00"	71' 06"	30' 02"
M-13	**McCULLOUGH CONSTRUCTION INC., PORT CLINTON, OH**							
	Manitou	TB	1934	D	19*	40' 00"	10' 00"	4' 06"
M-14	**McKEIL WORK BOATS LTD. (McKEIL MARINE LTD.), HAMILTON, ON**							
	Alouette Spirit	TK	1969	B	6,773*	415' 06"	74' 01"	29' 05"
	Built: Gulfport Shipbuilding Co., Port Arthur, TX (KTC 135 '69-'04, Lambert Spirit '04-'05)							
	Beaver D.	TB	1955	D	15*	36' 02"	14' 09"	4' 04"

Fleet #.	Fleet Name Vessel Name	Type of Vessel	Year Built	Type of Engine	Cargo Cap. or Gross*	Overall Length	Breadth	Depth or Draft*
	Bonnie B. III	TB	1969	D	308*	100' 03"	32' 00"	17' 00"
	(Esso Oranjestad '69-'85, Oranjestad '85-'86, San Nicolas '86-'87, San Nicolas I '87-'88)							
	Carrol C. I	TB	1969	D	291*	100' 03"	32' 00"	17' 00"
	(Launched as Esso Oranjestad II. Esso San Nicolas '69-'86, San Nicolas '86-'87, Carrol C '87-'88)							
	Daniele M.	TB	1984	D	251*	85' 01"	30' 00"	12' 07"
	(Smit Bonaire '84-'06)							
	Erie West	DB	1951	B	1,800	290' 00"	50' 00"	12' 00"
	(Dover Light)							
	Evans McKeil	TB	1936	D	284*	110' 07"	25' 06"	11' 06"
	(Alhajuela '36-'70, Barbara Ann {2} '70-'89)							
	Flo-Mac	TB	1960	D	15*	40' 00"	13' 00"	6' 00"
	Florence M.	TB	1961	D	236*	96' 03"	28' 00"	14' 06"
	(Foundation Vibert '61-'73, Point Vibert '73-'06)							
	Glenevis	TB	1944	D	91*	80' 06"	20' 00"	9' 07"
	(HMCS Glenevis [W-65 / YTM-502] '44-'77)							
	Greta V	TB	1951	D	14*	44' 00"	12' 00"	5' 00"
	Handy Andy	DB	1925	B	313*	95' 09"	43' 01"	10' 00"
	James E. McGrath	TB	1963	D	90*	77' 00"	20' 00"	10' 09"
	Jarrett M	TB	1945	D	96*	82' 00"	20' 00"	10' 00"
	(Atomic '45-'06)							
	Jarrett McKeil	TB	1956	D	197*	91' 08"	27' 04"	13' 06"
	(Robert B. No. 1 '56-'97)							
	Jean Raymond	DB	1941	B	6,800	409' 00"	57' 00"	18' 00"
	Jerry Newberry	TB	1956	D	244*	98' 00"	28' 02"	14' 04"
	(Foundation Victor '56-'73, Point Victor '73-'77, Kay Cole '77-'95)							
	John Spence	TB	1972	D	719*	171' 00"	38' 00"	15' 01"
	(Mary B. VI '72-'81, Mary B. '81-'82, Mary B. VI '82-'83, Artic Tuktu '83-'94)							
	Kathryn Spirit	GC	1967	D	12,497	503' 03"	66' 07"	36' 09"
	Built: Lindholmen Shipyard, Gothenburg, Sweden (Holmsund '67-'97, Menominee '97-'06)							
	Lac Como	TB	1944	D	63*	65' 00"	16' 10"	7' 10"
	(Tanac 74 '44-'64)							
	Lac Erie	TB	1944	D	65*	65' 00"	16' 10"	7' 07"
	(Tanmac '44-'74)							
	Lac Vancouver	TB	1943	D	65*	65' 00"	16' 10"	7' 07"
	(Vancouver '43-'74)							
	Molly M. 1	TB	1962	D	207*	98' 05"	26' 10"	13' 05"
	(Foundation Vigour '62-'74, Point Vigour '74-'07)							
	Nicole M.	TB	1984	D	251*	85' 01"	30' 00"	12' 07"
	(Smit Aruba '84-'06)							
	Ocean Hauler	TK	1943	B	4,540*	344' 00"	69' 00"	96' 00"
	Pacific Standard	TB	1967	D	451*	127' 08"	31' 00"	15' 06"
	(Irishman '67-'76, Kwakwani '76-'78, Lorna B. '78-'81)							
	Paul E. No. 1	TB	1945	D	97*	80' 00"	20' 00"	9' 07"
	(W.A.C. 4 '45-'46, E. A. Rockett '46-'76)							
	Salvor	TB	1963	D	426*	120' 00"	32' 09"	18' 09"
	(Esther Moran '63-'00)							
	Sault au Cochon	DH	1969	B	10,000	422' 11"	74' 10"	25' 07"
	St. Clair {2}	TF	1927	B	27 rail cars	400' 00"	54' 00"	22' 00"
	(Pere Marquette 12 '27-'70)							
	Stormont	TB	1953	D	108*	80' 00"	20' 00"	15' 00"
	Techno-Venture	TB	1939	D	469*	138' 03"	30' 06"	18' 09"
	(M.I.L. Venture)							
	Tony MacKay	TB	1973	D	366*	127' 00"	30' 05"	14' 05"
	(Point Carroll '73-'01)							
	Viateur's Spirit	DB	2004	D	253*	141' 01"	52' 03"	5' 01"
	(Traverse Rene Lavasseur '04-'06)							
	Wilf Seymour	TB	1961	D	429*	120' 00"	32' 09"	18' 09"
	(M. Moran '61-'70, Port Arthur '70-'72, M. Moran '72-'00, Salvager '00-'04)							

Avenger IV in the 2006
International Tugboat Race
at Detroit / Windsor.
(Roger LeLievre)

Fleet #.	Fleet Name Vessel Name	Type of Vessel	Year Built	Type of Engine	Cargo Cap. or Gross*	Overall Length	Breadth	Depth or Draft*
	Willmac	TB	1959	D	16*	40′ 00″	13′ 00″	3′ 07″
	Wyatt M	TB	1948	D	123*	86′ 00″	21′ 00″	10′ 00″

(P. J. Murer '48-'81, Michael D. Misner '81-'93, Thomas A. Payette '93-'96, Progress '96-'06)

REMORQUEURS & BARGES MONTREAL LTEE, SALABERRY-DE-VALLEYFIELD, QC A SUBSIDIARY OF McKEIL WORK BOATS LTD.

Fleet #.	Fleet Name Vessel Name	Type of Vessel	Year Built	Type of Engine	Cargo Cap. or Gross*	Overall Length	Breadth	Depth or Draft*
	Aldo H.	PB	1979	D	37*	56′ 04″	15′ 04″	6′ 02″
	Boatman No. 3	PB	1965	D	13*	33′ 08″	11′ 00″	6′ 00″
	Boatman No. 6	PB	1979	D	39*	56′ 07″	18′ 07″	6′ 03″
	Pilot 1	PB	1994	D	14*	32′ 01″	5′ 08″	2′ 06″
M-15	**McLEOD BROTHERS MECHANICAL, SAULT STE. MARIE, ON**							
	Kam	TB	1927	D	33*	52′ 00″	13′ 00″	5′ 06″

(North Shore Supply '27-'74)

Fleet #.	Fleet Name Vessel Name	Type of Vessel	Year Built	Type of Engine	Cargo Cap. or Gross*	Overall Length	Breadth	Depth or Draft*
M-16	**McMULLEN & PITZ CONSTRUCTION CO., MANITOWOC, WI**							
	Dauntless	TB	1937	D	25*	52′ 06″	15′ 06″	5′ 03″
	Erich	TB	1943	D	19*	45′ 00″	12′ 07″	5′ 09″
M-17	**McNALLY CONSTRUCTION INC., HAMILTON, ON**							
	Bagotville	TB	1964	D	65*	65′ 00″	18′ 06″	10′ 00″
	Canadian	DR	1954	B	1,087*	173′ 08″	49′ 08″	13′ 04″
	Canadian Argosy	DR	1978	B	951*	149′ 09″	54′ 01″	10′ 08″
	Carl M.	TB	1957	D	21*	47′ 00″	14′ 06″	6′ 00″
	Idus Atwell	DR	1962	B	366*	100′ 00″	40′ 00″	8′ 05″
	John Holden	DR	1954	B	148*	89′ 08″	30′ 01″	6′ 02″
	Le Taureau	TB	1985	D	25*	36′ 04″	14′ 07″	5′ 09″
	(George Bay)							
	Manistique	TB	1954	D	16*	38′ 00″	12′ 01″	3′ 02″
	Paula M.	TB	1959	D	12*	46′ 06″	16′ 01″	4′ 10″
	R. C. L. No. II	TB	1958	D	20*	42′ 09″	14′ 03″	5′ 09″
	Sandra Mary	TB	1962	D	97*	80′ 00″	21′ 00″	10′ 09″
	(Flo Cooper '62-'00)							
	Whitby	TB	1978	D	24*	45′ 00″	14′ 00″	5′ 00″

BEAVER MARINE LTD. – A SUBSIDIARY OF McNALLY CONSTRUCTION INC., HALIFAX, NS

Fleet #.	Fleet Name Vessel Name	Type of Vessel	Year Built	Type of Engine	Cargo Cap. or Gross*	Overall Length	Breadth	Depth or Draft*
	Beaver Delta II	TB	1959	D	14*	35′ 08″	12′ 00″	4′ 04″
	(Halcyon Bay)							
	Beaver Gamma	TB	1960	D	17*	37′ 01″	12′ 09″	6′ 00″
	(Burlington Bertie)							
	Beaver Kay	GC	1953	B	614*	115′ 01″	60′ 00″	9′ 05″
	Dapper Dan	TB	1948	D	21*	41′ 03″	12′ 07″	5′ 09″
	Jamie L.	TB	1988	D	25*	36′ 04″	14′ 07″	5′ 09″
	(Baie Ste-Anne II '88-'05)							
	Mister Joe	TB	1964	D	70*	61′ 00″	19′ 00″	7′ 02″
	Oshawa	TB	1969	D	24*	42′ 09″	13′ 08″	5′ 04″
	William B. Dilly	DR	1957	B	473*	116′ 00″	39′ 10″	9′ 01″
M-18	**MENASHA TUGBOAT CO., SARNIA, ON**							
	Charles XX	DB	1965	B	219*	109′ 7″	31′ 09″	7′ 01″
	Menasha {2}	TB	1949	D	147*	78′ 00″	24′ 00″	9′ 08″

(W. C. Harms '49-'54, Hamilton '54-'86, Ruby Casho '86-'88, W. C. Harms '88-'97)

Fleet #.	Fleet Name Vessel Name	Type of Vessel	Year Built	Type of Engine	Cargo Cap. or Gross*	Overall Length	Breadth	Depth or Draft*
M-19	**MERCURY CRUISE LINES, PALATINE, IL**							
	Chicago's First Lady	ES	1991	D	62*	96′ 00″	22′ 00″	9′ 00″
	Chicago's Little Lady	ES	1999	D	70*	69′ 02″	22′ 08″	7′ 00″
	Skyline Princess	ES	1956	D	56*	59′ 04″	16′ 00″	4′ 08″
	Skyline Queen	ES	1959	D	45*	61′ 05″	16′ 10″	6′ 00″
M-20	**MICHIGAN DEPARTMENT OF NATURAL RESOURCES, LANSING, MI**							
	Channel Cat	RV	1968	D	24*	46′ 00″	13′ 06″	4′ 00″

Fleet #.	Fleet Name / Vessel Name	Type of Vessel	Year Built	Type of Engine	Cargo Cap. or Gross*	Overall Length	Breadth	Depth or Draft*
	Chinook	RV	1947	D	26*	50' 00"	12' 00"	5' 00"
	Judy	RV	1950	D	41*	40' 00"	12' 00"	3' 06"
	Steelhead	RV	1967	D	70*	63' 00"	16' 04"	6' 06"
M-21	**MIDDLE BASS BOAT LINE, MIDDLE BASS, OH**							
	Victory	PA/CF	1960	D	14*	63' 07"	15' 03"	4' 08"
M-22	**MIDLAND TOURS INC., MIDLAND, ON**							
	Miss Midland	ES	1974	D	119*	68' 07"	19' 04"	6' 04"
	Serendipity Princess	ES	1982	D	93*	69' 00"	23' 00"	4' 03"
	(Trent Voyageur '82-'87, Serendipity Lady '87-'95)							
M-23	**MIDWEST MARITIME CORP., MILWAUKEE, WI**							
	Leona B.	TB	1972	D	99*	59' 08"	24' 01"	10' 03"
	(Kings Squire '72-'78, Juanita D. '78-'79, Katherine L. '79-'93, Mary Page Hannah {2} '93-'04)							
M-24	**MILLER BOAT LINE INC., PUT-IN-BAY, OH**							
	Islander {3}	PA/CF	1983	D	92*	90' 03"	38' 00"	8' 03"
	Put-In-Bay {3}	PA/CF	1997	D	95*	96' 00"	38' 06"	9' 06"
	South Bass	PA/CF	1989	D	95*	96' 00"	38' 06"	9' 06"
	Wm. Market	PA/CF	1993	D	95*	96' 00"	38' 06"	8' 09"
M-25	**MILWAUKEE BULK TERMINALS INC., MILWAUKEE, WI**							
	MBT 10	DH	1994	B	1,960	200' 00"	35' 00'	13' 00"
	MBT 20	DH	1994	B	1,960	200' 00"	35' 00'	13' 00"
	MBT 33	DH	1976	B	3,793	240' 00"	52' 06"	14' 06"
M-26	**MINISTER OF PUBLIC SAFETY & EMERGENCY PREPAREDNESS, OTTAWA, ON**							
	Simmonds		1995	D	56*	53' 10"	21' 09"	6' 06"
M-27	**MUSEUM SHIP WILLIS B. BOYER, TOLEDO, OH**							
	Willis B. Boyer	MU	1911	T	15,000	617' 00"	64' 00"	33' 01"
	Built: Great Lakes Engineering Works, Ecorse, MI; former Shenago Furance Co./Republic Steel Co./Cleveland-Cliffs Steamship Co. bulk carrier last operated in 1980; open to the public at Toledo, OH							
	(Col. James M. Schoonmaker '11-'69)							
M-28	**MUSKOKA STEAMSHIP & HISTORICAL SOCIETY, GRAVENHURST, ON**							
	Segwun	PA	1887	R	168*	128' 00"	24' 00"	7' 06"
	(Nipissing {2} 1887-'25)							
	Wanda III	PA	1915	R	60*	94' 00"	12' 00"	5' 00"
	Wenonah II	PA	2001	D	470*	127' 00"	28' 00"	6' 00"
N-1	**NADRO MARINE SERVICES LTD., PORT DOVER, ON**							
	Ecosse	TB	1979	D	146*	91' 00"	26' 01"	8' 06"
	(R & L No. 1 '79-'96)							
	Intrepid III	TB	1976	D	39*	66' 00"	17' 00"	7' 06"
	Lac Manitoba	TB	1944	D	65*	65' 00"	16' 10"	7' 07"
	(Tanac 75 '44-'52, Manitoba '52-'57)							
	Nadro Clipper	TB	1939	D	64*	70' 00"	23' 00"	6' 06"
	(Stanley Clipper '39-'94)							
	Seahound	TB	1941	D	60*	65' 06"	17' 00"	7' 00"
	([Unnamed] '41-'56, Sea Hound '56-'80, Carolyn Jo '80-'00)							
	Vac	TB	1942	D	37*	65' 00"	21' 00"	6' 06"
	Vigilant 1	TB	1944	D	111*	76' 08"	20' 09"	10' 02"
	(HMCS Glenlivet [W-43] '44-'75, Glenlivet II '75-'77, Canadian Franko '77-'82, Glenlivet II '82-'00)							
N-2	**NAUTICA QUEEN CRUISE DINING SHIP (NOW ACQUISITION LLC), CLEVELAND, OH**							
	Nautica Queen	ES	1981	D	95*	124' 00"	31' 02"	8' 10"
	(Bay Queen '81-'85, Arawanna Queen '85-'88, Star of Nautica '88-'92)							
N-3	**NAUTICAL ADVENTURES, TORONTO, ON**							
	Empire Sandy	ES/3S	1943	D/W	434*	140' 00"	32' 08"	14' 00"
	(Empire Sandy '43-'48, Ashford '48-'52, Chris M. '52-'79)							

JOHN D. LEITCH

Vessel Spotlight

Considered radical, innovative and just plain different when built, there is no doubt the *John D. Leitch* is unique on the Great Lakes. A product of Port Weller Dry Docks, St. Catharines, Ont., this self-unloading bulk carrier was designed with one cargo in mind: coal for Upper Lakes Shipping's first contract with the Hydro Electric Power Commission of Ontario. She was launched April 15, 1967, and christened *Canadian Century* in honor of Canada's centennial year.

With coal a less-dense commodity than ore, the cubic cargo capacity of the vessel was paramount. As a result, she was built with one gigantic hold with an inverted dome design at the floor. Even the wheelhouse and forward accommodations were placed as close to the bow as possible and stacked to increase the hold capacity. Her unloading equipment consisted of a single belt feeding a forward bucket-and-hopper elevator system (replaced in 1976 with a loop-belt elevator system) to the discharge

There's no mistaking the *John D. Leitch*, thanks to her towering superstructure. *(Jim Hoffman)*

boom. Unloading was assisted by a mechanical reclaimer, a first in the industry. Built to the maximum 730 x 75-foot Seaway dimensions of the time, the *Canadian Century* became the largest self-unloader on the Great Lakes.

Entering service, the *Canadian Century* immediately began setting coal cargo records. On Dec. 8, 1967, she set a Welland Canal coal mark with 28,283 tons from Conneaut to Hamilton. The vessel carried 1.7 million tons of coal in 63 trips during her first season of operation. A Conneaut dock record was set June 1, 1975, when 27,890 tons of coal was loaded in 3 hours, 40 minutes.

Canadian Century returned to Port Weller Dry Docks for the winter lay-up of 2001-02 to receive a $23 million midlife refit. Taking advantage of the new maximum allowed Seaway width of 78 feet, the self-unloader received a new mid-body from the keel to the deck, including new flat tank tops and two diesel-powered excavators replacing the reclaiming machine, increasing cargo handling flexibility and efficiency. Also included was the rebuilding of the propeller shaft and the installation of a larger, controllable-pitch propeller.

Canadian Century in the 1970s. *(Tom Manse)*

In a private ceremony held at the dry dock on May 15, 2002, the vessel was rededicated *John D. Leitch* in honor of Jack Leitch, the former president and current chairman of Upper Lakes Group. Even though purists scoff at her boxy design and office building-style forward cabin, she is truly one of a kind among lakers. **– George Wharton**

Fleet #.	Fleet Name Vessel Name	Type of Vessel	Year Built	Type of Engine	Cargo Cap. or Gross*	Overall Length	Breadth	Depth or Draft*
	Wayward Princess	ES	1976	D	325*	92' 00"	26' 00"	10' 00"
	(Cayuga II '76-'82)							
N-4	**NAVETTES MARITIMES DU SAINT-LAURENT INC., MONTREAL, QC**							
	Miss Olympia	ES	1972	D	29*	62' 08"	14' 00"	4' 08"
	(Miss Parry Sound)							
	Tandem I	PA	1991	D	108*	87' 01"	22' 00"	4' 05"
	Transit	PA	1992	D	120*	68' 00"	22' 09"	4' 05"
N-5	**NAVY MARINE CORPS RESERVE CENTER, BUFFALO, NY**							
	LCU 1680	TV	1943	D	170*	135' 00"	29' 00"	
N-6	**NEW YORK STATE MARINE HIGHWAY TRANSPORTATION LLC, TROY, NY**							
	Benjamin Elliot	TB	1960	D	27*	50' 00"	15' 06"	7' 00"
	(El Jean)							
	Margot	TB	1958	D	141*	90' 00"	25' 00"	10' 00"
	(Margot Moran)							
N-7	**NORLAKE TRANSPORTATION CO., PORT COLBORNE, ON**							
	Ours Polaire	TB	1997	D	9*	31' 00"	13' 00"	6' 00"
	Radium Yellowknife	TB	1948	D	235*	120' 00"	28' 00"	6' 06"
	Salvage Monarch	TB	1959	D	219*	97' 09"	28' 00"	14' 06"
	(Charlie S. '54-'75, Cathy McAllister '75-'02)							
	W. B. Indock	TB	1972	D		27' 39"	10' 33"	5' 05"
	(Mokka Fjord '72-'91)							
N-8	**NORTHEASTERN MARITIME HISTORICAL FOUNDATION INC., SUPERIOR, WI**							
	Islay	TB	1892	D	19*	60' 00"	13' 00"	5' 00"
	Scheduled to be moved from Milwaukee to Superior, WI (Islay 1892-'1947, Bayfield {1} '47-'83)							
	Mount McKay	TB	1908	D	99*	80' 00"	21' 06"	9' 00"
	(Walter F. Mattick '08-' 19, Merchant '19-'24, Marinette '24-'47, Esther S. '47-'66)							
	Nicole S.	TB	1949	D	146*	88' 06"	25' 06"	11' 00"
	(Evening Star '49-'86, Protector '86-'94)							
	Q.A. Gillmore	TB	1913	R	99*	80' 00"	20' 00"	12' 06"
	Former Reiss Steamship Co. tug last operated in 1969; scheduled to be moved from Saugatuck, MI, to Superior, WI (Q. A. Gillmore '13-'32, Reiss '32-'05)							
N-9	**NORTHERN MARINE TRANSPORTATION INC., SAULT STE. MARIE, MI**							
	David Allen	PB	1964	D	32*	56' 04"	13' 03"	6' 00"
	Linda Jean	PB	1950	D	17*	38' 00"	10' 00"	5' 00"
	Soo River Belle	PB	1961	D	25*	40' 00"	14' 00"	6' 00"
O-1	**OAK GROVE MARINE AND TRANSPORTATION INC., CLAYTON, NY**							
	Maple Grove	PK	1954	D	55*	73' 07"	20' 00"	9' 00"
O-2	**OLSON DREDGE & DOCK CO., ALGONAC, MI**							
	John Michael	TB	1913	D	41*	55' 04"	15' 01"	7' 06"
	(Colonel Ward, Ross Coddington, Joseph J. Olivieri)							
O-3	**OLYMPIA CRUISE LINES, THORNHILL, ON**							
	Enterprise 2000	ES	1998	D	370*	121' 06"	35' 00"	6' 00"
O-4	**ONTARIO MINISTRY OF TRANSPORTATION & COMMUNICATION, DOWNSVIEW, ON**							
	Frontenac II	PA/CF	1962	D	666*	181' 00"	45' 00"	10' 00"
	(Charlevoix {2} '62-'92)							
	Frontenac County Ferry	PF/CF	1974	D	62*	60' 00"	32' 00"	4' 01"
	Frontenac Howe Islander	PF/CF	2004	D	130*	100' 00"	32' 03"	5' 05"
	Glenora	PA/CF	1952	D	209*	127' 00"	33' 00"	9' 00"
	(The St. Joseph Islander '52-'74)							
	Jiimaan	PA/CF	1992	D	2,830*	176' 09"	42' 03"	13' 06"
	Pelee Islander	PA/CF	1960	D	334*	145' 00"	32' 00"	10' 00"

Fleet #.	Fleet Name / Vessel Name	Type of Vessel	Year Built	Type of Engine	Cargo Cap. or Gross*	Overall Length	Breadth	Depth or Draft*
	Quinte Loyalist	PA/CF	1954	D	209*	127' 00"	32' 00"	8' 00"
	Wolfe Islander III	PA/CF	1975	D	985*	205' 00"	68' 00"	6' 00"
O-5	**ONTARIO POWER GENERATION INC., TORONTO, ON**							
	Niagara Queen II	IB	1992	D	57*	56' 01"	18' 00"	6' 08"
O-6	**OSBORNE MATERIALS CO., GRAND RIVER, OH**							
	Emmet J. Carey	SC	1948	D	900	114' 00"	23' 00"	11' 00"
	(Beatrice Ottinger '48-'63, James B. Lyons '63-'88)							
	F. M. Osborne {2}	SC	1910	D	500	150' 00"	29' 00"	11' 03"
	(Grand Island {1} '10-'58, Lesco '58-'75)							
O-7	**OWEN SOUND TRANSPORTATION CO. LTD., OWEN SOUND, ON**							
	Chi-Cheemaun	PA/CF	1974	D	6,991*	365' 05"	61' 00"	21' 00"
	Built: Canadian Shipbuilding and Engineering Ltd., Collingwood, ON							
P-1	**PAUL VASSALL, DETROIT, MI**							
	Elizabeth	TB	1935	D	48*	65' 00"	18' 00"	7' 00"
	(Chester)							
P-2	**PENETANGUISHENE 30,000 ISLAND CRUISES, PENETANGUISHENE, ON**							
	Georgian Queen	ES	1918	D	249*	119' 00"	36' 00"	16' 06"
	(Victoria '18-'18, Murray Stewart '18-'48, David Richard '48-'79)							
P-3	**PERE MARQUETTE SHIPPING CO., LUDINGTON, MI**							
	Pere Marquette 41	SU	1941	B	4,545	403' 00"	58' 00"	23' 06"
	Built: Manitowoc Shipbuilding Co., Manitowoc, WI; converted from powered train/car ferry to a self-unloading barge in '97 (City of Midland 41 '41-'97)							
	Undaunted	AT	1944	DE	860*	143' 00"	33' 01"	18' 00"
	Built: Gulfport Boiler/Welding, Port Arthur, TX							
	(USS Undaunted [ATR-126, ATA-199] '44-'63, USMA Kings Pointer '63-'93, Krystal K. '93-'97)							
	[ATB Undaunted / PM 41 OA dimensions together]					493' 06"	58' 00"	23' 06"
P-4	**PETERSEN STEAMSHIP CO., DOUGLAS, MI**							
	Keewatin {2}	MU	1907	Q	3,856*	346' 00"	43' 08"	26' 06"
	Built: Fairfield Shipbuilding, Govan, Scotland; former Canadian Pacific Railway Co. passenger vessel last operated Nov. 29, 1965; open to the public at Douglas, MI; celebrating its 100th birthday in 2007							
P-5	**PICTURED ROCKS CRUISES INC., MUNISING, MI**							
	Grand Island {2}	ES	1989	D	51*	68' 00"	16' 01"	5' 01"
	Miners Castle	ES	1974	D	72*	68' 00"	17' 00"	5' 00"
	Miss Superior	ES	1984	D	76*	68' 00"	17' 00"	5' 00"
	Pictured Rocks	ES	1972	D	47*	60' 00"	14' 00"	4' 04"
P-6	**PIER WISCONSIN, MILWAUKEE, WI**							
	Denis Sullivan	TV/ES	1994	W/D	99*	138' 00"	24' 00"	8' 09"
P-7	**PLAUNT TRANSPORTATION CO. INC., CHEBOYGAN, MI**							
	Kristen D.	CF	1988	D	83*	64' 11"	36' 00"	6' 05"
P-8	**POLOVIC CONSTRUCTION & LEASING, MENTOR, OH**							
	Arthur	TB	1930	D	31*	49' 08"	14' 01"	6' 00"
	(Dover '29-'75, Margaret Barker '75-8?, Julie Dee '8?-'92)							
P-9	**PORT CITY PRINCESS CRUISES INC., MUSKEGON, MI**							
	Port City Princess	ES	1966	D	79*	64' 09"	30' 00"	5' 06"
	(Island Queen {1} '66-'87)							
P-10	**PORT DALHOUSIE VITALIZATION CORP., ST. CATHARINES, ON**							
	Dalhousie Princess	ES	1975	D	281*	106' 00"	24' 00"	8' 02"
	(Island Queen {3} '75-'79, Miss Kingston II '79-'84, M/V Montreal '84-'01)							

P-11   PORT HURON MUSEUM OF ARTS & HISTORY, PORT HURON, MI

	Bramble	MU	1944	DE	1,025*	180' 00"	37' 00"	17' 04"

Built: Zenith Dredge Co., Duluth, MN; former U.S. Coast Guard bouy tender/icebreaker was retired in 2003; open to the public at Port Huron, MI (USCGC Bramble [WLB-392] '44-'03)

	Huron	MU	1920	D	392*	96' 05"	24' 00"	10' 00"

Built: Charles L. Seabury Co., Morris Heights, NY; former U.S. Coast Guard lightship WLV-526 was retired Aug. 25, 1970; open to the public at Port Huron, MI

P-12   PORT OF INDIANA HARBOR, BURNS HARBOR, IN

	Oconto	MU	1953	D	23*	45' 00"	13' 00"	7' 00"

Retired tug is on display ashore as museum at Burns Harbor, IN (ST-2162 '53-'62)

P-13   PORTOFINO ON THE RIVER, WYANDOTTE, MI

	Friendship	ES	1968	D	110*	85' 00"	30' 06"	7' 03"

(Peche Island V '68-'71, Papoose V '71-'82)

P- 14   PROJECT H.M.S. DETROIT, AMHERSTBURG, ON

	His Majesty's Ship Detroit	ES	2006	3M/D	235*	131' 02"	30' 06"	9' 10"

P-15   PURVIS MARINE LTD., SAULT STE. MARIE, ON

	Adanac	TB	1913	D	108*	80' 03"	19' 02"	10' 06"

(Edward C. Whalen '13-'66, John McLean '66-'95)

	Anglian Lady	TB	1953	D	398*	136' 06"	30' 00"	14' 01"

(Hamtun '53-'72, Nathalie Letzer '72-'88)

	Avenger IV	TB	1962	D	293*	120' 00"	30' 05"	17' 05"

(Avenger '62-'85)

	Chief Wawatam	DB	1911	B	4,500	347' 00"	62' 03"	15' 00"

Converted from a powered train ferry to a barge in '88

	G.L.B. No. 1	DB	1953	B	3,215	305' 00"	50' 00"	12' 00"
	G.L.B. No. 2	DB	1953	B	3,215	305' 02"	50' 00"	12' 00"
	Malden	DB	1946	B	1,075	150' 00"	41' 09"	10' 03"

U.S. Coast Guard cutter *Biscayne Bay* breaking ice as night falls. *(Chris Winters)*

Fleet #.	Fleet Name / Vessel Name	Type of Vessel	Year Built	Type of Engine	Cargo Cap. or Gross*	Overall Length	Breadth	Depth or Draft*
	Martin E. Johnson	TB	1959	D	26*	46' 00"	16' 00"	5' 09"
	P.M.L. Alton	DB	1951	B	150	93' 00"	30' 00"	8' 00"
	P.M.L. 357	DB	1944	B	600	138' 00"	38' 00"	11' 00"
	P.M.L. 2501	TK	1980	B	1,954*	302' 00"	52' 00"	17' 00"
	(CTCO 2505 '80-'96)							
	P.M.L. 9000	TK	1968	B	4,285*	400' 00"	76' 00"	20' 00"
	(Palmer '68-'00)							
	Reliance	TB	1974	D	708*	148' 04"	35' 07"	21' 06"
	(Sinni '74-'81, Irving Cedar '81-'96, Atlantic Cedar '96-'02)							
	Rocket	TB	1901	D	39*	70' 00"	15' 00"	8' 00"
	Tecumseh II	DB	1976	B	2,500	180' 00"	54' 00"	12' 00"
	(U-727 '76-'94)							
	Wilfred M. Cohen	TB	1948	D	284*	104' 00"	28' 00"	14' 06"
	(A. T. Lowmaster '48-'75)							
	W. I. Scott Purvis	TB	1938	D	206*	96' 06"	26' 04"	10' 04"
	(Orient Bay '38-'75, Guy M. No. 1 '75-'90)							
	W. J. Ivan Purvis	TB	1938	D	191*	100' 06"	25' 06"	9' 00"
	(Magpie '38-'66, Dana T. Bowen '66-'75)							
	Waub Nav. No. 1	TB	1941	D	14*	38' 06"	10' 06"	6' 00"
	Yankcanuck {2}	CS	1963	D	4,760	324' 03"	49' 00"	26' 00"
	Built: Collingwood Shipyards, Collingwood, ON							
P-16	**PUT-IN-BAY BOAT LINE CO., PORT CLINTON, OH**							
	Jet Express	PF/CA	1989	D	93*	92' 08"	28' 06"	8' 04"
	Jet Express II	PF/CA	1992	D	85*	92' 06"	28' 06"	8' 04"
	Jet Express III	PF/CA	2001	D	70*	78' 02"	27' 06"	8' 02"
R-1	**RANKIN CONSTRUCTION INC., ST. CATHARINES, ON**							
	Judique Flyer	DB	1967	D	67.7*	60' 00"	29' 08"	3' 09"
	(Sweep Scow No. 4 '67-'03)							
R-2	**RIGEL SHIPPING CANADA INC., SHEDIAC, NB**							
	VESSELS CHARTERED TO PETRO-NAV INC., MONTREAL, QC							
	Diamond Star	TK	1992	D	10,511	405' 11"	58' 01"	34' 09"
	Built: MTW Shipyards, Wismar, Germany (Elbestern '92-'93)							
	Emerald Star	TK	1992	D	10,511	405' 11"	58' 01"	34' 09"
	Built: MTW Shipyards, Wismar, Germany (Emsstern '92-'93)							
	Jade Star	TK	1993	D	10,511	405' 11"	58' 01"	34' 09"
	Built: MTW Shipyards, Wismar, Germany (Jadestern '93-'94)							
R-3	**ROCKPORT BOAT LINE LTD., ROCKPORT, ON**							
	Ida M.	ES	1970	D	29*	55' 00"	14' 00"	3' 00"
	Ida M. II	ES	1973	D	116*	63' 02"	22' 02"	5' 00"
	Sea Prince II	ES	1978	D	172*	83' 00"	24' 02"	6' 08"
R-4	**ROEN SALVAGE CO., STURGEON BAY, WI**							
	Chas. Asher	TB	1967	D	10*	50' 00"	18' 00"	8' 00"
	John R. Asher	TB	1943	D	93*	70' 00"	20' 00"	8' 06"
	(U. S. Army ST-71 '43-'46, Russell 8 '46-'64, Reid McAllister '64-'67, Donegal '67-'85)							
	Louie S.	TB	1956	D	43*	37' 00"	12' 00"	5' 00"
	Spuds	TB	1944	D	19*	42' 00"	12' 06"	6' 00"
	Stephan M. Asher	TB	1954	D	60*	65' 00"	19' 01"	5' 04"
	(Captain Bennie '54-'82, Dumar Scout '82-'87)							
	Timmy A.	TB	1953	D	12*	33' 06"	10' 08"	5' 02"
R-5	**ROYAL CANADIAN YACHT CLUB, TORONTO, ON**							
	Elsie D.	PA	1958	D	9*	34' 07"	10' 08"	3' 06"
	Esperanza	PA	1953	D	14*	38' 06"	11' 02"	4' 06"
	Hiawatha	PA	1895	D	46*	56' 01"	14' 04"	6' 02"
	Kwasind	PA	1912	D	47*	70' 08"	15' 09"	5' 05"

ALGOVILLE

A unique lake boat from the outset, *Algoville* was launched Oct. 15, 1967, as *Senneville* for Montreal's Mohawk Navigation Co. She was one of only a handful of vessels built for Great Lakes service by the St. John Shipbuilding and Dry Dock Co. of St. John, N.B., and also one of only two lakers built around this time with all accommodations, wheelhouse and machinery aft (the other being the 1963 built fleet-mate *Silver Isle*). Less noticeable – the *Senneville* was built with the lightest weight steel possible to save weight and increase cargo capacity. The Seaway-sized vessel could carry up to 28,200 tons and took her name from the community of Senneville, Que., located at the western end of Montreal Island.

Vessel Spotlight

In 1970, *Senneville* came under management of the Misener group of companies but retained her Mohawk colors, a green hull with blue forecastle. The vessel set a couple of Great Lakes cargo records, with a load of rye from Thunder Bay, Ont., to Sorel, Que., in 1975 followed by a load of soybeans from Superior, Wis., to Sorel in 1977. In 1980, the *Senneville* and *Silver Isle* were purchased by Pioneer Shipping Ltd. Remaining under Misener management, the vessels soon sported dramatic orange hulls with yellow forecastles and white cabins. A white billboard-style "PIONEER" was painted on the sides of the hulls.

Beginning with the 1991 season, the *Senneville* began sailing under the management consortium Great Lakes Bulk Carriers, St. Catharines, Ont., which combined the bulker fleets of Canada Steamship Lines, Misener and Pioneer Shipping. With the collapse of the consortium, *Senneville* and *Silver Isle* were acquired by Algoma Central Corp. for $5.7 million (Can.) in 1994. *Senneville* was renamed *Algoville* and began sailing that year for her new owners. October 1996 saw the *Algoville* return to service following a $6.4 million (Can.) midlife refit that included widening of her hull, increasing her midsummer capacity to 31,250 tons.

The *Algoville* has sailed every season since her launch, a feat not often achieved by some Canadian bulkers due to fluctuations in the bulk agricultural industry. Engine problems forced the vessel to lay up in May 2006. However Algoma has installed a new energy-efficient diesel that should see the vessel back in service by late spring 2007. – **George Wharton**

Algoville in the St. Clair River. *(John Meyland);* **Inset, as Senneville** *(Tom Manse Coll.)*

R-6	**RUSSELL ISLAND TRANSIT CO., ALGONAC, MI**							
	Islander {2}	PA/CF	1967	D	38*	41' 00"	15' 00"	3' 06"
R-7	**RYBA MARINE CONSTRUCTION CO., CHEBOYGAN, MI**							
	Alcona	TB	1957	D	18*	40' 00"	12' 06"	5' 06"
	Amber Mae	TB	1922	D	67*	65' 00"	14' 01"	10' 00"
	(E. W. Sutton '22-'52, Venture '52- '00)							
	Jarco 1402	CS	1981	B	473*	140' 00"	39' 00"	9' 00"
	Kathy Lynn	TB	1944	D	140*	85' 00"	24' 00"	9' 06"
	(U. S. Army ST-693 '44-'79, Sea Islander '79-'91)							
	Rochelle Kaye	TB	1963	D	52*	51' 06"	19' 04"	7' 00"
	(Jaye Anne '63-?, Katanni ?-'97)							
	Tenacious	TB	1960	D	149*	90' 00"	26' 04"	12' 00"
	(Mobil 8 '60-'91, Tatarrax '91-'93, Nan McKay '93-'95)							
S-1	**SABLE POINT MARINE LLC, LUDINGTON, MI**							
	Snohomish		1943	DE	195*	110' 00"	26' 06"	12' 06"
	(Former U.S. Coast Guard WYTM-98 Snohomish)							
S-2	**SCOTLUND STIVERS, MARINETTE, WI**							
	Arthur K. Atkinson	PA	1917	D	3,241*	384' 00"	56' 00"	20' 06"
	Built: Great Lakes Engineering Company of Ecorse , MI; last operated in April 1982; laid up at DeTour, MI							
	(Ann Arbor No. 6 '17-'59)							
S-3	**SEA SERVICE LLC, SUPERIOR, WI**							
	Sea Colt	TB	1984	D	23*	38' 00"	11' 06"	8' 00"
	SEAWAY MARINE TRANSPORT, ST. CATHARINES, ON *PARTNERSHIP BETWEEN ALGOMA CENTRAL CORP. (A-6) AND UPPER LAKES GROUP (U-15) SEE RESPECTIVE FLEETS FOR VESSELS INVOLVED.*							
S-4	**SELVICK MARINE TOWING CORP., STURGEON BAY, WI**							
	Carla Anne Selvick	TB	1908	D	191*	96' 00"	23' 00"	11' 02"
	(S.O. Co. No. 19 '08-'16, S.T. Co. No. 19 '16-'18, Socony 19 '18-'47, Esso Tug No. 4 '47-'53, McAllister 44 '53-'55, Roderick McAllister '55-'84)							
	Cameron O.	TB	1955	D	26*	50' 00"	15' 00"	7' 03"
	(Escort II '55-'06)							
	Jacquelyn Nicole	TB	1913	D	96*	81' 00"	20' 00"	12' 06"
	(Michigan {4} '13-'78, Ste. Marie II '78-'81, Dakota '81-'92, Ethel E. '92-'02)							
	Jimmy L.	TB	1939	D	148*	110' 00"	25' 00"	13' 00"
	(USCGC Naugatuck [WYT / WYTM-92] '39-'80, Timmy B. '80-'84)							
	Mary Page Hannah {1}	TB	1950	DE	461*	143' 00"	33' 01"	14' 06"
	(U. S. Army ATA-230 '49-'72, G. W. Codrington '72-'73, William P. Feeley {2} '73-'73, William W. Stender '73-'78)							
	Sharon M. Selvick	TB	1945	D	28*	45' 00"	13' 00"	7' 00"
	(USACE Judson)							
	Susan L.	TB	1944	D	163*	86' 00"	23' 00"	10' 04"
	(U. S. Army ST-709 '44-'47, USCOE Stanley '47-'99)							
	William C. Selvick	TB	1944	D	142*	85' 00"	22' 11"	10' 04"
	(U. S. Army ST-500 '44-'49, Sherman H. Serre '49-'77)							
S-5	**SHAMROCK CHARTERING CO., GROSSE POINTE, MI**							
	Helene	ES	1927	D	99*	96' 09"	17' 00"	8' 00"
S-6	**SHELL PRODUCTS CANADA, MONTREAL, QC**							
	Arca	RT	1963	D	1,296	175' 00"	36' 00"	14' 00"
	Built: Port Weller Drydocks, Port Weller, ON (Imperial Lachine '63-'03, Josee M. '03-'03)							
S-7	**SHEPARD MARINE CONSTRUCTION, ST. CLAIR SHORES, MI**							
	Geraldine	TW	1988	D	26*	42' 00"	19' 00"	5' 00"
	Robin Lynn	TB	1952	D	146*	85' 00"	25' 00"	11' 00"
	(Bonita '52-'85, Susan Hoey {2} '85'-'95, Blackie B '95-'97, Susan Hoey {3 } '97-'98)							

Fleet #.	Fleet Name Vessel Name	Type of Vessel	Year Built	Type of Engine	Cargo Cap. or Gross*	Overall Length	Breadth	Depth or Draft*
S-8	**SHEPLER'S MACKINAC ISLAND FERRY SERVICE, MACKINAW CITY, MI**							
	Capt. Shepler	PF	1986	D	71*	84' 00"	21' 00"	7' 10"
	Felicity	PF	1972	D	84*	65' 00"	18' 01"	8' 03"
	Sacre Bleu	PK	1959	D	92*	94' 10"	31' 00"	9' 09"
	(Put-In-Bay {2} '59-'94)							
	The Hope	PF	1975	D	87*	77' 00"	20' 00"	8' 03"
	The Welcome	PF	1969	D	66*	60' 06"	16' 08"	8' 02"
	Wyandot	PF	1979	D	99*	77' 00"	20' 00"	8' 00"
S-9	**SHIPWRECK TOURS INC., MUNISING, MI**							
	Miss Munising	ES	1967	D	50*	60' 00"	14' 00"	4' 04"
S-10	**SHORELINE CHARTERS, GILLS ROCK, WI**							
	The Shoreline	ES	1973	D	12*	33' 00"	11' 4"	3' 00"
S-11	**SHORELINE CONTRACTORS INC., CLEVELAND, OH**							
	Eagle	TB	1943	D	31*	57' 09"	14' 05"	6' 10"
S-12	**SHORELINE SIGHTSEEING CO., CHICAGO, IL**							
	Cap Streeter	ES	1987	D	28*	63' 06"	24' 04"	7' 07"
	Evening Star	ES	2001	D	93*	83' 00"	23' 00"	7' 00"
	Shoreline II	ES	1987	D	89*	75' 00"	26' 00"	7' 01"
	Star of Chicago {2}	ES	1999	D	73*	64' 10"	22' 08"	7' 05"
	Voyager	CF	1960	D	98*	65' 00"	35' 00"	8' 00"
S-13	**SOCIETÉ DES TRAVERSIERS DU QUEBEC, QUEBEC, QC**							
	Alphonse Desjardins	CF	1971	D	1,741*	214' 00"	71' 06"	20' 00"
	Armand Imbeau	CF	1980	D	1,285*	203' 07"	72' 00"	18' 04"
	Camille Marcoux	CF	1974	D	6,122*	310' 09"	62' 09"	39' 00"
	Catherine Legardeur	CF	1985	D	1,348*	205' 09"	71' 10"	18' 10"
	Felix Antoine Savard	CF	1997	D	2,489*	272' 00"	70' 00"	21' 09"
	Grue des Iles	CF	1981	D	447*	155' 10"	41' 01"	12' 06"
	Jos Deschenes	CF	1980	D	1,287*	203' 07"	72' 00"	18' 04"
	Joseph Savard	CF	1985	D	1,445*	206' 00"	71' 10"	18' 10"
	Lomer Gouin	CF	1971	D	1,741*	214' 00"	71' 06"	20' 00"
	Lucien L.	CF	1967	D	867*	220' 10"	61' 06"	15' 05"
	Radisson {1}	CF	1954	D	1,043*	164' 03"	72' 00"	10' 06"
S-14	**SOCIETE DU PORT DE MONTREAL, MONTREAL, QC**							
	Beaupre	TB	1952	D	13*	37' 05"	10' 49"	4' 08"
	Maisonneuve	TB	1972	D	103*	63' 10"	20' 07"	9' 03"
	Denis M	TB	1942	D	21*	46' 07"	12' 08"	4' 01"
S-15	**SOO LOCKS BOAT TOURS, SAULT STE. MARIE, MI**							
	Bide-A-Wee {3}	ES	1955	D	99*	64' 07"	23' 00"	7' 11"
	Hiawatha {2}	ES	1959	D	99*	64' 07"	23' 00"	7' 11"
	Holiday	ES	1957	D	99*	64' 07"	23' 00"	7' 11"
	Le Voyageur	ES	1959	D	70*	65' 00"	25' 00"	7' 00"
	Nokomis	ES	1959	D	70*	65' 00"	25' 00"	7' 00"
S-16	**SOUTH SHORE DREDGE AND DOCK INC., LORAIN, OH**							
	Cojak	TB	1954	D	11*	31' 07	10' 09"	6' 00"
S-17	**SPIRIT CRUISE LINE LTD., TORONTO, ON**							
	Northern Spirit I	ES	1983	D	489*	136' 00"	31' 00"	9' 00"
	(New Spirit '83-'89, Pride of Toronto '89-'92)							
	Oriole	ES	1987	D	200*	75' 00"	23' 00"	9' 00"
S-18	**SPIRIT CRUISES LLC, CHICAGO, IL**							
	Spirit of Chicago	ES	1988	D	92*	156' 00"	35' 00"	7' 01"

Mesabi Miner loading taconite at Escanaba in 2006. *(Lee Rowe)*

S-19	**SPIRIT OF THE SOUND SCHOONER CO., PARRY SOUND, ON**							
	Chippewa III	PA	1954	D	47*	65' 00"	16' 00"	6' 06"
	(Maid of the Mist III '54–'56, Maid of the Mist '56–'92)							
S-20	**S.S. CITY OF MILWAUKEE-NATIONAL HISTORIC LANDMARK, MANISTEE, MI**							
	City of Milwaukee	MU	1931	R	26 cars	360' 00"	56' 03"	21' 06"
	Built: Manitowoc Shipbuilding Co., Manitowoc, WI; train ferry sailed for the Grand Trunk Railroad '31–'78 and the Ann Arbor Railroad '78–'81; open to the public at Manistee, MI							
S-21	**S.S. METEOR WHALEBACK SHIP MUSEUM, SUPERIOR, WI**							
	Meteor {2}	MU	1896	R	40,100	380' 00"	45' 00"	26' 00"
	Built: American Steel Barge Co., Superior, WI; former ore carrier/auto carrier/tanker is the last vessel of "whaleback" design surviving on the Great Lakes. The Cleveland Tankers vessel last operated in 1969; open to the public at Superior, WI (Frank Rockefeller 1896–'28, South Park '28–'43)							
S-22	**S.S. NORISLE HERITAGE MUSEUM, MANITOWANING, ON**							
	Norisle	MU	1946	R	1,668*	215' 09"	36' 03"	16' 00"
	Built: Collingwood Shipyards, Collingwood, ON; former Ontario Northland Transportation Commission passenger vessel last operated in 1974; open to the public at Manitowaning, Manitoulin Island, ON							
S-23	**ST. JAMES MARINE CO., BEAVER ISLAND, MI**							
	American Girl	PK	1922	D	67*	62' 00"	14' 00"	6' 00"
	Oil Queen	TK	1949	B	50*	64' 08"	16' 00"	6' 00"
S-24	**ST. LAWRENCE CRUISE LINES INC., KINGSTON, ON**							
	Canadian Empress	PA	1981	D	463*	108' 00"	30' 00"	8' 00"
S-25	**ST. LAWRENCE SEAWAY DEVELOPMENT CORP., MASSENA, NY**							
	Koziol	TB	1973	D	356*	109' 00"	30' 06"	16' 03"
	(USS Chetek [YTB-827] '73–'96, Chetek '96–'00)							
	McCauley	CS	1948	B		112' 00"	52' 00"	3' 00"
	Robinson Bay	TB	1958	DE	213*	103' 00"	26' 10"	14' 06"
	Performance	TB	1997	D		50' 00"	16' 06"	7' 05"
S-26	**ST. LAWRENCE SEAWAY MANAGEMENT CORP., CORNWALL, ON**							
	VM/S Hercules	GL	1962	D	2,107*	200' 00"	75' 00"	18' 08"
	VM/S Maisonneuve	TB	1974	D	56*	58' 03"	20' 03"	6' 05"
	VM/S St. Lambert	TB	1974	D	20*	30' 08"	13' 01"	6' 05"
	VM/S St. Louis III	TB	1977	D	15*	34' 02"	11' 08"	4' 00"
S-27	**ST. MARYS CEMENT INC. (CANADA), TORONTO, ON**							
	Sea Eagle II	ATB	1979	D	560*	132' 00"	35' 00"	19' 00"
	Built: Modern Marine Power Co., Houma, LA; (Sea Eagle '79–'81, Canmar Sea Eagle '81–'91)							
	St. Marys Cement	CC	1986	B	9,400	360' 00"	60' 00"	23' 03"
	Built: Merce Industries East, Cleveland, OH							
	St. Marys Cement II	CC	1978	B	19,513	496' 06"	76' 00"	35' 00"
	Built: Galveston Shipbuilding Co., Galveston, TX (Velasco '78–'81, Canmar Shuttle '81–'90)							
	St. Marys Cement III	CC	1980	B	4,800	335' 00"	76' 08"	17' 09"
	Built: Robin Shipyard Pte Ltd., Singapore, China; last operated Sept. 1, '00; in use as a cement storage barge at Green Bay, WI (Bigorange XVI '80–'84, Says '84–'85, Al-Sayb-7 '85–'86, Clarkson Carrier '86–'94)							

THE FOLLOWING THREE VESSELS MANAGED BY HMC SHIP MANAGEMENT LTD., LEMONT, IL – AN AFFILIATE OF HANNAH MARINE CORP.

	C.T.C. No. 1	CC	1943	R	16,300	620' 06"	60' 00"	35' 00"
	Built: Great Lakes Engineering Works, River Rouge, MI; last operated Nov. 12, 1981; in use as a cement storage/transfer vessel in S. Chicago, IL							
	(Launched as McIntyre. Frank Purnell {1} '43–'64, Steelton {3} '64–'78, Hull No. 3 '78–'79, Pioneer {4} '79–'82)							
	St. Marys Challenger	CC	1906	S	10,250	552' 01"	56' 00"	31' 00"
	Built: Great Lakes Engineering Works, Ecorse, MI; repowered in '50; converted to a self-unloading cement carrier in '67; celebrated its 100th season in 2006 (William P. Snyder '06–'26, Elton Hoyt II {1} '26–'52, Alex D. Chisholm '52–'66, Medusa Challenger '66–'99, Southdown Challenger '99–'04)							

Fleet #.	Fleet Name / Vessel Name	Type of Vessel	Year Built	Type of Engine	Cargo Cap. or Gross*	Overall Length	Breadth	Depth or Draft*
	St. Marys Conquest	CC	1937	B	8,500	437' 06"	55' 00"	28' 00"

Built: Manitowoc Shipbuilding Co., Manitowoc, WI; converted from a powered tanker to a self-unloading cement barge in '87

(Red Crown '37-'62, Amoco Indiana '62-'87, Medusa Conquest '87-'99, Southdown Conquest '99-'04)

THE FOLLOWING VESSEL CHARTERED BY ST. MARYS CEMENT CO. FROM GREAT LAKES & INTERNATIONAL TOWING & SALVAGE CO., BURLINGTON, ON

	Petite Forte	TB	1969	D	368*	127' 00"	32' 00"	14' 06"

Built: Cochrane and Sons Ltd., Selby, England

(E. Bronson Ingram '69-'72, Jarmac 42 '72-'73, Scotsman '73-'81, Al Battal '81-'86)

S-28	**ST. MARYS RIVER MARINE CENTRE, SAULT STE. MARIE, ON**							
	Norgoma	MU	1950	D	1,477*	188' 00"	37' 06"	22' 06"

Built: Collingwood Shipyards, Collingwood, ON; former Ontario Northland Transportation Commission passenger vessel last operated in 1974; open to the public at Sault Ste. Marie, ON

S-29	**STANTON CRUISE LINES, THUNDER BAY, ON**							
	Pioneer II	ES	1959	D	28*	52' 01"	11' 08"	3' 09"

(Witte-De-With '59-'72, Miss Algonquin Park '72-'74, David H. Simpson '74-'90, London Princess '90-'02)

S-30	**STAR LINE MACKINAC ISLAND FERRY, ST. IGNACE, MI**							
	Cadillac {5}	PF	1990	D	73*	64' 07"	20' 00"	7' 07"
	Joliet {3}	PF	1993	D	83*	64' 08"	22' 00"	8' 03"
	LaSalle {4}	PF	1983	D	55*	65' 00"	20' 00"	7' 05"
	Marquette II {2}	PF	2005	D	65*	74' 00"	23' 06"	8' 00"
	Radisson {2}	PF	1988	D	97*	80' 00"	23' 06"	7' 00"

S-31	**STATE OF NEW YORK POWER AUTHORITY, LEWISTON, NY**							
	Breaker	TB	1962	D	29*	43' 03"	14' 03"	5' 00"
	Daniel Joncaire	TB	1979	D	25*	43' 03"	15' 00"	5' 00"

S-32	**STE. CLAIRE FOUNDATION, CLEVELAND, OH**							
	Ste. Claire	PA	1910	R	870*	197' 00"	65' 00"	14' 00"

Built: Detroit Dry Dock Co, Detroit, MI; former Detroit-Bob-Lo Island passenger steamer last operated Sept. 2, 1991; restoration underway at Toledo, OH; may be sold to a Detroit group in 2007

S-33	**STEAMER COLUMBIA FOUNDATION, DETROIT, MI**							
	Columbia {2}	PA	1902	R	968*	216' 00"	60' 00"	13' 06"

Built: Detroit Dry Dock Co, Detroit, MI; former Detroit-Bob-Lo Island passenger steamer last operated Sept. 2, 1991; laid up at Ecorse, MI

T-1	**TALISMAN ENERGY INC., CALGARY, AB**							
	Vessels are engaged in oil and gas exploration on Lake Erie							
	Dr. Bob	DV	1973	B	1,022*	160' 01"	54' 01"	11' 01"
	(Mr. Chris '73-'03)							
	J.R. Rouble	DV	1958	D	562*	123' 06"	49' 08"	16' 00"
	(Mr. Neil)							
	Miss Libby	DV	1972	B	924*	160' 01"	54' 01"	11' 01"
	Sarah No. 1	TB	1969	D	43*	72' 01"	17' 03"	6' 08"
	Timesaver II	DB	1964	B	510*	91' 08"	70' 08"	9' 01"

T-2	**TGL MARINE HOLDINGS LLC, PLYMOUTH, MI**							
	PURVIS MARINE LTD., SAULT STE. MARIE, ON – OPERATOR							
	Jane Ann IV	ATB	1978	D	954*	137' 06"	42' 08"	21' 04"

Built: Mitsui Engineering, Fujinagat, Japan (Ouro Fino '78-'81, Bomare '81-'93, Tignish Sea '93-'98)

	Sarah Spencer	SU	1959	B	23,200	611' 03"	72' 00"	40' 00"

Built: Manitowoc Shipbuilding Co., Manitowoc, WI; engine removed, converted to a self-unloading barge in '89 (Adam E. Cornelius {3} '59-'89, Capt. Edward V. Smith '89-'91, Sea Barge One '91-'96)

	[Jane Ann IV / Sarah Spencer OA dimensions together]					729' 03"	72' 00"	40' 00"

T-3	**THOMAS A. KOWAL (APALACHEE MARINE), ROCHESTER, NY**							
	Apalachee	TB	1943	DE	224*	104' 03"	26' 04"	15' 01"
	(Apalachee WYTM-71)							

Fleet #.	Fleet Name Vessel Name	Type of Vessel	Year Built	Type of Engine	Cargo Cap. or Gross*	Overall Length	Breadth	Depth or Draft*
T-4	**THOUSAND ISLANDS AND SEAWAY CRUISES, BROCKVILLE, ON**							
	Alouette	ES	1954	D	7*	31' 00"	10' 05"	3' 02"
	General Brock III	ES	1977	D	56*	50' 05"	15' 04"	5' 02"
	(Miss Peterborough)							
	Island Heritage	ES	1929	D	21*	63' 09"	9' 08"	4' 09"
	(Miss Ivy Lea No. 1)							
	Sea Fox II	ES	1988	D	55*	39' 08"	20' 00"	2' 00"
T-5	**THUNDER BAY MARINE SERVICE LTD., THUNDER BAY, ON**							
	Coastal Cruiser	TB	1939	D	29*	65' 00"	18' 00"	12' 00"
	Robert W.	TB	1949	D	48*	60' 00"	16' 00"	8' 06"
	Rosalee D.	TB	1943	D	22*	55' 00"	16' 00"	10' 00"
T-6	**THUNDER BAY TUG SERVICES LTD., THUNDER BAY, ON**							
	Glenada	TB	1943	D	107*	80' 06"	25' 00"	10' 01"
	(HMCS Glenada [W-30] '43-'45)							
	Miseford	TB	1915	D	116*	85' 00"	20' 00"	10' 06"
	Point Valour	TB	1958	D	246*	97' 08"	28' 02"	13' 10"
	(Foundation Valour '58-'83)							
T-7	**TNT DREDGING INC., GRAND RAPIDS, MI**							
	Bonnie G.	TB	1928	D	95*	86' 00"	21' 00"	12' 00"
	(E. James Fucik '28-'77, Bonnie G. Selvick '77-'04)							
	Joyce Marie	TB	1960	D	36*	46' 02"	15' 02"	6' 03"
	(Kendee '60-'71, Morelli '71-?, Michelle B ?-'98, Debra Ann '98-'03)							
	Wolverine	TB	1952	D	22*	42' 05"	14' 00"	7' 00"
T-8	**TOBERMORY ADVENTURE TOURS, TOBERMORY, ON**							
	Dawn Light	TB	1891	D	64*	75' 00"	24' 00"	12' 00"
	(Le Roy Brooks 1891-'25, Henry Stokes '25-'54, Aburg '54-'81)							
T-9	**TORONTO DRYDOCK CORP., TORONTO, ON**							
	M. R. Kane	TB	1945	D	51*	60' 06"	16' 05"	6' 07"
	(Tanac V-276 '45-'47)							
	Menier Consol	FD	1962	B	2,575*	304' 05"	49' 06"	25' 06"
T-10	**TORONTO FIRE DEPARTMENT, TORONTO, ON**							
	Wm. Lyon Mackenzie	FB	1964	D	102*	81' 01"	20' 00"	10' 00"
T-11	**TORONTO PADDLEWHEEL CRUISES LTD., NORTH YORK, ON**							
	Pioneer Princess	ES	1984	D	74*	56' 00"	17' 01"	3' 09"
	Pioneer Queen	ES	1968	D	110*	85' 00"	30' 06"	7' 03"
	(Peche Island III '68-'71, Papoose IV '71-'96)							
T-12	**TORONTO PARKS & RECREATION DEPARTMENT, TORONTO, ON**							
	Ongiara	PF	1963	D	180*	78' 00"	12' 04"	9' 09"
	P. & P. No. 1	TB	1984	D	14*	37' 03"	36' 00"	3' 07"
	Sam McBride	PF	1939	D	412*	129' 00"	34' 11"	6' 00"
	Thomas Rennie	PF	1950	D	419*	129' 00"	32' 11"	6' 00"
	Trillium	PF	1910	R	611*	150' 00"	30' 00"	8' 04"
	William Inglis	PF	1935	D	238*	99' 00"	24' 10"	6' 00"
	(Shamrock {2} '35-'37)							
T-13	**TORONTO PORT AUTHORITY, TORONTO, ON**							
	Brutus I	TB	1992	D	10*	36' 01"	11' 09"	4' 04"
	Fred Scandrett	TB	1963	D	52*	62' 00"	17' 00"	8' 00"
	(C. E. "Ted" Smith '63-'70)							
	Maple City	PA/CF	1951	D	135*	70' 06"	36' 04"	5' 11"
	TCCA 1	PA/CF	2006	D	219*	95' 10"	37' 07"	7' 05"
	William Rest	TB	1961	D	62*	65' 00"	18' 06"	10' 06"
	Windmill Point	PA/CF	1954	D	118*	65' 00"	36' 00"	10' 00"

CSL Niagara, seen from the saltie *Gunay-A*, approaching the Port Weller piers on the Welland Canal. *(Alain Gindroz)*

Fleet #.	Fleet Name / Vessel Name	Type of Vessel	Year Built	Type of Engine	Cargo Cap. or Gross*	Overall Length	Breadth	Depth or Draft*
T-14	**TORONTO PUBLIC WORKS DEPARTMENT, TORONTO, ON**							
	Ned Hanlan II	TB	1966	D	26*	41' 06"	14' 01"	5' 05"
T-15	**TORONTO TOURS LTD., TORONTO, ON**							
	Miss Kim Simpson	ES	1960	D	33*	90' 02"	13' 04"	3' 09"
	New Beginnings	ES	1961	D	28*	41' 09"	13' 01"	4' 09"
	Shipsands	ES	1972	D	23*	58' 03"	12' 01"	4' 07"
T-16	**TRANSPORT DESGAGNÉS INC., QUEBEC, QC**							
	SUBSIDIARY OF GROUPE DESGAGNÉS INC., QUEBEC CITY, QC							
	Amelia Desgagnés	GC	1976	D	7,126	355' 00"	49' 00"	30' 06"

Built: Collingwood Shipyards, Collingwood, ON (Soodoc {2} '76-'90)

	Anna Desgagnés	RR	1986	D	17,850	565' 00"	75' 00"	45' 00"

Built: Kvaerner Warnow Werft GmbH, Rostock, Germany; re-registered in the Bahamas 2006
(Truskavets '86-'96, Anna Desgagnes '96-'98, PCC Panama '98-'99)

	Camilla Desgagnés	GC	1982	D	7,000	436' 00"	68' 05"	22' 06"

Built: Kroeger Werft GmbH & Co. KG, Rendsburg, Germany (Camilla 1 '82-'04)

	Catherine Desgagnés	GC	1962	D	8,350	410' 03"	56' 04"	31' 00"

Built: Hall, Russel and Co., Aberdeen, Scotland (Gosforth '62-'72, Thorold {4} '72-'85)

	Cecelia Desgagnés	GC	1971	D	7,875	374' 10"	54' 10"	34' 06"

Built: Hollming Oy, Rauma, Finland (Carl Gorthon '71-'81, Federal Pioneer '81-'85)

	Melissa Desgagnés	GC	1975	D	7,000	355' 00"	49' 00"	30' 06"

Built: Collingwood Shipyards, Collingwood, ON (Ontadoc {2} '75-'90)

	Nordik Passeur	PF	1962	D	3,723*	271' 01"	60' 00"	20' 01"

Built: Halifax Shipyard Ltd., Halifax, NS; laid up at Quebec, QC (Confederation {1} '62-'93, Hull 28 '93-'94)

THE FOLLOWING FOUR VESSELS CHARTERED TO PETRO-NAV INC., MONTREAL QC, A SUBSIDIARY OF GROUPE DESGAGNÉS INC.

	Maria Desgagnés	TK	1999	D	14,335	393' 08"	68' 11"	40' 04"

Built: Qiuxin Shipyard, Shanghai, PRC (Kilchem Asia '99-'99)

	Petrolia Desgagnés	TK	1975	D	9,712	441' 05"	56' 06"	32' 10"

Built: Ankerlokken Verft Glommen, Fredrikstad, Norway (Jorvan '75-'79, Lido '79-'84, Ek-Sky '84-'98)

	Thalassa Desgagnés	TK	1976	D	9,748	441' 05"	56' 06"	32' 10"

Built: Ankerlokken Verft Glommen, Fredrikstad, Norway (Joasla '76-'79, Orinoco '79-'82, Rio Orinoco '82-'93)

	Vega Desgagnés	TK	1982	D	11,548	461' 11"	69' 08"	35' 01"

Built: Kvaerner Masa-Yards, Helsinki, Finland (Shelltrans '82-'94, Acila '94-'99, Bacalan '99-'01)

THE FOLLOWING VESSEL CHARTERED TO RELAIS NORDIC INC., RIMOUSKI, QC A SUBSIDIARY OF GROUPE DESGAGNÉS INC.

	Nordik Express	CF	1974	D	1,697	219' 11"	44' 00"	16' 01"

Built: Todd Pacific Shipyards Corp., Seattle, WA (Theriot Offshore IV '74-'77, Scotoil 4 '77-'79, Tartan Sea '79-'87)

T-17	**TRANSPORT IGLOOLIK INC., MONTREAL, QC**							
	Aivik	HL	1980	D	4,860	359' 08"	63' 08"	38' 09"

Built: ACH - Construction Navale, Le Havre, France (Mont Ventoux '80-'90, Aivik '90-'91, Unilifter '91-'92)

T-18	**TRANSPORT NANUK INC., MONTREAL, QC**							
	Umiavut	GC	1988	D	9,682	371' 02"	63' 01"	37' 00"

Built: Miho Shipbuilding Co. Ltd., Shimizu Shizuoka Prefecture, Japan
(Completed as Newca. Kapitan Silin '88-'92, Lindengracht '92-'00)

T-19	**TRAVERSE TALL SHIP CO., TRAVERSE CITY, MI**							
	Manitou {1}	ES/2S	1983	W	78*	114' 00"	21' 00"	9' 00"
T-20	**30,000 ISLANDS CRUISE LINES INC., PARRY SOUND, ON**							
	Island Queen V {3}	ES	1990	D	526*	130' 00"	35' 00"	6' 06"
U-1	**UNCLE SAM BOAT TOURS, ALEXANDRIA, NY**							
	Alexandria Belle	ES	1988	D	92*	82' 00"	32' 00"	8' 00"
	Island Duchess	ES	1988	D	73*	90' 03"	27' 08"	9' 00"
	Island Wanderer	ES	1971	D	57*	62' 05"	22' 00"	7' 02"
	Uncle Sam 7	ES	1976	D	55*	60' 04"	22' 00"	7' 01"

Fleet #.	Fleet Name / Vessel Name	Type of Vessel	Year Built	Type of Engine	Cargo Cap. or Gross*	Overall Length	Breadth	Depth or Draft*
U-2	**U.S. ARMY CORPS OF ENGINEERS, CHICAGO, IL – GREAT LAKES / OHIO RIVER DIV.**							
	U.S. ARMY CORPS OF ENGINEERS, BUFFALO, NY – BUFFALO DISTRICT							
	Cheraw	TB	1970	D	356*	109′ 00″	30′ 06″	16′ 03″
	(USS Cheraw [YTB-802] '70-'96)							
	Simonsen	CS	1954	B		142′ 00″	58′ 00″	5′ 00″
	U.S. ARMY CORPS OF ENGINEERS, CHICAGO, IL – CHICAGO DISTRICT							
	Kenosha	TB	1954	D	82*	70′ 00″	20′ 00″	9′ 08″
	(U. S. Army ST-2011 '54-'65)							
	Manitowoc	CS	1976	B		132′ 00″	44′ 00″	8′ 00″
	Racine	TB	1931	D	61*	66′ 03″	18′ 05″	7′ 08″
	U.S. ARMY CORPS OF ENGINEERS, DETROIT, MI – DETROIT DISTRICT							
	D. L. Billmaier	TB	1968	D	356*	109′ 00″	30′ 06″	16′ 03″
	(USS Natchitoches [YTB-799] '68-'95)							
	Demolen	TB	1974	D	356*	109′ 00″	30′ 06″	16′ 03″
	(USS Metacom [YTB-829] '74-'01, Metacom '01-'02)							
	Fairchild	TB	1953	D	23*	45′ 00″	13′ 00″	7′ 00″
	Hammond Bay	TB	1953	D	23*	45′ 00″	13′ 00″	7′ 00″
	H. J. Schwartz	CS	1995	B		150′ 00″	48′ 00″	11′ 00″
	Harvey	CS	1961	B		122′ 00″	40′ 00″	
	Huron	CS	1954	B		100′ 00″	34′ 00″	4′ 06″
	Michigan	CS	1971	B		120′ 00″	33′ 00″	3′ 06″
	Nicolet	CS	1971	B		120′ 00″	42′ 00″	5′ 00″
	Owen M. Frederick	TB	1942	D	56*	65′ 00″	17′ 00″	7′ 06″
	Paul Bunyan	GL	1945	B		150′ 00″	65′ 00″	12′ 06″
	Veler	CS	1991	B	613*	150′ 00″	46′ 00″	10′ 06″
	Whitefish Bay	TB	1953	D	23*	45′ 00″	13′ 00″	7′ 00″
U-3	**U.S. COAST GUARD 9TH COAST GUARD DISTRICT, CLEVELAND, OH**							
	Alder **[WLB-216]**	BT	2004	D	2,000*	225′ 09″	46′ 00″	19′ 08″
	Built: Marinette Marine Corp., Marinette, WI; stationed at Duluth, MN							
	Bristol Bay **[WTGB-102]**	IB	1979	D	662*	140′ 00″	37′ 06″	12′ 00″
	Built: Tacoma Boatbuilding Co., Tacoma, WA; stationed at Detroit, MI							
	Buckthorn **[WLI-642]**	BT	1963	D	200*	100′ 00″	24′ 00″	4′ 08″
	Built: Mobile Ship Repair, Inc., Mobile, AL; stationed at Sault Ste. Marie, MI							
	CGB-12000	BT	1991	B	700*	120′ 00″	50′ 00″	6′ 00″
	CGB-12001	BT	1991	B	700*	120′ 00″	50′ 00″	6′ 00″
	Hollyhock **[WLB-214]**	BT	2003	D	2,000*	225′ 09″	46′ 00″	19′ 08″
	Built: Marinette Marine Corp., Marinette, WI; stationed at Port Huron, MI							
	Katmai Bay **[WTGB-101]**	IB	1978	D	662*	140′ 00″	37′ 06″	12′ 00″
	Built: Tacoma Boatbuilding Co., Tacoma, WA; stationed at Sault Ste. Marie, MI							
	Mackinaw **[WLBB-30]**	IB	2005	D	15′06″*	240′ 00″	58′ 00″	15′ 05″
	Built: Marinette Marine Corp., Marinette, WI; stationed at Cheboygan, MI							
	Mobile Bay **[WTGB-103]**	IB	1979	D	662*	140′ 00″	37′ 06″	12′ 00″
	Built: Tacoma Boatbuilding Co., Tacoma, WA; stationed at Sturgeon Bay, WI							
	Neah Bay **[WTGB-105]**	IB	1980	D	662*	140′ 00″	37′ 06″	12′ 00″
	Built: Tacoma Boatbuilding Co., Tacoma, WA; stationed at Cleveland, OH							
U-4	**U.S. DEPARTMENT OF THE INTERIOR, ANN ARBOR, MI – GREAT LAKES SCIENCE CENTER**							
	Grayling	RV	1977	D	198*	75′ 00″	22′ 00″	9′ 10″
	Kaho	RV	1961	D	83*	64′ 10″	17′ 10″	9′ 00″
	Kiyi	RV	1999	D	290*	107′ 00″	27′ 00″	12′ 02″
	Musky II	RV	1960	D	25*	45′ 00″	14′ 04″	5′ 00″
	Sturgeon	RV	1977	D	325*	100′00″	25′ 05″	10′ 00″
U-5	**U.S. ENVIRONMENTAL PROTECTION AGENCY, DULUTH, MN & CHICAGO, IL**							
	Bluewater	RV	1970	D	22*	50′ 00″	14′ 00″	3′ 0″
	Lake Guardian	RV	1981	D	282*	180′ 00″	40′ 00″	11′ 00″
	(Marsea Fourteen '81-'90)							

Michipicoten departs Marquette with a load of iron ore pellets. *(Rod Burdick)*

Fleet #.	Fleet Name / Vessel Name	Type of Vessel	Year Built	Type of Engine	Cargo Cap. or Gross*	Overall Length	Breadth	Depth or Draft*
U-6	**U.S. FISH & WILDLIFE SERVICE, JORDAN RIVER NATIONAL FISH HATCHERY, ELMIRA, MI**							
	Spencer F. Baird	RV	2006	D		95' 00"	30' 00"	
	Togue	RV	1975	D	95*	73' 00"	22' 00"	10' 00"
U-7	**U.S. NATIONAL PARK SERVICE-ISLE ROYALE NATIONAL PARK, HOUGHTON, MI**							
	Greenstone II	TK	2003	B	114*	70' 01"	24' 01"	8' 00"
	Ranger III	PK	1958	D	648*	152' 08"	34' 00"	13' 00"
	Shelter Bay	TB	1953	D	23*	45' 00"	13' 00"	7' 00"
U-8	**U.S. NAVAL SEA CADET CORPS**							
	Grayfox [TWR-825]	TV	1985	D	213*	120' 00"	25' 00"	12' 00"
	Built: Marinette Marine, Marinette, WI; based at Port Huron, MI (USS TWR-825 '85-'97)							
	Manatra [YP-671]	TV	1974	D	67*	80' 05"	17' 09"	5' 04"
	Based at Chicago, IL; name stands for MArine NAvigation and TRaining Association (USS YP-671 '74-'89)							
	Pride of Michigan [YP-673]	TV	1977	D	70*	80' 06"	17' 08"	5' 03"
	Built: Peterson Builders Inc., Sturgeon Bay, WI; based at Mount Clemens, MI (USS YP-673 '77-'89)							
	Roy R. Love	TB	1908	D	55*	72' 00"	16' 02"	7' 08"
	Based at Joliet, IL (Herbert '08-'18, H. Ewig '18-'39, Roy R. Love '39-'68, Charlevoix '68-'92)							
U-9	**UNIVERSITÉ DU QUÉBEC A RIMOUSKI, RIMOUSKI, QC**							
	Coriolis II	RV	1990	D	836*	163'10"	36' 01"	22' 11"
U-10	**UNIVERSITY OF MICHIGAN, CENTER FOR GREAT LAKES & AQUATIC SCIENCES, ANN ARBOR, MI**							
	Laurentian	RV	1977	D	129*	80' 00"	21' 06"	11' 00"
U-11	**UNIVERSITY OF MINNESOTA-DULUTH, DULUTH, MN**							
	Blue Heron	RV	1985	D	175*	119' 06"	28' 00"	15' 06"
	(Fairtry '85-'97)							
U-12	**UNIVERSITY OF WISCONSIN, GREAT LAKES WATER INSTITUTE, MILWAUKEE, WI**							
	Neeskay	RV	1952	D	75*	71' 00"	17' 06"	7' 06"
U-13	**UNIVERSITY OF WISCONSIN, SUPERIOR, WI**							
	L. L. Smith Jr.	RV	1950	D	38*	57' 06"	16' 06"	6' 06"
U-14	**UPPER GREAT LAKES MANAGEMENT UNIT, ONTARIO MINISTRY OF NATURAL RESOURCES**							
	Atigamayg	RV	1954	D	82*	43' 09"	20' 02"	5' 07"
	Erie Explorer	RV	1981	D	72*	53' 05"	20' 01"	4' 08"
	Keenosay	RV	1957	D	68*	51' 04"	20' 07"	2' 07"
	Namaycush	RV	1954	D	28*	65' 03"	12' 00"	4' 01"
	Nipigon Osprey	RV	1990	D	33*	42' 04"	14' 09"	6' 08"
	Wonda Goldie	RV	1950	D	12*	46' 08"	12' 00"	3' 09"
U-15	**UPPER LAKES GROUP INC., TORONTO, ON**							
	DISTRIBUTION GRANDS LACS/ST-LAURENT LTEE, TROIS RIVIERES, QC – A DIVISION OF UPPER LAKES GROUP INC.							
	Barge Laviolette	BC	1965	B	7,573	498' 00"	75' 00"	39' 03"
	Grain storage barge built from bow / cargo sections of powered vessel Canadian Explorer in '01							
	BIG 503	BC	2000	B	902*	190' 06"	35' 00"	14' 00"
	BIG 543	BC	2003	B	916*	191' 00"	35' 00"	14' 00"
	BIG 546	BC	2003	B	916*	191' 00"	35' 00"	14' 00"
	BIG 548	BC	2003	B	916*	191' 00"	35' 00"	14' 00"
	BIG 549	BC	2003	B	916*	191' 00"	35' 00"	14' 00"
	BIG 551	BC	2003	B	916*	191' 00"	35' 00"	14' 00"
	BIG 9708 B	BC	1996	B	958*	191' 09"	35' 00"	14' 00"
	BIG 9917 B	BC	1999	B	958*	191' 09"	35' 00"	14' 00"
	Canadian Mariner	BC	1963	T	27,700	730' 00"	75' 00"	39' 03"
	Built: St. John Shipbuilding and Drydock Co., St. John, NB; last sailed in 2003; laid up at Trois-Rivieres, QC (Newbrunswicker '63-'68, Grande Hermine '68-'72)							
	Commodore Straits	TB	1966	D	566*	130' 00"	34' 01"	15' 07"
	Built: Dominion Steel & Coal Corp., Halifax, NS (Haida Brave '66-'79)							

Fleet #.	Fleet Name / Vessel Name	Type of Vessel	Year Built	Type of Engine	Cargo Cap. or Gross*	Overall Length	Breadth	Depth or Draft*
	Doc Morin	TB	1954	D	225*	101' 10"	26' 00"	13' 08"
	(Seven Sisters '54-'05)							

PROVMAR FUELS INC., HAMILTON, ON – A DIVISION OF UPPER LAKES GROUP INC.

	Hamilton Energy	TK	1965	D	1,282	201' 05"	34' 01"	14' 09"
	Built: Grangemouth Dockyard Co., Grangemouth, Scotland (Partington '65-'79, Shell Scientist '79-'81, Metro Sun '81-'85)							
	Provmar Terminal	TK	1959	B	7,300	403' 05"	55' 06"	28' 05"
	Built: Sarpsborg Mek, Verksted, Greater Norway; last operated in 1984; in use as a fuel storage barge at Hamilton, ON (Varangnes '59-'70, Tommy Wiborg '70-'74, Ungava Transport '74-'85)							
	Provmar Terminal II	TK	1948	B	6,832	408' 08"	53' 00"	26' 00"
	Built: Collingwood Shipyards, Collingwood, ON; last operated 1986; in use as a fuel storage barge at Hamilton, ON (Imperial Sarnia {2} '48-'89)							

UPPER LAKES SHIPPING LTD., CALGARY, AB – DIVISION OF UPPER LAKES GROUP INC.
* VESSELS OPERATED & MANAGED BY SEAWAY MARINE TRANSPORT, ST. CATHARINES, ON, A PARTNERSHIP BETWEEN ALGOMA CENTRAL CORP. AND UPPER LAKES GROUP INC.

	Canadian Enterprise*	SU	1979	D	35,100	730' 00"	75' 08"	46' 06"
	Built: Port Weller Drydocks, Port Weller, ON							
	Canadian Leader*	BC	1967	T	28,300	730' 00"	75' 00"	39' 08"
	Built: Collingwod Shipyards, Collingwood, ON (Feux-Follets '67-'72)							
	Canadian Miner*	BC	1966	D	28,050	730' 00"	75' 00"	39' 01"
	Built: Canadian Vickers, Montreal, QC (Maplecliffe Hall '66-'88, Lemoyne {2} '88-'94)							
	Canadian Navigator*	SU	1967	D	30,925	728' 11"	75' 10"	40' 06"
	Built: J. Readhead & Sons, South Shields, England; converted from a saltwater bulk carrier in '80; converted to a self-unloader in '97 (Demeterton '67-'75, St. Lawrence Navigator '75-'80)							
	Canadian Olympic*	SU	1976	D	35,100	730' 00"	75' 00"	46' 06"
	Built: Port Weller Drydocks, Port Weller, ON							
	Canadian Progress*	SU	1968	D	32,700	730' 00"	75' 00"	46' 06"
	Built: Port Weller Drydocks, Port Weller, ON							
	Canadian Prospector*	BC	1964	D	30,500	730' 00"	75' 10"	40' 06"
	Built: Short Brothers Ltd., Sunderland, England; converted from a saltwater bulk carrier in '79 (Carlton '64-'75, St. Lawrence Prospector '75-'79)							
	Canadian Provider*	BC	1963	T	27,450	730' 00"	75' 00"	39' 02"
	Built: Collingwood Shipyards, Collingwood, ON (Murray Bay {3} '63-'94)							
	Canadian Ranger*	SU	1943/67	D	25,900	729' 10"	75' 00"	39' 03"
	Canadian Ranger was built by joining the stern section (pilothouse, engine room, machinery) of the former coastal package freighter Chimo with the bow and mid-body of the laker Hilda Marjanne in '84; converted to a self- unloader in '88)							
	*([**Fore Section**] Grande Ronde '43-'48, Kate N. L. '48-'61, Hilda Marjanne '61-'84) Coverted from a saltwater bulk carrier in '61 ([**Stern Section**] Chimo '67-'83)*							
	Canadian Transfer*	SU	1943/67	D	22,204	650' 06"	60' 00"	35' 00"
	Built: Great Lakes Engineering Works, Ashtabula, OH; Canadian Transfer was built by joining the stern section of Canadian Explorer (engine room, machinery) with the bow and mid-body of the World War II-era laker Hamilton Transfer in '98							
	*([**Fore Section**] J. H. Hillman Jr. '43-'74, Crispin Oglebay {2} '74-'95, Hamilton Transfer '95-'98) Converted to a self-unloader in '74 ([**Stern Section**] Cabot {1} '65-'83, Canadian Explorer '83-'98)*							
	Canadian Transport* {2}	SU	1979	D	35,100	730' 00"	75' 08"	46' 06"
	Built: Port Weller Drydocks, Port Weller, ON							
	Gordon C. Leitch* {2}	BC	1968	D	29,700	730' 00"	75' 00"	42' 00"
	Built: Canadian Vickers, Montreal, QC; converted from a self-unloader to a bulk carrier in '77 (Ralph Misener '68-'94)							
	James Norris*	SU	1952	S	18,600	663' 06"	67' 00"	35' 00"
	Built: Midland Shipyards, Midland, ON; converted to a self-unloader, '81							
	John D. Leitch*	SU	1967	D	31,600	730' 00"	78' 00"	45' 00"
	Built: Port Weller Drydocks, Port Weller, ON; rebuilt with new mid-body, widened by 3' in '02 (Canadian Century '67-'02)							
	Montrealais*	BC	1962	T	27,800	730' 00"	75' 00"	39' 00"
	Built: Canadian Vickers, Montreal, QC (Launched as Montrealer)							

Fleet #.	Fleet Name Vessel Name	Type of Vessel	Year Built	Type of Engine	Cargo Cap. or Gross*	Overall Length	Breadth	Depth or Draft*
	Quebecois*	BC	1963	T	27,800	730' 00"	75' 00"	39' 00"
	Built: Canadian Vickers, Montreal, QC							
U-16	**UPPER LAKES TOWING CO., ESCANABA, MI**							
	Joseph H. Thompson	SU	1944	B	21,200	706' 06"	71' 06"	38' 06"
	Built: Sun Shipbuilding & Drydock Co., Chester, PA; converted from a saltwater vessel to a Great Lakes bulk							
	carrier in '52; converted to a self-unloading barge in '91 (USNS Marine Robin '44-'52)							
	Joseph H. Thompson Jr.	ATB	1990	D	841*	146' 06"	38' 00"	35' 00"
	Built: At Mainette, WI, from steel left over from the conversion of Joseph H. Thompson (see above)							
U-17	**USLHS MAPLE LLC, WAUWATOSA, WI**							
	Maple	MU	1939	D	350*	122' 03"	27' 00"	7' 06"
	Former U.S. Coast Guard "122-Foot" class lighthouse tender [WLI / WAGL-234] / EPA vessel							
	(USCGC Maple [WLI / WAGL-234] '39-'73, Roger R. Simons '73-'94)							
V-1	**VAN ENKEVORT TUG & BARGE INC., BARK RIVER, MI**							
	Great Lakes Trader	SU	2000	B	39,600	740' 00"	78' 00"	45' 00"
	Built: Halter Marine, Pearlington, MS							
	Joyce L. VanEnkevort	AT	1998	D	1,179*	135' 04"	50' 00"	26' 00"
	Built: Bay Shipbuilding Co., Sturgeon Bay, WI							
	[ATB VanEnkevort / GL Trader OA dimensions together]					844' 10"	78' 00"	45' 00"
V-2	**VERREAULT NAVIGATION INC., LES MECHINS, QC**							
	Nindawayma	PA/CF	1976	D	6,197*	333' 06"	55' 00"	36' 06"
	Last operated in 1992; laid up at Montreal, QC (Monte Cruceta '76-'76, Monte Castillo '76-'78,							
	Manx Viking '78-'87, Manx '87-'88, Skudenes '88-'89, Ontario No.1 {2} '89-'89)							
V-3	**VINCENT KLAMERUS, DRUMMOND ISLAND, MI**							
	Lime Island	PA	1953	D	24*	42' 08"	12' 00"	6' 00"
V-4	**VISTA FLEET, DULUTH, MN**							
	Vista King	ES	1978	D	60*	78' 00"	23' 00"	5' 02"
	Vista Queen	ES	1987	D	97*	64' 00"	16' 00"	6' 02"
	Vista Star	ES	1987	D	95*	91' 00"	24' 09"	5' 02"
	(Island Empress '87-'88)							
V-5	**VOIGHT'S MARINE SERVICES LTD., ELLISON BAY & GILLS ROCK, WI**							
	Island Clipper {2}	ES	1987	D	71*	65' 00"	20' 00"	8' 00"
	Yankee Clipper	ES	1971	D	41*	46' 06"	17' 00"	6' 00"
V-6	**VOYAGEUR MARINE TRANSPORT LTD., RIDGEVILLE, ON**							
	Voyageur Independent	BC	1952	D	20,668	642' 03"	67' 00"	35' 00"
	Built: DeFoe Shipbuilding Co., Bay City, MI; converted from steam power to diesel in '05							
	(Charles L. Hutchinson {3} '52-'62, Ernest R. Breech '62-'88, Kinsman Independent '88-'05)							
	VOYAGEUR MARITIME TRADING INC., OWNER							
	Maritime Trader	BC	1967	D	19,093	607' 10"	62' 00"	36' 00"
	Built: Collingwood Shipyards, Collingwood, ON (Mantadoc '67-'02, Teakglen '02-'05)							
	VOYAGEUR PIONEER MARINE INC., OWNER							
	Voyageur Pioneer	BC	1983	D	33,824	730' 00"	75' 09"	48' 00"
	Built: Govan Shipyards, Glasgow, Scotland (Saskatchewan Pioneer '83-'95, Lady Hamilton '95-'06)							
W-1	**WASHINGTON ISLAND FERRY LINE INC., WASHINGTON ISLAND, WI**							
	Arni J. Richter	PA/CF	2003	D	92*	104' 00"	38' 06"	10' 11"
	C. G. Richter	PA/CF	1950	D	82*	70' 06"	25' 00"	9' 05"
	Eyrarbakki	PA/CF	1970	D	95*	87' 00"	36' 00"	7' 06"
	Robert Noble	PA/CF	1979	D	97*	90' 04"	36' 00"	8' 03"
	Washington {2}	PA/CF	1989	D	93*	100' 00"	37' 00"	9' 00"
W-2	**WENDELLA BOAT TOURS, CHICAGO, IL**							
	Sunliner	ES	1959	D	41*	67' 00"	20' 00"	4' 00"

Fleet #.	Fleet Name / Vessel Name	Type of Vessel	Year Built	Type of Engine	Cargo Cap. or Gross*	Overall Length	Breadth	Depth or Draft*
	Wendella	ES	1961	D	35*	68' 00"	17' 00"	6' 05"
	Wendella LTD	ES	1992	D	66*	68' 00"	20' 00"	4' 09"
W-3	**WINDY OF CHICAGO LTD., CHICAGO, IL**							
	Windy	ES/4S	1996	W	75*	148' 00"	25' 00"	8' 00"
	Windy II	ES/4S	2000	W	99*	150' 00"	25' 00"	8' 05"
W-4	**WISCONSIN DEPARTMENT OF NATURAL RESOURCES, BAYFIELD & STURGEON BAY, WI**							
	Hack Noyes	RV	1947	D	50*	56' 00"		4' 00"
	Barney Devine	RV	1937	D	42*	50' 00"	14' 05"	6' 00"
W-5	**WISCONSIN MARITIME MUSEUM, MANITOWOC, WI**							
	Cobia	MU	1944	D/V	1,500*	311' 09"	27' 03"	33' 09"

Built: Manitowoc Shipbuilding Co., Manitowoc, WI; former U. S. Navy "Gato" class submarine AGSS-245 is open to the public at Manitowoc, WI

Fleet #.	Fleet Name / Vessel Name	Type of Vessel	Year Built	Type of Engine	Cargo Cap. or Gross*	Overall Length	Breadth	Depth or Draft*
Y-1	**YALMER MATTILA CONTRACTING INC., HANCOCK, MI**							
	J. E. Colombe	TB	1954	D	23*	45' 00"	13' 00"	7' 00"
	Oshkosh # 15	DB	1944	B	238*	137' 00"	21' 06"	9' 00"
Z-1	**ZENITH TUGBOAT CO., DULUTH, MN**							
	Anna Marie Altman	TB	1950	D	146*	88' 06"	25' 06"	11' 00"

(Navajo {1} '50-'52, Seaval '52-'63, Mary T. Tracy '63-'69, Yankee '69-'70, Minn '70-'74, William S. Bell '74-'83, Newcastle '83-'93, Laura Lynn '93-'99, Susan Hoey {3} '99-'06)

	Park State	TB	1938	D	16*	45' 00"	12' 00"	5' 00"

(Hoosier State '49-'62, Tommy B. '62-'06)

	Lacey 3	TB	1957	D	214*	100' 00"	27' 00"	12' 00"
	Seneca	TB	1939	DE	132*	94' 20"	22' 00"	9' 00"

(General {1} '39-'39, Raymond Card '39-'40, USS Keshena '40-'47, Mary L. McAllister '47-'81)

	Sioux	TB	1921	D	96*	81' 00"	20' 00"	12' 06"

(Oregon {1} '21-'78, Ste. Marie I '78-'81, Sioux {2} '81-'91, Susan E. '91-'05)

Tug *Sioux* under tow on Lake Superior.
(Franz VonRidel)

VESSEL ENGINE DATA

bhp: brake horsepower, a measure of diesel engine output measured at the crankshaft before entering gearbox or any other power take-out device

ihp: indicated horsepower, based on an internal measurement of mean cylinder pressure, piston area, piston stroke and engine speed. Used for reciprocating engines

shp: shaft horsepower, a measure of engine output at the propeller shaft at the output of the reduction gearbox. Used for steam and diesel-electric engines

cpp: controllable pitch propeller

Vessel Name	Engine Manufacturer & Model #	Engine Type	Total Engines	Total Cylinders	Rated HP	Total Props	Speed MPH
Adam E. Cornelius	GM - Electro-Motive Div. - 20-645-E7B	Diesel	2	20	7,200 bhp	1 cpp	16.1
Agawa Canyon	Fairbanks Morse - 10-38D8-1/8	Diesel	4	10	6,662 bhp	1 cpp	13.8
Algobay	Pielstick - 10PC2-3V-400	Diesel	2	10	10,700 bhp	1 cpp	13.8
Algocape	Sulzer - 6RND76	Diesel	1	6	9,600 bhp	1 cpp	17.3
Algoeast	B&W - 6K45GF	Diesel	1	6	5,300 bhp	1 cpp	15.8
Algoisle	M.A.N. - K6Z78/155	Diesel	1	6	9,000 bhp	1 cpp	19.3
Algolake	Pielstick - 10PC2-2V-400	Diesel	2	10	9,000 bhp	1 cpp	17.3
Algomarine	Sulzer - 6RND76	Diesel	1	6	9,600 bhp	1 cpp	17.0
Algonorth	Werkspoor - 9TM410	Diesel	2	9	12,000 bhp	1 cpp	16.1
Algontario	B&W - 7-74VTBF-160	Diesel	1	7	8,750 bhp	1 cpp	14.4
Algoport	Pielstick - 10PC2-3V-400	Diesel	2	10	10,700 bhp	1 cpp	13.8
Algorail	Fairbanks Morse - 10-38D8-1/8	Diesel	4	10	6,662 bhp	1 cpp	13.8
Algosar	Alco - 16V251E	Diesel	2	16	5,150 bhp	2	14.4
Algoscotia	Wartsila - 6L46C	Diesel	1	6	8,445 bhp	1 cpp	16.0
Algosoo	Pielstick - 10PC2-V-400	Diesel	2	10	9,000 bhp	1 cpp	15.0
Algosea	Wartsila - 6L46A	Diesel	1	6	6,434 bhp	1 cpp	15.0
Algosteel	Sulzer - 6RND76	Diesel	1	6	9,599 bhp	1	17.0
Algoville	MaK model 8M43C	Diesel	1	8	10,750 bhp	1 cpp	
Algoway	Fairbanks Morse - 10-38D8-1/8	Diesel	4	10	6,662 bhp	1 cpp	13.8
Algowood	MaK - 6M552AK	Diesel	2	6	10,200 bhp	1 cpp	13.8
Alpena	De Laval Steam Turbine Co.	Turbine	1	**	4,400 shp	1	14.1
Amelia Desgagnes	Allen - 12PVBCS12-F	Diesel	2	12	4,000 bhp	1 cpp	16.1
American Century	GM - Electro-Motive Div. - 20-645-E7B	Diesel	4	20	14,400 bhp	2 cpp	17.3
American Courage	GM - Electro-Motive Div. - 20-645-E7	Diesel	2	20	7,200 bhp	1 cpp	16.1
American Fortitude	General Electric Co.	Turbine	1	**	7,700 shp	1	16.7
American Integrity	GM - Electro-Motive Div. - 20-645-E7	Diesel	4	20	14,400 bhp	2 cpp	18.4
American Valor	Westinghouse Elec. Corp.	Turbine	1	**	7,700 shp	1	19.0
American Victory	Bethlehem Steel Co.	Turbine	1	**	7,700 shp	1	16.1
American Mariner	GM - Electro-Motive Div. - 20-645-E7	Diesel	2	20	7,200 bhp	1 cpp	15.0
American Republic	GM - Electro-Motive Div. - 20-645-E7	Diesel	2	20	7,200 bhp	2 cpp	15.0
American Spirit	Pielstick - 16PC2-2V-400	Diesel	2	16	16,000 bhp	2 cpp	17.3
Anglian Lady	*(Tug / Barge, usually paired with PML2501)*						
	Deutz	Diesel	2	12	3,480 bhp	2 cpp	15.5
Anna Desgagnes	M.A.N. - K5SZ70/125B	Diesel	1	5	10,332 bhp	1	17.8
Arctic	M.A.N. 14V52/55A	Diesel	1	14	14,770 bhp	1 cpp	17.8
Arthur M. Anderson	Westinghouse Elec. Corp.	Turbine	1	**	7,700 shp	1	16.1
Atlantic Erie	Sulzer - 6RLB66	Diesel	1	6	11,100 bhp	1 cpp	16.1
Atlantic Huron	Sulzer - 6RLB66	Diesel	1	6	11,094 bhp	1 cpp	17.3
Atlantic Superior	Sulzer - 6RLA66	Diesel	1	6	11,095 bhp	1 cpp	17.3
Avenger IV	*(Tug / Barge, usually paired with Chief Wawatam or PML9000)*						
	British Polar	Diesel	1	9	2,700 bhp	1 cpp	12.0
Badger	Skinner Engine Co.	Steeple Compound Uniflow	2	4	8,000 ihp	2	18.4
Barbara Andrie	*(Tug / Barge, usually paired with A-390)*						
	GM Electro-Motive Div. 16-645-EF	Diesel	1	16	2,000 bhp	1	
Birchglen	Sulzer 4RLB76	Diesel	1	4	10,880 bhp	1cpp	13.8
Buffalo	GM - Electro-Motive Div. - 20-645-E7	Diesel	2	20	7,200 bhp	1 cpp	16.1
Burns Harbor	GM - Electro-Motive Div. - 20-645-E7	Diesel	4	20	14,400 bhp	2 cpp	18.4
Calumet	Nordberg FS-1316-HSC	Diesel	1	16	4,234 bhp	1	12.1
Canadian Enterprise	M.A.N. - 7L40/45	Diesel	2	7	8,804 bhp	1 cpp	13.8
Canadian Leader	Canadian General Electric Co. Ltd.	Turbine	1	**	9,900 shp	1	19.0
Canadian Mariner	General Electric Co.	Turbine	1	**	9,900 shp	1	19.0
Canadian Miner	Fairbanks Morse - 12-38D8-1/8	Diesel	4	12	8,000 bhp	1 cpp	15.0
Canadian Navigator	Doxford Engines Ltd. - 76J4	Diesel	1	4	9,680 bhp	1	16.7
Canadian Olympic	M.A.N. - 8L40/54A	Diesel	2	8	10,000 bhp	1 cpp	15.0

Vessel Name	Engine Manufacturer & Model #	Engine Type	Total Engines	Total Cylinders	Rated HP	Total Props	Speed MPH
Canadian Progress	Caterpillar - 3612-TA	Diesel	2	12	9,000 bhp	1 cpp	15.5
Canadian Prospector	Gotaverken - 760/1500VGS6U	Diesel	1	6	7,500 bhp	1	16.1
Canadian Provider	John Inglis Co. Ltd.	Turbine	1	**	10,000 shp	1	17.3
Canadian Ranger	Sulzer - 5RND68	Diesel	1	5	6,100 bhp	1 cpp	19.6
Canadian Transfer	Sulzer - 5RND68	Diesel	1	5	6,100 bhp	1 cpp	18.4
Canadian Transport	M.A.N. - 8L40/45	Diesel	2	8	10,000 bhp	1 cpp	13.8
Capt. Henry Jackman	MaK - 6M552AK	Diesel	2	6	9,465 bhp	1 cpp	17.3
Cason J. Callaway	Westinghouse Elec. Corp.	Turbine	1	**	7,700 bhp	1	16.1
Catherine Desgagnes	Sulzer - 6SAD60	Diesel	1	6	3,841 bhp	1	15.5
Cecelia Desgagnes	B&W - 6S50LU	Diesel	1	6	3,840 bhp	1 cpp	17.3
Cedarglen	B&W - 7-74TVBF-160	Diesel	1	7	8,750 bhp	1 cpp	15.5
Charles M. Beeghly	General Electric Co.	Turbine	1	**	9,350 shp	1	17.8
Chi-Cheemaun	Ruston Paxman Diesels Ltd. - 16RKCM	Diesel	2	16	7,000 bhp	2	18.7
Cleveland	*(Tug / Barge, usually paired with Cleveland Rocks)*						
	Caterpillar 3516-B	Diesel	2	16	5,000 bhp	2	
CSL Laurentien	Pielstick - 10PC2-2V-400	Diesel	2	10	9,000 bhp	1 cpp	16.1
CSL Assiniboine	Pielstick - 10PC2-2V-400	Diesel	2	10	9,000 bhp	1 cpp	15.0
CSL Niagara	Pielstick - 10PC2-2V-400	Diesel	2	10	9,000 bhp	1 cpp	15.0
CSL Tadoussac	Sulzer - 6RND76	Diesel	1	6	9,600 bhp	1	17.0
Cuyahoga	Caterpillar - 3608	Diesel	1	8	3,000 bhp	1 cpp	12.6
David Z. Norton	Alco - 16V251E	Diesel	2	16	5,600 bhp	1	16.1
Diamond Star	B&W - 6L35MC	Diesel	1	6	5,030 bhp	1 cpp	14.4
Dorothy Ann	*(Articulated Tug / Barge, paired with Pathfinder)*					2 Ulstein	
	GM - Electro-Motive Div. - 20-645-E7B	Diesel	2	20	7,200 bhp	Z-Drive	16.1
E. M. Ford	Cleveland Ship Building Co.	Quad. Exp	1	4	1,500 ihp	1	11.5
Earl W. Oglebay	Alco - 16V251E	Diesel	2	16	5,600 bhp	1	16.1
Edgar B. Speer	Pielstick - 18PC2-3V-400	Diesel	2	18	19,260 bhp	2 cpp	17.0
Edward L. Ryerson	General Electric Co.	Turbine	1	**	9,900 shp	1	19.0
Edwin H. Gott	Enterprise - DMRV-16-4	Diesel	2	16	19,500 bhp	2 cpp	16.7
Emerald Star	B&W - 6L35MC	Diesel	1	6	5,030 bhp	1 cpp	14.4
English River	Werkspoor - TMAB-390	Diesel	1	8	1,850 bhp	1 cpp	13.8
Everlast	*(Articulated Tug / Barge, paired with Norman McLeod)*						
	Daihatsu - 8DSM-32	Diesel	2	8	6,000 bhp	2	16.5
Frontenac	Sulzer - 6RND76	Diesel	1	6	9,600 bhp	1 cpp	17.0
G.L. Ostrander	*(Articulated Tug / Barge, paird with Integrity)*						
	Caterpillar - 3608-DITA	Diesel	2	8	6,008 bhp	2	17.3
Gordon C. Leitch	Sulzer - 6RND76	Diesel	1	6	9,600 bhp	1 cpp	17.3
H. Lee White	GM - Electro-Motive Div. - 20-645-E7B	Diesel	2	20	7,200 bhp	1 cpp	15.0
Halifax	John Inglis Co. Ltd.	Turbine	1	**	10,000 shp	1	19.6
Herbert C. Jackson	General Electric Co.	Turbine	1	**	6,600 shp	1	16.0
Indiana Harbor	GM - Electro-Motive Div. - 20-645-E7	Diesel	4	20	14,400 bhp	2 cpp	16.1
Invincible	*(Articulated Tug / Barge, paired with McKee Sons)*						
	GM - Electro-Motive Div. - 16-645-E7B	Diesel	2	16	5,750 bhp	2	13.8
J. A. W. Iglehart	De Laval Steam Turbine Co.	Turbine	1	**	4,400 shp	1	15.0
J. B. Ford	American Ship Building Co.	Triple Exp.	1	3	1,500 ihp	1	
J. S. St. John	GM - Electro-Motive Div. - 8-567	Diesel	1	8	850 bhp	1	11.5
Jade Star	B&W - 6L35MC	Diesel	1	6	5,030 bhp	1 cpp	14.4
James Norris	Canadian Vickers Ltd.	Uniflow	1	5	4,000 ihp	1	16.1
James R. Barker	Pielstick - 16PC2-2V-400	Diesel	2	16	16,000 bhp	2 cpp	15.5
Jane Ann IV	*(Articulated Tug / Barge, paired with Sarah Spencer)*						
	Pielstick - 8PC2-2L-400	Diesel	2	8	8,000 bhp	2	15.8
Jiimaan	Ruston Paxman Diesels Ltd. - 6RK215	Diesel	2	6	2,839 bhp	2 cpp	15.0
John B. Aird	MaK - 6M552AK	Diesel	2	6	9,460 bhp	1 cpp	13.8
John D. Leitch	B&W - 5-74VT2BF-160	Diesel	1	5	7,500 bhp	1 cpp	16.1
John G. Munson	General Electric Co.	Turbine	1	**	7,700 shp	1	17.3
John J. Boland	GM - Electro-Motive Div. - 20-645-E7B	Diesel	2	20	7,200 bhp	1 cpp	15.0
John Sherwin	De Laval Steam Turbine Co.	Turbine	1	**	9,350 shp	1	16.7
John Spence	*(Tug / Barge, usually paired with McAsphalt 401)*						
	GM Electro-Motive Div. 16-567-C	Diesel	2	16	3,280 bhp	2	13.8
Joseph H. Thompson Jr.	*(Articulated Tug / Barge, paired with Joseph H. Thompson)*						
	Caterpillar	Diesel	2			1	
Joseph L. Block	GM - Electro-Motive Div. - 20-645-E7	Diesel	2	20	7,200 bhp	1 cpp	17.3
Joyce L. Van Enkevort	*(Articulated Tug / Barge, paired with Great Lakes Trader)*						
	Caterpillar - 3612	Diesel	2	12	10,200 bhp	2 cpp	
Karen Andrie	*(Tug / Barge, usually paired with A-397)*						
	GM Electro-Motive Div. 16-567-BC	Diesel	2	16	3,600 bhp	2	19
Kathryn Spirit	Pielstick 10PC2-V-400	Diesel	2		8,000 bhp	1 ccp	19

Vessel Name	Engine Manufacturer & Model #	Engine Type	Total Engines	Total Cylinders	Rated HP	Total Props	Speed MPH
Kaye E. Barker	De Laval Steam Turbine Co.	Turbine	1	**	7,700 shp	1	17.3
Lee A. Tregurtha	Rolls-Royce Bergen B32:40L6P	Diesel	2	6	8,160 bhp	1 ccp	17.0
Manistee	GM - Electro-Motive Div.- 20-645-E6	Diesel	1	20	2,950 bhp	1	
Maria Desgagnes	B&W - 6S42MC	Diesel	1	6	8,361 bhp	1 cpp	16.1
Maritime Trader	Fairbanks Morse -8-38D8-1/8	Diesel	4	8	5,332 bhp	1 cpp	16.1
Maumee	Nordberg - FS-1312-H5C	Diesel	1	12	3,240 bhp	1	11.5
Melissa Desgagnes	Allen - 12PVBCS12-F	Diesel	2	12	4,000 bhp	1 cpp	13.8
Mesabi Miner	Pielstick - 16PC2-2V-400	Diesel	2	16	16,000 bhp	2 cpp	15.5
Michigan	*(Articulated Tug / Barge, paired with Michigan)*						
	GM - Electro-Motive Div.- 20-645-E6	Diesel	2	16	3,900 bhp	2	13.2
Michipicoten	Bethlehem Steel Co.	Turbine	1	**	7,700 shp	1	17.3
Mississagi	Caterpillar - 3612-TA	Diesel	1	12	4,500 bhp	1 cpp	13.8
Montrealais	Canadian General Electric Co. Ltd.	Turbine	1	**	9,900 shp	1	19.0
Nanticoke	Pielstick - 10PC2-2V-400	Diesel	2	10	10,700 bhp	1 cpp	13.8
Nordik Express	GM Electro-Motive Div. 20-645-E7	Diesel	2	20	7,200 bhp	2 ccp	16.0
Nordik Passeur	Paxman 12YLCM	Diesel	2	12	6,000 bhp		15.0
Olive L. Moore	*(Tug / Barge, usually paired with Lewis J. Kuber)*						
	Alco 16V251	Diesel	2	16	5,830 bhp	1	
Paul H. Townsend	Nordberg TSM-216	Diesel	1	6	2,150 bhp	1	12.1
Paul R. Tregurtha	Pielstick - 16PC2-3V-400	Diesel	2	16	17,120 bhp	2 cpp	15.5
Peter R. Cresswell	MaK - 6M552AK	Diesel	2	6	9,460 bhp	1 cpp	13.8
Petite Forte	*(Tug / Barge, usually paired with St. Marys Cement)*						
	Ruston 8ATC	Diesel	2	8	4,200 bhp	2	15.5
Petrolia Desgagnes	B&W - 8K42EF	Diesel	1	8	5,000 bhp	1 cpp	16.4
Philip R. Clarke	Westinghouse Elec. Corp.	Turbine	1	**	7,700 shp	1	16.1
Pineglen	MaK - 6M601AK	Diesel	1	6	8,158 bhp	1 cpp	15.5
Presque Isle	*(Integrated Tug / Barge paired with Presque Isle)*						
	Mirrlees Blackstone Ltd. - KVMR-16	Diesel	2	16	14,840 bhp	2 cpp	
Quebecois	Canadian General Electric Co. Ltd.	Turbine	1	**	9,900 shp	1	19.0
Rebecca Lynn	*Tug / Barge, usually paired with A-410)*						
	GM - Electro-Motive Div. 16-567-BC	Diesel	2	16	3,600 bhp	2	
Reliance	*(Tug / Barge, usually paired with PML9000)*						
	A.B. Nohab SVI 16VS-F	Diesel	2	16	5,600 bhp	1 cpp	17.6
Reserve	Westinghouse Elec. Corp.	Turbine	1	**	7,700 shp	1	19.0
Roger Blough	Pielstick - 16PC2V-400	Diesel	2	16	14,200 bhp	1 cpp	16.7
Rt. Hon. Paul J. Martin	Pielstick - 10PC2-V-400	Diesel	2	10	9,000 bhp	1 cpp	15.0
Saginaw	De Laval Steam Turbine Co.	Turbine	1	**	7,700 shp	1	16.1
Sam Laud	GM - Electro-Motive Div.- 20-645-E7	Diesel	2	20	7,200 bhp	1 cpp	16.1
Samuel de Champlain	*(Articulated Tug / Barge, paired with Innovation)*						
	GM - Electro-Motive Div. - 20-645-E5	Diesel	2	20	7,200 bhp	2 cpp	17.3
Sauniere	MaK - 6M552AK	Diesel	2	6	8,799 bhp	1 cpp	15.0
Sea Eagle II	*(Tug / Barge, usually paired with St. Marys Cement II)*						
	GM Electro-Motive Div. 20-645-E7	Diesel	2	20	7,200 bhp	2	13.8
Spruceglen	Sulzer 4RLB76	Diesel	1	4	10,880 bhp	1cpp	13.8
St. Clair	GM - Electro-Motive Div.- 20-645-E7	Diesel	3	20	10,800 bhp	1 cpp	16.7
St. Marys Challenger	Skinner Engine Co.	Uniflow	1	4	3,500 ihp	1	12.0
Ste. Claire	Toledo Ship Building Co.	Triple Exp.	1	3	1,083 ihp	1	
Stephen B. Roman (Total)		Diesel			5,996 bhp	1 cpp	18.4
Stephen B. Roman (Center)	Fairbanks Morse - 10-38D8-1/8	Diesel	2	10	3,331 bhp		
Stephen B. Roman (Wing)	Fairbanks Morse - 8-38D8-1/8	Diesel	2	8	2,665 bhp		
Stewart J. Cort	GM - Electro-Motive Div.- 20-645-E7	Diesel	4	20	14,400 bhp	2 cpp	18.4
Susan W. Hannah	*(Articulated Tug / Barge, paired with St. Marys Conquest)*						
	GM - Electro-Motive Div.- 12-645-E5	Diesel	2	12	4,320 bhp	2	11.5
Thalassa Desgagnes	B&W - 8K42EF	Diesel	1	8	5,000 bhp	1 cpp	16.4
Undaunted	*(Articulated Tug / Barge, paired with Pere Marquette 41)*						
	GM - Cleveland Diesel Div.- 12-278A	Diesel	1	12	2,400 bhp	1	11.5
Vega Desgagnes	Wartsila - 9R32	Diesel	2	9	7,560bhp	1 cpp	16.1
Victory	*(Articulated Tug)*						
	MaK - 6MU551AK	Diesel	2	6	3,940 bhp	2	16.1
Voyageur Independent	2005 GE 7FDM EFI	Diesel	1	16	4,100 bhp	1 cpp	
Vogageur Pioneer	Sulzer 4RLB76	Diesel	4	4	10,880 bhp	1cpp	15.5
Walter J. McCarthy Jr.	GM - Electro-Motive Div.- 20-645-E7B	Diesel	4	20	14,400 bhp	2 cpp	16.1
Wilfred Sykes	Westinghouse Elec. Corp.	Turbine	1	16	7,700 shp	1	16.1
William J. Moore	*(Tug / Barge, usually paired with McLeary's Spirit)*						
	GM Electro-Motive Div. 16-645-E	Diesel	2	16	4,000 bhp	2 cpp	15.5
Wolf River	Fairbanks Morse - 10-38D8-1/8	Diesel	1	10	1,880 bhp	1	10.4
Yankcanuck	Cooper-Bessemer Corp.	Diesel	1	8	1,860 bhp	1	11.5

Saltwater Fleets

Diezeborg in the
MacArthur Lock
at Sault Ste. Marie.
(Glenn Blaskiewicz)

Listed after each vessel in order are: Type of Vessel, Year Built, Type of Engine, Maximum Cargo Capacity (at midsummer draft in long tons) or Gross Tonnage*, Overall Length, Breadth and Depth (from the top of the keel to the top of the upper deck beam). This list reflects vessels whose primary trade routes are on saltwater but which also regularly visit Great Lakes and St. Lawrence Seaway ports. It is not meant to be a complete listing of every saltwater vessel that could potentially visit the Great Lakes and St. Lawrence Seaway. To attempt to do so, given the sheer number of world merchant vessels, would be space prohibitive. Fleets listed may operate other vessels worldwide than those included herein. Former names listed in boldface type indicate the vessel visited the system under that name.

Fleet #.	Fleet Name Vessel Name	Type of Vessel	Year Built	Type of Engine	Cargo Cap. or gross*	Overall Length	Breadth	Depth or Draft*
IA-1	**ADRICO SHIPPING CO., ATHENS, GREECE**							
	Nobility	BC	1981	D	30,900	617' 06"	76' 00"	47' 07"
	*(**Nosira Lin** '81-'89, **Dan Bauta** '89-'89, **Kristianiafjord** '89-'93, **Federal Vibeke** '93-'00, **Kalisti** '00-'02)*							
IA-2	**ALENDAL REDERI AS, HAUGESUND, NORWAY**							
	Queen Trader	TK	1980	D	3,726	293' 08"	46' 00"	27' 11"
	*(**Proof Gallant** '80-'98)*							
IA-3	**ALLROUNDER MARITIME CO. INC., MANILA, PHILIPPINES**							
	Sir Walter	BC	1996	D	18,315	486' 03"	74' 10"	40' 00"
	*(**Rubin Stork** '96-'03)*							
IA-4	**ALVARGONZALEZ NAVIGATION, GIJON, SPAIN**							
	Covadonga	TK	2005	D	6,967	390' 09"	55' 05"	27' 07"
IA-5	**AMALTHIA MARINE INC., ATHENS, GREECE**							
	Antikeri	BC	1984	D	28,788	606' 11"	75' 09"	48' 02"
	*(**LT Argosy** '84-'98, **Millenium Hawk** '98-'02, **Cashin** '02-'05)*							
	Seneca	BC	1983	D	28,788	606' 11"	75' 09"	48' 02"
	*(**Mangal Desai** '83-'98, **Millenium Eagle** '98-'02, **Stokmarnes** '02-'05)*							
	Tuscarora	BC	1983	D	28,031	639' 09"	75' 09"	46' 11"
	*(Manila Spirit '83-'86, **Rixta Oldendorff** '86-'06)*							
IA-6	**AMERICAN CANADIAN CARIBBEAN LINE INC., WARREN, RI, USA**							
	Grande Caribe	PA	1997	D	97*	182' 07"	39' 01"	9' 10"
	Grande Mariner	PA	1998	D	97*	182' 07"	39' 01"	9' 10"
	Niagara Prince	PA	1994	D	99*	174' 00"	40' 00"	9' 00"
IA-7	**ANBROS MARITIMA S.A, PIRAEUS, GREECE**							
	Ypermachos	BC	1983	D	9,653	584' 08"	75' 09"	48' 07"
	*(**Socrates** '88-'92, **Union** '92-'97, **Mecta Sea** '97-'05)*							
IA-8	**ANDERS UTKILENS REDERI AS, BERGEN, NORWAY**							
	Sundstraum	TK	1993	D	4,737	316' 01"	50' 04"	26' 05"
	(Maj-Britt Terkol '93-'96)							
IA-9	**ATHENA MARINE CO. LTD., LIMASSOL, CYPRUS**							
	FOLLOWING VESSELS UNDER CHARTER TO FEDNAV LTD.							
	Federal Danube	BC	2003	D	37,372	652' 11"	78' 05"	50' 02"
	Federal Elbe	BC	2003	D	37,372	652' 11"	78' 05"	50' 02"
	Federal Ems	BC	2002	D	37,372	652' 11"	78' 05"	50' 02"
	Federal Leda	BC	2003	D	37,372	652' 11"	78' 05"	50' 02"
	Federal Patroller	BC	1999	D	17,477	469' 02"	74' 10"	43' 08"
	*(Atlantic Pride '99-'01, Seaboard Rover '01-'02, **Atlantic Patroller** '02-'05, African Patroller '05-'06)*							
	Federal Pride	BC	2000	D	17,477	469' 02"	74' 10"	43' 08"
	*(Atlantic Pride '00-'01, Seaboard Rover '01-'02, **Atlantic Pride** '02-'05, Seabord Chile II '05-'06)*							
	Federal Weser	BC	2002	D	37,372	652' 11"	78' 05"	50' 02"
IA-10	**ATLANTSKA PLOVIDBA D.D., DUBROVNIK, CROATIA**							
	Mljet	BC	1982	D	29,643	622' 01"	74' 11"	49' 10"
	FOLLOWING VESSEL UNDER CHARTER TO FEDNAV LTD.							
	Orsula	BC	1996	D	34,372	656' 02"	77' 01"	48' 10"
	*(**Federal Calumet** {2} '96-'97)*							

Fleet #.	Fleet Name / Vessel Name	Type of Vessel	Year Built	Type of Engine	Cargo Cap. or gross*	Overall Length	Breadth	Depth or Draft*
IA-11	**AURORA SHIPPING INC., MANILA, PHILIPPINES**							
	Aurora Topaz	BC	1982	D	28,268	639' 09"	75' 10"	46' 11"
	*(Launched as Haifu, **Sea Fortune** '82-'85, **Miss Aliki** '85-'93)*							
IB-1	**B & N MOORMAN BV, RIDDERKERK, NETHERLANDS**							
	Andromeda	GC	1999	D	6,663	388' 09"	49' 10"	27' 06"
	Capricorn	GC	2000	D	6,715	388' 09"	49' 08"	27' 02"
IB-2	**BARU DELTA MARITIME INC., PIRAEUS, GREECE**							
	Doxa D	BC	1984	D	30,820	617' 05"	76' 01"	47' 06"
	*(**Alberta** '84-'93, **Nea Doxa** '93-'02)*							
IB-3	**BELUGA SHIPPING GMBH, BREMEN, GERMANY**							
	BBC India	BC	1998	D	17,539	468' 06"	70' 06"	43' 08"
	*(**Maria Green** '98-'04)*							
	Beluga Elegance	BC	2004	D	12,782	452' 09"	68' 11"	36' 01"
	Beluga Emotion	BC	2004	D	12,782	452' 09"	68' 11"	36' 01"
	Beluga Endurance	BC	2005	D	12,782	452' 09"	68' 11"	36' 01"
	Beluga Eternity	BC	2004	D	12,782	452' 09"	68' 11"	36' 01"
	Beluga Federation	BC	2006	D	11,380	452' 11"	70' 01"	36' 01"
	Beluga Fusion	BC	2000	D	11,380	452' 11"	70' 01"	36' 01"
	Beluga Indication	BC	2005	D	11,380	452' 11"	70' 01"	36' 01"
	Beluga Recognition	BC	2005	D	11,380	452' 11"	70' 01"	36' 01"
	Beluga Recommendation	BC	2005	D	10,536	439' 04"	70' 06"	30' 06"
	Beluga Resolution	BC	2005	D	10,536	439' 04"	70' 06"	30' 06"
	Beluga Revolution	BC	2005	D	10,536	439' 04"	70' 06"	30' 06"
	Magdalena Green	BC	2001	D	17,538	465' 10"	70' 06"	43' 10"
	Makiri Green	BC	1999	D	17,538	465' 10"	70' 06"	43' 10"
	Margaretha Green	BC	2000	D	17,538	465' 10"	70' 06"	43' 10"
	*(**Margaretha Green** '00-'00, Coral Green '00-'01, Nirint Voyager '01-'02, **Margaretha Green** '02-'04, Newpac Cumulus '04-'05)*							
	Marinus Green	BC	2000	D	17,538	465' 10"	70' 06"	43' 10"
	Marion Green	BC	1999	D	17,538	465' 10"	70' 06"	43' 10"
IB-4	**BIGLIFT SHIPPING BV, ROOSENDAAL, NETHERLANDS**							
	Enchanter	HL	1998	D	16,069	452' 09"	74' 10"	31' 03"
	Happy Ranger	HL	1998	D	15,065	454' 01"	74' 10"	42' 04"
	Happy River	HL	1998	D	15,700	452' 09"	74' 10"	31' 03"
	Happy Rover	HL	1997	D	15,700	452' 09"	74' 10"	31' 03"
	Tracer	HL	2000	D	8,874	329' 09"	73' 06"	26' 11"
	Tramper	HL	2000	D	8,874	329' 09"	73' 06"	26' 11"
	Transporter	HL	1999	D	8,469	329' 09"	80' 01"	36' 05"
	Traveller	HL	2000	D	8,874	329' 09"	73' 06"	26' 11"
IB-5	**BLYSTAD TANKERS INC., OSLO, NORWAY**							
	FOLLOWING VESSELS UNDER CHARTER TO SONGA OFFSHORE							
	Songa Aneline	TK	1998	D	8,941	378' 03"	61' 00"	33' 08"
	(Alexander '98-'04, Garonne '04-'04, Gironde '04-'05)							
	Songa Defiance	TK	2001	D	17,396	442' 11"	74' 10"	41' 00"
	*(**North Defiance** '01-'06)*							
	Sichem Maya	TK	1988	D	17,485	496' 01"	73' 06"	39' 08"
	*(Kapitan Rudynev '88-'94, **Kapitan Rudnev** '94-'03, **Lake Maya** '03-'06, Songa Maya '06-'06)*							
IB-6	**BOOMSMA SHIPPING BV, SNEEK, NETHERLANDS**							
	Frisian Spring	GC	2006	D	5,023	390' 01"	44' 00"	29' 10"
IB-7	**BRIESE SCHIFFAHRTS GMBH & CO. KG, LEER, GERMANY**							
	Bavaria	GC	1996	D	3,500	288' 09"	42' 00"	23' 04"
	(Geise '96-'96)							
	BBC Asia	GC	2003	D	7,000	391' 09"	63' 03"	32' 02"
	(Embse '03-'03)							

Marinus Green, seen from her sister ship, the *Margaretha Grreen,* on Lake St. Clair. *(Alain Gindroz)*

Fleet #.	Fleet Name Vessel Name	Type of Vessel	Year Built	Type of Engine	Cargo Cap. or gross*	Overall Length	Breadth	Depth or Draft*
	BBC Atlantic	GC	2005	D	6,090	380' 05"	54' 02"	26' 01"
	(Westerriede '05-'05)							
	BBC Canada	GC	1999	D	4,798	330' 01"	54' 06"	26' 07"
	BBC Ems	GC	2006	D	14,000	469' 02"	75' 06"	23' 04"
	BBC Finland	GC	2000	D	8,760	353' 06"	59' 09"	33' 02"
	(Norderney '00-'00)							
	BBC France	GC	2005	D	4,309	324' 06"	45' 03"	24' 03"
	BBC Germany	GC	2003	D	8,469	329' 09"	80' 01"	36' 05"
	BBC Holland	GC	2002	D	4,303	330' 00"	54' 06"	26' 07"
	BBC Iceland	GC	1999	D	4,806	330' 01"	54' 06"	26' 07"
	(Industrial Accord '99-'02)							
	BBC Northsea	GC	2000	D	7,820	353' 06"	59' 09"	33' 02"
	(Northsea '00-'04)							
	BBC Scotland	GC	2002	D	4,713	330' 01"	54' 06"	26' 07"
	BBC Shanghai	GC	2001	D	4,900	330' 01"	54' 06"	26' 07"
	(Baltic Sea '01-'01, BBC Shanghai '01-'03, TLI Aquila '03-'03)							
	BBC Singapore	GC	1990	D	4,900	328' 01"	54' 06"	26' 07"
	(Randzel '90-'97, Bremer Timber '97-'04)							
	BBC Texas	GC	1992	D	7,520	351' 01"	62' 04"	34' 09"
	(Paula '92-'00, Tina '00-'00)							
	BBC Venezuela	GC	1999	D	5,240	324' 10"	51' 11"	26' 07"
	(Fockeburg '99-'00, Global Africa '00-'01)							
	Borkum	GC	1994	D	18,355	486' 07"	74' 10"	40' 00"
	(Erna Oldendorff *'94-'05)*							
	Santiago	GC	1997	D	3,525	280' 10"	42' 00"	23' 04"
	Skaftafell	GC	1997	D	4,900	328' 01"	54' 06"	26' 07"
	(Launched as Torum, Industrial Harmony '97-'00, **BBC Brazil** *'00-'03, Brake '03-'03, BBC Brazil '04-'04)*							
IB-8	**BROVIG CHEMICAL TANKERS, FARSUND, NORWAY**							
	Brovig Fjord	TK	2006	D	12,956	417' 04"	66' 11"	37' 09"
	(Launched as Songa Pearl)							
	Brovig Ocean	TK	2006	D	12,956	417' 04"	66' 11"	37' 09"
	(Launched as Songa Onyx)							
IC-1	**CAMILLO EITZEN & CO. AS, LYSAKER, NORWAY**							
	Sichem Padua	TK	1993	D	9,214	382' 06"	62' 04"	33' 02"
	(Anne Sif '93-'01, Sichem Anne '01-'02)							
	Sichem Palace	TK	2004	D	8,807	367' 05"	62' 04"	32' 10"
	Sichem Peace	TK	2005	D	8,807	367' 05"	62' 04"	32' 10"
	Sichem Princess Marie-Chantal	TK	2003	D	7,930	370' 09"	60' 00"	31' 06"
	Sichem Singapore	TK	2006	D	13,141	421' 11"	66' 11"	37' 09"
IC-2	**CANADIAN FOREST NAVIGATION (CANFORNAV) LTD., MONTREAL, QUEBEC, CANADA**							

IC-2 **CANADIAN FOREST NAVIGATION (CANFORNAV) LTD., MONTREAL, QUEBEC, CANADA**
At press time, Canadian Forest Navigation Co. Ltd. had the following vessels under long or short-term charter. Please consult their respective fleets for details: Apollon, Bluebill, Bluewing, Cinnamon, Eider, Goldeneye, Greenwing, Mandarin, Milo, Pintail, Orna, Pochard, Puffin, Redhead, Scoter, Toro, Woody

Fleet #.	Fleet Name / Vessel Name	Type of Vessel	Year Built	Type of Engine	Cargo Cap. or gross*	Overall Length	Breadth	Depth or Draft*
IC-3	**CANSHIP LTD., ST. JOHN'S, NEWFOUNDLAND, CANADA**							
	Astron	RR	1971	D	1,910	278' 08"	45' 03"	21' 03"
	(Atlantic Bermudian '71-'75, Londis '75-'76, Merzario Sardinia '76-'78)							
IC-4	**CARISBROOKE SHIPPING PLC, COWES, ISLE OF WIGHT, UNITED KINGDOM**							
	Jill-C	GC	1998	D	4,900	311' 08"	43' 03"	23' 07"
	Vectis Harrier	BC	1997	D	8,130	380' 07"	54' 02"	30' 02"
	(Viscount '97-'04)							
IC-5	**CATSAMBIS SHIPPING LTD., PIRAEUS, GREECE**							
	Calypso	GC	1977	D	30,880	600' 00"	75' 02"	47' 06"
	(Hercegovina *'77-'98,* **Adimon** *'98-'04)*							

Fleet #.	Fleet Name / Vessel Name	Type of Vessel	Year Built	Type of Engine	Cargo Cap. or gross*	Overall Length	Breadth	Depth or Draft*
IC-6	**CANDLER SCHIFFAHRT GMBH, BREMEN, GERMANY**							
	Glory	BC	2005	D	7,378	381' 04"	59' 01"	34' 01"
	(FCC Glory '05-'06)							
IC-7	**CHARTWORLD SHIPPING CORP., ATHENS, GREECE**							
	Chem Bothnia	TK	1985	D	6,730	351' 01"	55' 10"	27' 11"
	(Ace '85-'85, Ace Chemi '85-'91, Kilchem Bothnia '91-'99)							
	Chem Oceania	TK	1984	D	6,748	370' 09"	59' 01"	20' 09"
	(Shoun Maru No. 11 '84-'89, Oceania Glory '89-'90, Kilchem Oceania '90-'00)							
IC-8	**CHINA OCEAN SHIPPING CO. (COSCO), BEIJING, PEOPLE'S REPUBLIC OF CHINA**							
	Yick Hua	BC	1984	D	28,086	584' 08"	75' 09"	48' 07"
	(Santa Lucia '84-'84, Pacific Defender '84-'85, Lori '85-'91)							
IC-9	**CLIPPER DENMARK APS, HUMLEBAEK, DENMARK**							
	Clipper Eagle	BC	1994	D	16,906	490' 02"	75' 04"	39' 08"
	Clipper Falcon	BC	1994	D	16,906	490' 02"	75' 04"	39' 08"
IC-10	**CLIPPER ELITE CARRIERS AS, COPENHAGEN, DENMARK**							
	CEC Fantasy	GC	1994	D	7,121	331' 08"	61' 08"	30' 06"
	(Arktis Fantasy '94-'00)							
	CEC Fighter	GC	1994	D	7,121	331' 08"	61' 08"	30' 06"
	(Arktis Fighter '94-'94, Ville de Rodae '94-'96, Arktis Fighter '96-'02)							
	CEC Future	GC	1994	D	7,121	331' 08"	61' 08"	30' 06"
	(Arktis Future '01-'01)							
	CEC Oceanic	RR	1997	D	5,085	331' 00"	61' 00"	31' 10"
	*(**Scan Oceanic** '97-'05)*							
	CEC Polaris	RR	1996	D	5,100	331' 00"	61' 00"	31' 10"
	*(**Scan Polaris** '96-'05)*							
	CEC Spring	GC	1993	D	4,110	290' 00"	49' 03"	24' 07"
	(Arktis Spring '93-'94, Mekong Spring '94-'95, Arktis Spring '95-'01, CEC Spring '01-'01, Anking '01-'02 CEC Spring '02-'03, Sofrana Bligh '03-'04)							
	Thor Sofia	BC	1984	D	4,281	288' 09"	50' 09"	27' 03"
IC-11	**CLIPPER WONSILD TANKERS AS, COPENHAGEN, DENMARK**							
	Clipper Golfito	TK	2006	D	14,227	440' 02"	67' 03"	38' 01"
	Clipper Kristin	TK	2006	D	11,316	382' 03"	65' 07"	38' 05"
	Clipper Leader	TK	2004	D	10,098	388' 04"	62' 04"	33' 02"
	*(**Panam Trinity** '04-'06)*							
	Clipper Legacy	TK	2005	D	10,098	388' 04"	62' 04"	33' 02"
	Clipper Legend	TK	2004	D	10,098	388' 04"	62' 04"	33' 02"
	Clipper Tobago	TK	1999	D	8,834	367' 05"	61' 08"	31' 08"
	(Botany Treasure '99-'06)							
	Clipper Trinidad	TK	1998	D	5,483	370' 09"	61' 08"	31' 08"
	(Botany Trust '98-'06)							
	Clipper Trojan	TK	1996	D	9,553	452' 09"	71' 06"	39' 08"
	(Botany Trojan '96-'98, Stolt Trojan '98-'04, Botany Trojan '04-'06)							
IC-12	**COASTAL SHIPPING LTD., GOOSE BAY, NEWFOUNDLAND, CANADA**							
	Tuvaq	TK	1977	D	15,955	539' 08"	72' 10"	39' 04"
	(Tiira '02)							
IC-13	**COLUMBIA SHIPMANAGEMENT BV, SPIJKENISSE, NETHERLANDS**							
	Alioth Star	TK	1985	D	16,421	495' 05"	73' 06"	39' 11"
	(Bolshevik Kamo '85-'93, Kobuleti '93-'00)							
IC-14	**COMMERCIAL FLEET OF DONBASS LLC, DONETSK, UKRAINE**							
	Avdeevka	BC	1977	D	26,398	570' 11"	75' 03"	47' 07"
	(Goldensari '77-'80, Bogasari Tiga '80-'86)							
	Berdyansk	BC	1977	D	27,559	584' 04"	75' 02"	48' 03"
	(Baltic Skou '77-'85)							

Fleet #.	Fleet Name / Vessel Name	Type of Vessel	Year Built	Type of Engine	Cargo Cap. or gross*	Overall Length	Breadth	Depth or Draft*
	General Blazhevich	BC	1981	D	7,805	399' 09"	67' 00"	27' 03"
	(Traun '81-'85, **General Blazhevich** '85-'00, **Regina** '00-'03)							
	Dobrush	BC	1982	D	28,136	644' 08"	75' 09"	46' 11"
	(**World Goodwill** '82-'85)							
	Makeevka	BC	1982	D	28,136	644' 08"	75' 09"	46' 11"
	(**World Shanghai** '82-'85)							
	Mariupol	BC	1977	D	27,559	584' 04"	75' 02"	48' 03"
	(**Arctic Skou** '77-'85, Zdhanov '85-'89)							
IC-15	**COMMERCIAL TRADING & DISCOUNT CO. LTD., ATHENS, GREECE**							
	Ira	BC	1979	D	26,697	591' 02"	75' 10"	45' 08"
	Ivi	BC	1979	D	26,697	591' 04"	75' 10"	45' 08"
IC-16	**COMMON PROGRESS COMPANIA NAVIERA SA, PIRAEUS, GREECE**							
	Kastor P	BC	1983	D	22,713	528' 03"	75' 07"	45' 07"
	(Sea Augusta '83-'85, Jovian Lily '85-'91)							
	Polydefkis P	BC	1982	D	22,713	528' 03"	75' 07"	45' 07"
	(Sea Astrea '82-'85, Jovian Luzon '85-'91)							
IC-17	**COPENHAGEN TANKERS AS, GENTOFTE, DENMARK**							
	Panam Linda	TK	1998	D	10,300	410' 01"	61' 08"	32' 06"
	Panam Sol	TK	1998	D	12,756	406' 10"	66' 03"	36' 09"
	(Opal Sun '98-'02)							
IC-18	**CRUISE WEST, SEATTLE, WA, USA**							
	Nantucket Clipper	PA	1984	D	96*	207' 00"	37' 00"	11' 06
IC-19	**CSL INTERNATIONAL INC., BEVERLY, MA, USA**							
	CSL Asia	BC	1999	D	45,729	609' 05"	99' 09"	54' 02"
	CSL Atlas	SU	1990	D	67,308	746' 01"	105' 00"	63' 01"
	CSL Cabo	SU	1971	D	31,364	596' 00"	84' 02"	49' 10"
	(Bockenheim '71-'80, Cabo San Lucas '80-'95)							
	CSL Pacific	SU	1977	D	31,921	596' 05"	81' 06"	47' 06"
	(Selwyn Range '77-'85, River Torrens '85-'00)							
	CSL Spirit	SU	2000	D	70,037	738' 03"	105' 07"	64' 00"
	CSL Trailblazer	SU	1978	D	26,608	583' 11"	85' 00"	46' 03"
	(Gold Bond Trailblazer '78-'98)							
	Sheila Ann	SU	1999	D	70,037	738' 03"	105' 07"	64' 00"
	MARBULK SHIPPING INC. – MANAGED BY CSL INTERNATIONAL INC.							
	PARTNERSHIP BETWEEN CSL INTERNATIONAL INC. AND ALGOMA CENTRAL CORP.							
	Ambassador	SU	1983	D	37,448	730' 00"	75' 10"	50' 00"
	(**Canadian Ambassador** '83-'85, **Ambassador** '85-'00, **Algosea** {2} '00-'00)							
	Pioneer	SU	1981	D	37,448	730' 00"	75' 10"	50' 00"
	(**Canadian Pioneer** '81-'86)							
IC-20	**CRESCENT MARINE SERVICES, COPENHAGEN, DENMARK**							
	Panam Atlantico	TK	2001	D	14,003	439' 08"	67' 03"	38' 01"
	Panam Felice	TK	1999	D	11,616	384' 10"	65' 07"	36' 09"
	Panam Flota	TK	1999	D	11,642	384' 06"	65' 07"	36' 09"
	Panam Oceanica	TK	2005	D	12,000	406' 10"	65' 07"	36' 09"
	Panam Trinity	TK	2004	D	10,048	388' 04"	62' 04"	33' 02"
IC-21	**CYPRUS MARITIME CO. LTD., ATHENS, GREECE**							
	Lake Superior	BC	1982	D	30,670	617' 04"	76' 00"	47' 07"
	(**Broompark** '82-'99, **Millenium Raptor** '99-'02, Cardinal '02-'02)							
ID-1	**DAITOH TRADING CO. LTD., TOKYO, JAPAN**							
	Shamrock Moon	TK	1997	D	10,303	410' 01"	62' 05"	32' 06"
ID-2	**DOUN KISEN CO. LTD., OCHI EHIME PREFECTURE, JAPAN**							
	Bright Laker	BC	2001	D	30,778	606' 11"	77' 05"	48" 11"

Fleet #.	Fleet Name Vessel Name	Type of Vessel	Year Built	Type of Engine	Cargo Cap. or gross*	Overall Length	Breadth	Depth or Draft*
	FOLLOWING VESSEL UNDER CHARTER TO FEDNAV LTD.							
	Federal Kushiro	BC	2003	D	32,787	624' 08"	77' 05"	49' 10"
IE-1	**EASTWIND SHIP MANAGEMENT, SINGAPORE, SINGAPORE**							
	Arabian Wind	TK	1987	D	17,484	496' 05"	73' 06"	39' 10"
	*(Akademik Vekua '87-'94, **Vekua** '94-'00, **Gali** '00-'05)*							
	Yarmouth	BC	1985	D	29,462	600' 04"	76' 01"	48' 10"
	*(**Paolo Pittaluga** '85-'91, **Federal Oslo** '91-'00)*							
	Yellowknife	BC	1984	D	29,651	622' 00"	74' 08"	49' 08"
	*(**Bihac** '84-'93, **La Boheme** '93-'95, Lindsey M. '98-'99, Med Pride '99-'01)*							
	Yosemite	BC	1985	D	28,019	584' 08"	75' 11"	48' 05"
	*(**Astral Mariner** '85-'90, **Lake Challenge** '90-'97, **Manila Angus** '97-'98, **Darya Devi** '98-'06)*							
	Yucatan	BC	1996	D	30,838	606' 11"	77' 05"	48' 11"
	(Golden Laker '96-'04)							
IE-2	**ELDER SHIPPING LTD., LONDON, UNITED KINGDOM**							
	Balticland	BC	1977	D	17,161	511' 10"	73' 10"	45' 11"
	(Pollux '77-'88, Baltikum '88-'89, Pollux '89-'90, Nomadic Pollux '90-'04)							
IE-3	**EMIRATES TRADING AGENCY LLC, DUBAI, UNITED ARAB EMIRATES**							
	Siam Star	BC	1984	D	29,617	587' 03"	75' 11"	47' 07"
	*(**Trident Mariner** '84-'01, **Taxideftis** '01-'06)*							
IE-4	**EMPROS LINES SHIPPING CO., ATHENS, GREECE**							
	Adamastos	BC	1986	D	17,792	479' 00"	74' 10"	40' 01"
	*(**Clipper Bueno** '86-'93, Clipper Atria '93-'95)*							
IE-5	**ENZIAN SHIPPING AG, BERNE, SWITZERLAND**							
	Alessia	BC	1999	D	5,647	311' 03"	42' 09"	23' 02"
	Celine	BC	2001	D	8,600	423' 03"	52' 00"	32' 00"
	Claudia	BC	1999	D	5,647	311' 06"	42' 09"	23' 02"
	Kathrin	BC	1999	D	5,647	311' 04"	42' 11"	23' 03"
	Marie-Jeanne	BC	1999	D	5,049	311'11"	43' 04"	23' 05"
	Sabina	BC	2000	D	9,231	419' 06"	52' 05"	32' 00"
	SCL Bern	BC	2005	D	12,680	459' 03"	70' 06"	38' 03"
	(SCL Bern '05-'05, SITC Bern '05-'06)							
IE-6	**ER DENIZCILIK SANAYI NAKLIYAT VE TICARET AS, ISTANBUL, TURKEY**							
	Balaban I	BC	1979	D	25,651	562' 08"	75' 02"	45' 11"
	*(**Ocean Glory** '79-'83, **Serafim** '83-'91)*							
IE-7	**EXECUTIVE SHIP MANAGEMENT LTD., SINGAPORE, SINGAPORE**							
	Chemical Trader	TK	2005	D	8,801	367' 05"	61' 04"	32' 10"
IF-1	**FAIRPLAY TOWAGE, HAMBURG, GERMANY**							
	Fairplay XIV	TB	1971	D	814	162' 04"	37' 02"	23' 04"
	(Rega 1 '71-'78, Hanseatic '78-'79)							
IF-2	**FAR EASTERN SHIPPING CO. (FESCO), VLADIVOSTOK, RUSSIA**							
	Grigoriy Aleksandrov	BC	1986	D	24,105	605' 08"	75' 02"	46' 07"
	Khudozhnik Kraynev	BC	1986	D	24,105	605' 08"	75' 02"	46' 07"
IF-3	**FEDNAV LTD., MONTREAL, QUEBEC, CANADA** **FEDNAV INTERNATIONAL LTD. - DIVISION OF FEDNAV LTD.**							
	Federal Agno	BC	1985	D	29,643	599' 09"	76' 00"	48' 07"
	*(**Federal Asahi** {1} '85-'89)*							
	Federal Asahi {2}	BC	2000	D	36,563	656' 02"	77' 11"	48' 09"
	Federal Hudson {3}	BC	2000	D	36,563	656' 02"	77' 11"	48' 09"
	Federal Hunter {2}	BC	2001	D	36,563	656' 02"	77' 11"	48' 09"
	Federal Katsura	BC	2005	D	32,787	624' 08"	77' 05"	49' 10"
	Federal Kivalina	BC	2000	D	36,563	656' 02"	77' 11"	48' 09"
	Federal Maas {2}	BC	1997	D	34,372	656' 02"	77' 01"	48' 10"

Fleet #.	Fleet Name Vessel Name	Type of Vessel	Year Built	Type of Engine	Cargo Cap. or gross*	Overall Length	Breadth	Depth or Draft*
	Federal Mackinac	BC	2004	D	27,000	606' 11"	77' 09"	46' 25"
	Federal Margaree	BC	2005	D	27,000	606' 11"	77' 09"	46' 25"
	Federal Nakagawa	BC	2005	D	36,563	656' 02"	77' 11"	48' 09"
	Federal Oshima	BC	1999	D	36,563	656' 02"	77' 11"	48' 09"
	Federal Progress (Northern Progress '89-'02)	BC	1989	D	38,130	580' 07"	86' 07"	48' 08"
	Federal Rhine {2}	BC	1997	D	34,372	656' 02"	77' 01"	48' 10"
	Federal Rideau	BC	2000	D	36,563	656' 02"	77' 11"	48' 09"
	Federal Saguenay {2}	BC	1996	D	34,372	656' 02"	77' 01"	48' 10"
	Federal Sakura	BC	2005	D	32,787	624' 08"	77' 05"	49' 10"
	Federal Schelde {3}	BC	1997	D	34,372	656' 02"	77' 01"	48' 10"
	Federal Seto	BC	2004	D	36,563	656' 02"	77' 11"	48' 09"
	Federal St. Laurent {3}	BC	1996	D	34,372	656' 02"	77' 01"	48' 10"
	Federal Venture (Northern Venture '89-'02)	BC	1989	D	38,130	580' 07"	86' 07"	48' 08"
	Federal Welland	BC	2000	D	36,563	656' 02"	77' 11"	48' 09"
	Federal Yukon	BC	2000	D	36,563	656' 02"	77' 11"	48' 09"
	Lake Erie (**Federal Ottawa** '80-'95)	BC	1980	D	38,294	730' 00"	76' 01"	47' 03"
	Lake Michigan (**Federal Maas** {1} '81-'95)	BC	1981	D	38,294	730' 00"	76' 01"	47' 03"
	Lake Ontario (**Federal Danube** '80-'95)	BC	1980	D	38,294	730' 00"	76' 01"	47' 03"
	Lake Superior (**Federal Thames** '81-'95)	BC	1981	D	38,294	730' 00"	76' 01"	47' 03"
	Umiak I	BC	2006	D	31,992	619' 04"	87' 02"	51' 50"

At press time, FedNav Ltd. also had the following vessels under charter. Please consult their respective fleets for details: Calliroe Patronicola, Daviken, Federal Asahi, Federal Danube, Federal Elbe, Federal Ems, Federal Fuji, Federal Kumano, Federal Kushiro, Federal Leda, Federal Manitou, Federal Matane, Federal Mattawa, Federal Miramichi, Federal Patroller, Federal Pride, Federal Polaris, Federal Pride, Federal Seto, Federal Shimanto, Federal Weser, Federal Yoshino, Goviken, Inviken, Olympic Melody, Olympic Mentor, Olympic Merit, Olympic Miracle, Orsula, Sandviken, Spar Garnet, Spar Jade, Spar Opal, Spar Ruby, Utviken, Yarmouth.

Fleet #.	Fleet Name Vessel Name	Type of Vessel	Year Built	Type of Engine	Cargo Cap. or gross*	Overall Length	Breadth	Depth or Draft*
IF-4	**FISSER & V. DOORNUM KG GMBH & CO., HAMBURG, GERMANY**							
	Okapi (Imela Fisser '72-'75, Boca Tabla '75-'82, Tabla '82-'86)	GC	1972	D	6,364	332' 10"	52' 07"	30' 03"
	Pyrgos (Elisabeth Fisser '72-'79, Villiers '79-'86)	GC	1972	D	6,364	332' 10"	52' 07"	30' 03"
IF-5	**FLINTER GRONINGEN BV (ANCORA AFS MGRS.), GRONINGEN, THE NETHERLANDS**							
	Flinterbaltica	GC	2004	D	3,400	270' 06"	41' 03"	21' 06"
	Flinterbelt	GC	2004	D	3,400	270' 06"	41' 03"	21' 06"
	Flinterbjorn	GC	2004	D	3,400	270' 06"	41' 03"	21' 06"
	Flinterborg	GC	2004	D	3,400	270' 06"	41' 03"	21' 06"
	Flinterbothnia	GC	2004	D	3,480	270' 06"	41' 03"	21' 06"
	Flinterdam	GC	1996	D	4,506	325' 07"	44' 06"	23' 06"
	Flinterdijk	GC	2000	D	6,250	366' 07"	48' 08"	26' 09"
	Flinterduin	GC	2000	D	6,359	364' 01"	49' 02"	26' 09"
	Flintereems	GC	2000	D	6,200	366' 07"	48' 08"	26' 09"
	Flinterhaven	GC	1997	D	6,067	366' 07"	48' 08"	26' 09"
	Flinterland	GC	1995	D	4,216	300' 01"	44' 08"	23' 07"
	Flintermaas	GC	2000	D	6,200	366' 05"	48' 10"	26' 10"
	Flinterspirit	GC	2001	D	6,358	366' 07"	48' 08"	26' 09"
	Flinterstar	GC	2002	D	9,200	424' 06"	55' 05"	32' 10"
	Flinterzee	GC	1997	D	6,075	366' 07"	48' 08"	26' 09"
	Flinterzijl	GC	1996	D	4,540	325' 09"	44' 09"	23' 07"
IF-6	**FORTUM OIL AND GAS OY, FORTUM, FINLAND**							
	Purha	TK	2003	D	25,000	556' 01"	78' 00"	48' 11"

Vamand Wave about to get a visit from the pilot boat *Juleen 1* at Port Weller in the Welland Canal. *(Paul Beesley)*

Fleet #.	Fleet Name / Vessel Name	Type of Vessel	Year Built	Type of Engine	Cargo Cap. or gross*	Overall Length	Breadth	Depth or Draft*
IF-7	**FRANCO COMPANIA NAVIERA SA, ATHENS, GREECE**							
	Stefania I	BC	1985	D	28,269	584' 08"	75' 11"	48' 05"
	(*Astral Ocean* '85-'95, Sea Crystal '95-'97, **Stefania** '97-'98)							
IF-8	**FRANK DAHL SHIPPING, CUXHAVEN, GERMANY**							
	Finex	GC	2001	D	9,857	433' 10"	52' 01"	31' 08"
	(**Volmeborg** '01-'06)							
	Matfen	GC	1998	D	8,664	433' 10"	52' 01"	31' 08"
	(**Veerseborg** '98-'04)							
	Morpeth	GC	2000	D	8,737	433' 10"	52' 01"	31' 08"
	(Vossborg '01-'04)							
IF-9	**FUKUJIN KISEN CO. LTD., OCHI EHIME PREFECTURE, JAPAN**							
	FOLLOWING VESSELS UNDER CHARTER TO FEDNAV LTD.							
	Federal Kumano	BC	2001	D	32,787	624' 08"	77' 05"	49' 10"
	Federal Shimanto	BC	2001	D	32,787	624' 08"	77' 05"	49' 10"
	Federal Yoshino	BC	2001	D	32,787	624' 08"	77' 05"	49' 10"
IG-1	**GALATIA SHIPPING CO. SA, PIRAEUS, GREECE**							
	Panos G.	BC	1996	D	10,100	370' 09"	63' 08"	34' 01"
	(Ayutthaya Ruby '96-'06)							
IG-2	**GENESIS SEATRADING CORP., PIRAEUS, GREECE**							
	Rio Glory	BC	1981	D	30,900	617' 04"	76' 00"	47' 07"
	(**Darya Kamal** '81-'01)							
IG-3	**GULMAR DENIZCILIK NAKLIYAT TICARET LTD., ISTANBUL, TURKEY**							
	Gulmar	BC	1981	D	27,048	627' 07"	75' 07"	44' 03"
	(Oakstar '81-'82, **Soren Toubro** '82-'98, **Millenium Falcon** '98-'02, Giant '02-'04, Atlas Sun '04-'04)							
IH-1	**HALFDAN DITLEV-SIMONSEN & CO. AS, BILLINGSTAD, NORWAY**							
	Viscaya	TK	1982	D	26,328	569' 00"	75' 00"	46' 07"
	(**Lake Anina** '82-'90, Jo Breid '90-'99)							
IH-2	**HAPAG-LLOYD GMBH, HAMBURG, GERMANY**							
	Bravery	CO	1978	D	33,869	717' 02"	101' 11"	54' 03"
	(Dart Canada '78-'81, Canadian Explorer '83-'90, OOCL Bravery '90-'98, CanMar Bravery '98-'99, Cast Privilege '99-'01, CanMar Bravery '01-'05, CP Bravery '05-'06)							
	Endurance	CO	1983	D	32,424	727' 02"	105' 08"	49' 03"
	(Tokyo Maru '83-'90, Alligator Joy '90-'95, CanMar Endeavour '96-'98, Contship Endeavour '98-'99, Cast Performance '99-'03, CanMar Endurance '03-'05, CP Endurance '05-'06)							
	Glory	CO	1979	D	18,643	580' 10"	88' 09"	44' 03"
	(Seatrain Saratoga '79-'80, TFL Jefferson '80-'86, Jefferson '86-'88, Asian Senator '88-'90, CMB Monarch '90-'91, Sea Falcon '91-'94, CanMar Glory '94-'05, CP Glory '05-'06)							
	Lisbon Express	CO	1995	D	34,330	709' 01"	105' 10"	62' 04"
	(CanMar Fortune '95-'03, Cast Prospect '03-'05, CP Prospector '05-'06)							
	Mississauga Express	CO	1998	D	40,879	803' 10"	105' 08"	62' 05"
	(CanMar Pride '98-'05, CP Pride '05-'06)							
	Montreal Express	CO	2003	D	47,840	964' 11"	106' 00"	60' 00"
	(CanMar Spirit '03-'05, CP Spirit '05-'06)							
	Ottawa Express	CO	1998	D	40,879	803' 10"	105' 11"	62' 05"
	(CanMar Honour '98-'05, CP Honour '05-'06)							
	Power	CO	1982	D	32,207	730' 00"	105' 10"	61'08"
	(America Maru '82-'90, Alligator Excellence '90-'95, CanMar Success '98-98, Contship Success '98-'99, Cast Power '99-'03, Montreal Senator '03-'05, CP Power '05-'06)							
	Toronto Express	CO	2003	D	47,840	964' 11"	106' 00"	60' 00"
	(CanMar Venture '03-'05, CP Venture '05-'06)							
	Triumph	CO	1978	D	18,643	580' 10"	88' 10"	44' 04"
	(Seatrain Independence '78-'81, Dart Americana '81-'87, American Senator '87-'89, CMB Marque '89-'90, CanMar Triumph '90-'05, CP Triumph '05-'06)							

Fleet #.	Fleet Name Vessel Name	Type of Vessel	Year Built	Type of Engine	Cargo Cap. or gross*	Overall Length	Breadth	Depth or Draft*
	Valencia Express	CO	1996	D	34,330	709' 01"	105' 10"	62' 04"
	(CanMar Courage '96-'03, Cast Prominence '96-'05, CP Performer '05-'06)							
	Victory	CO	1979	D	18,643	580' 10"	88' 10"	44' 04"
	(Seatrain Chesapeake '79-'81, Dart Atlantica '81-'87, Singapore Senator '87-'89, American Senator '89-'90, CanMar Victory '79-'05, CP Victory '05-'06)							

THE FOLLOWING VESSEL OPERATED BY CONTI REEDEREI MANAGEMENT GMBH

	C. Columbus	PA	1997	D	14,903*	475' 09"	70' 06"	43' 06"

IH-3	**HARBOR SHIPPING & TRADING CO. SA., CHIOS, GREECE**							
	Chios Charity	BC	1981	D	29,002	589' 11"	76' 01"	47' 07"
	(Violetta '81-'86, Capetan Yiannis '86-'88, Federal Nord '88-'96, Nordic Moor '96-'98)							
	Chios Pride	BC	1981	D	28,500	627' 07"	75' 03"	44' 04"
	(Regent Palm '81-'87, Protoporos III '87-'89, Crystal B. '89-'95, Ocean Leader '95-'97)							
	Chios Sailor	BC	1984	D	30,850	617' 04"	75' 11"	47' 07"
	(Radnik '84-'96, Grant Carrier '96-'01)							

IH-4	**HARREN & PARTNER SCHIFFAHRTS GMBH, BREMEN, GERMANY**							
	Palawan	RR	1996	D	5,085	331' 00"	61' 00"	31' 10"
	(Palawan '96-'96, Scan Partner '97-'01, Palawan '01-'01, Fret Meuse '02-'03)							
	Palessa	HL	2000	D	7,069	387' 02"	64' 08"	31' 00"
	(Pantaleon '00-'00, Fret Moselle '00-'04)							
	Pancaldo	HL	2000	D	7,069	387' 02"	64' 08"	31' 00"

FOLLOWING VESSELS UNDER CHARTER TO CANADIAN FOREST NAVIGATION LTD.

	Pochard	BC	2003	D	35,200	631' 04"	77' 09"	50' 02"
	Puffin	BC	2003	D	35,200	629' 09"	77' 05"	50' 00"

IH-5	**HELIKON SHIPPING ENTERPRISES LTD., LONDON, UNITED KINGDOM**							
	Elikon	BC	1980	D	16,106	582' 00"	75' 02"	44' 04"
	(Bailey '80-'89)							

IH-6	**HERMANN BUSS GMBH, LEER, GERMANY**							
	Bornholm	BC	2006	D	7,869	388' 11"	49' 10"	27' 11"

IH-7	**HERNING SHIPPING AS, HERNING, DENMARK**							
	Ditte Theresa	TK	1977	D	4,501	301' 10"	47' 07"	29' 10"
	(Bravado '77-'96)							

II-1	**ILVA SERVIZI MARITIME., MILAN, ITALY**							
	Sagittarius	BC	1987	D	29,365	613' 06"	75' 11"	46' 11"

II-2	**INTERSEE SCHIFFAHRTS-GESELLSCHAFT MBH & CO. , HAREN-EMS, GERMANY**							
	Aachen	GC	2004	D	5,780	348' 02"	47' 03"	20' 01"
	(Lea '04-'04)							
	Amanda	GC	2005	D	5,780	348' 02"	47' 03"	20' 01"
	Anja	GC	1999	D	9,200	419' 06"	52' 00"	32' 00"
	(Anja '99-'01, TMC Brazil '01-'02)							
	Annalisa	GC	2000	D	8,894	433' 09"	52' 01"	31' 08"
	(Malte Rainbow '00-'03)							
	Carola	GC	2000	D	9,000	424' 08"	52' 00"	32' 00"
	(Beatrice '00-'00)							
	Jana	GC	2001	D	8,994	433' 09"	52' 01"	31' 08'
	(Chandra Kirana '01-'01)							
	Julietta	GC	2002	D	10,500	423' 03"	52' 00"	33' 04"
	Katja	GC	2000	D	9,000	424' 08"	52' 00"	32' 00"
	(Katja '00-'01, MSC Apapa '01-'02)							
	Lara	GC	1998	D	5,726	329' 09"	49' 03"	27' 07"
	Nicola	GC	2000	D	5,050	312' 02"	43' 02"	23' 05"
	Nina	GC	1998	D	5,726	329' 09"	49' 03"	27' 07"
	(Nina '98-'98, Melody '98-'02)							
	Rebecca	GC	2002	D	10,450	468' 02"	59' 10"	33' 04"
	Sofia	GC	2005	D	5,780	348' 02"	47' 03"	26' 07"

Greenwing, bound for Windsor from Mexico with flurospar. *(Alain Gindroz)*

Fleet #.	Fleet Name / Vessel Name	Type of Vessel	Year Built	Type of Engine	Cargo Cap. or gross*	Overall Length	Breadth	Depth or Draft*
	Tatjana	GC	2000	D	9,000	424' 08"	52' 00"	32' 00"
	(Tatjana '00-'02, TMC Brazil '02-'02)							
	Thekla	GC	2003	D	8,994	433' 09"	52' 01"	31' 08'
	(Suryawati '03-'03)							
	Victoria	GC	2004	D	10,450	468' 02"	59' 10"	33' 04"
	Winona	GC	2003	D	10,000	433' 09"	52' 06"	32' 10"
	(Vermontborg '03-'03)							
	Xenia	GC	2003	D	10,500	468' 08"	59' 10"	33' 04"
II-3	**INTERSHIP NAVIGATION CO. LTD., LIMASSOL, CYPRUS**							
	BBC Korea	BC	2003	D	17,477	469' 02"	74' 10"	43' 08"
	(Atlantic Pendant *'03-'05)*							
	BBC Russia	BC	2002	D	17,477	469' 02"	74' 10"	43' 08"
	(Atlantic Progress '02-'03)							
II-4	**IONIA MANAGEMENT SA, PIRAEUS, GREECE**							
	Alkyon	BC	1981	D	18,277	487' 05"	73' 06"	38' 05"
	(Rich Arrow '81-'89, Pisagua '89-'95)							
II-5	**ISKO MARINE SHIPPING CO., ISTANBUL, TURKEY**							
	Global Carrier	HL	1982	D	9,864	403' 06"	67' 08"	33' 10"
	(Titan Scan *'82-'02, Scan Trader '02-'03, Global Traveller '03-'04, Taipan Scan '04-'05)*							
IJ-1	**JADROPLOV DD, SPLIT, CROATIA**							
	Hope	BC	1982	D	30,900	617' 01"	76' 01"	47' 07"
	(Nosira Madeleine *'82-'89, Bella Dan '89-'93,* **Hope 1** *'93-'02)*							
IJ-2	**JO TANKERS BV, SPIJKENISSE, NETHERLANDS**							
	Jo Spirit	TK	1998	D	6,248	352' 02"	52' 02"	30' 02"
IJ-3	**JSM SHIPPING GMBH & CO., JORK, GERMANY**							
	BBC England	GC	2003	D	10,300	465' 10"	59' 10"	33' 04"
	(Frida '03-'04)							
	S Pacific	GC	2004	D	10,385	468' 02"	59' 10"	24' 02"
	Ile de Molene '03-'04)							
IJ-4	**JUMBO SHIPPING CO. SA, ROTTERDAM, NETHERLANDS**							
	Daniella	HL	1989	D	7,600	322' 09"	60' 03"	37' 02"
	(Stellaprima '89-'90)							
	Fairlane	HL	2000	D	7,123	361' 03"	68' 05"	44' 03"
	Fairlift	HL	1990	D	7,780	330' 08"	68' 10"	43' 08"
	Fairload	HL	1995	D	5,198	314' 00"	60' 03"	37' 02"
	Fairmast	HL	1983	D	6,375	360' 11"	67' 09"	34' 05"
	Fairpartner	HL	2004	D	10,975	469' 06"	86' 11"	44' 03"
	Jumbo Challenger	HL	1983	D	6,375	360' 11"	63' 10"	34' 05"
	Jumbo Javelin	HL	2004	D	10,975	469' 06"	86' 11"	44' 03"
	Jumbo Spirit	HL	1995	D	5,198	314' 00"	60' 03"	37' 02"
	Jumbo Vision	HL	2000	D	7,123	361' 03"	68' 05"	44' 03"
	Stellanova	HL	1996	D	5,198	314' 00"	60' 03"	37' 02"
	Stellaprima	HL	1991	D	7,780	330' 08"	68' 10"	43' 08"
IK-1	**KARL SCHLUTER GMBH, RENDSBURG, GERMANY**							
	Atlantic Castle	BC	2001	D	24,765	574' 02"	75' 09"	44' 09"
	(Cedar *'01 -'03)*							
IK-2	**KNUTSEN O.A.S. SHIPPING AS, HAUGESUND, NORWAY**							
	Ellen Knutsen	TK	1992	D	17,071	464' 03"	75' 07"	38' 09"
	Sidsel Knutsen	TK	1993	D	22,625	533' 03"	75' 06"	48' 07"
	Synnove Knutsen	TK	1992	D	17,071	464' 03"	75' 07"	38' 09"
	Torill Knutsen	TK	1990	D	14,910	464' 08"	75' 07"	38' 09"
	Turid Knutsen	TK	1993	D	22,625	533' 03"	75' 06"	48' 07"

Fleet #.	Fleet Name Vessel Name	Type of Vessel	Year Built	Type of Engine	Cargo Cap. or gross*	Overall Length	Breadth	Depth or Draft*
IK-3	**KREY SCHIFFAHRTS GMBH & CO. KG, SIMONSWOLDE, GERMANY**							
	BBC Ontario	GC	2004	D	12,711	248' 10"	68' 11"	36' 01"
IL-1	**LATVIAN SHIPPING CO., RIGA, LATVIA**							
	Zanis Griva	TK	1985	D	17,585	497' 00"	73' 07"	39' 11"
	(Zhan Griva '85 -'91)							
IL-2	**LAURIN MARITIME (AMERICA) INC., HOUSTON, TEXAS, USA**							
	Mountain Blossom	TK	1986	D	19,993	527' 07"	74' 11"	39' 04"
	Nordic Blossom	TK	1981	D	19,954	505' 03"	74' 07"	45' 04"
	*(**Nordic Sun** '81-'89, **Nordic** '89 -'94)*							
	Swan Lake	TK	1982	D	10,579	445' 04"	62' 04"	33' 02"
	*(**Aurum** '82-'97)*							
IL-3	**LIETUVOS JURU LAIVININKYSTE (LITHUANIAN SHIPPING CO.), KLAIPEDA, LITHUANIA**							
	Kapitonas A. Lucka	BC	1980	D	14,550	479' 08"	67' 11"	42' 04"
	(Ivan Nesterov '80-'91)							
	Kapitonas Domeika	BC	1979	D	14,550	479' 08"	67' 11"	42' 04"
	*(Kapitan Valvilov '79-'92, **Kapitonas Valvilov** **'92-'95**)*							
	Kapitonas Kaminskas	BC	1978	D	14,550	479' 08"	67' 11"	42' 04"
	*(Kapitan Gudin '78-'92, **Kapitonas Gudin** '92-'95)*							
	Kapitonas Serafinas	BC	1980	D	14,550	479' 08"	67' 11"	42' 04"
	*(Kapitan Stulov '80-'91, **Kapitonas Stulov** '91-'97)*							
	Kapitonas Stulpinas	BC	1981	D	14,550	479' 08"	67' 11"	42' 04"
	(Yustas Paleckis '81-'92)							
	Staris	BC	1985	D	9,650	403' 06"	65' 08"	50' 09"
	*(Abitibi Concord '85-'92, Concord '92-'94, Abitibi Concord '94-'96, **Concord** '96-'02)*							
IL-4	**LOSINJSKA PLOVIDBA BRODARSTVO, RIJEKA, REPUBLIC OF CROATIA**							
	Liski	BC	1983	D	8,556	392' 01"	60' 08"	31' 02"
	(Vinuesa '83-'88, Lux Conqueror '88-'89)							
IL-5	**LYDIA MAR SHIPPING CO. SA, ATHENS, GREECE**							
	Dorothea	BC	1984	D	22,025	508' 05"	74' 08"	44' 06"
	(Garnet Star '84-'94)							
IM-1	**MADRIGAL-WAN HAI LINES CORP., MANILA, PHILIPPINES**							
	National Honor	BC	1980	D	19,407	534' 09"	75' 09"	4' 03"
	(Galleon Diamond '80 -'83, Galleon Honor '83 -'84)							
IM-2	**MALAYSIA INTERNATIONAL SHIPPING CORP., SELANGOR, SINGAPORE**							
	Manora Naree	BC	1980	D	29,159	590' 10"	75' 09"	47' 06"
	*(**High Peak** '84 -'90, **Federal Bergen** '90 -'92, Thunder Bay '92-'93, **Federal Bergen** '93-'04)*							
IM-3	**MARLOW SHIP MANAGEMENT DEUTSCHLAND GMBH, HAMBURG, GERMANY**							
	Emsmoon	GC	2000	D	6,359	366' 08"	49' 01"	32' 02"
	(Morgenstond III '00-'05)							
IM-4	**MURMANSK SHIPPING CO., MURMANSK, RUSSIA**							
	Aleksandr Suvorov	BC	1979	D	19,885	531' 06"	75' 02"	44' 05"
	Kolguev	BC	1987	D	28,358	590' 07"	75' 10"	48' 07"
	*(Green Laker '87-'94, **Great Laker** '94-'02)*							
	Mikhail Strekalovskiy	BC	1981	D	19,252	531' 06"	75' 02"	44' 05"
	Pavel Vavilov	BC	1981	D	19,252	531' 06"	75' 02"	44' 05"
IN-1	**NAVARONE SA MARINE ENTERPRISES, LIMASSOL, CYPRUS**							
	FOLLOWING VESSELS UNDER CHARTER TO CANADIAN FOREST NAVIGATION LTD.							
	Bluebill	BC	2004	D	37,200	632' 10"	77' 09"	50' 10"
	Bluewing	BC	2002	D	26,747	611' 00"	77' 09"	46' 07"
	Cinnamon	BC	2002	D	26,747	611' 00"	77' 09"	46' 07"
	Greenwing	BC	2002	D	26,747	611' 00"	77' 09"	46' 07"
	Mandarin	BC	2003	D	26,747	611' 00"	77' 09"	46' 07"

Fleet #.	Fleet Name / Vessel Name	Type of Vessel	Year Built	Type of Engine	Cargo Cap. or gross*	Overall Length	Breadth	Depth or Draft*
	Pintail	BC	1983	D	25,035	647' 08"	75' 09"	46' 11"
	(Punica '83-'95)							
	Scoter	BC	1982	D	27,995	647' 08"	75' 10"	46' 11"
	(Peonia '82-'04)							
IN-2	**NAVIGATION MARITIME BULGARE LTD., VARNA, BULGARIA**							
	Bogdan	BC	1997	D	14,011	466' 02"	72' 08"	36' 04"
	Kamenitza	BC	1980	D	24,150	605' 08"	75' 00"	46' 05"
	Kapitan Georgi Georgiev	BC	1980	D	24,150	605' 08"	75' 00"	46' 05"
	Kom	BC	1997	D	13,971	466' 02"	72' 10"	36' 05"
	Koznitsa	BC	1984	D	24,100	605' 08"	75' 02"	46' 07"
	Malyovitza	BC	1982	D	24,456	605' 08"	75' 02"	46' 07"
	Milin Kamak	BC	1979	D	25,857	607' 07"	75' 02"	46' 07"
	Okoltchitza	BC	1982	D	24,148	605' 08"	75' 05"	46' 06"
	Perelik	BC	1998	D	13,887	466' 02"	72' 10"	36' 05"
	Persenk	BC	1998	D	13,900	466' 02"	72' 08"	36' 04"
	Shipka	BC	1978	D	24,385	607' 07"	75' 02"	46' 07"
IN-3	**NOVOROSSIYSK SHIPPING CO. (NOVOSHIP), NOVOROSSIYSK, RUSSIA**							
	Ilya Erenburg	TK	1987	D	16,970	497' 01"	73' 07"	39' 10"
	Leonid Utesov	TK	1989	D	16,970	497' 01"	73' 07"	39' 10"
	Vladimir Vysotskiy	TK	1988	D	16,970	497' 01"	73' 07"	39' 10"
IO-1	**OCEAN FREIGHTERS LTD., PIRAEUS, GREECE**							
	Pontokratis	BC	1981	D	28,738	590' 02"	75' 11"	47' 07"
	Pontoporos	BC	1984	D	29,155	590' 02"	75' 11"	47' 07"
IO-2	**OCEANEX INC., MONTREAL, QUEBEC, CANADA**							
	ASL Sanderling	RR	1977	D	15,195	364' 01"	88' 05"	57' 07"
	(Rauenfels '77-'80, Essen '80-'81, Kongsfjord '81-'83, Onno '83-'87)							
	Cabot {2}	RR	1979	D	7,132	564' 09"	73' 11"	45' 09"
	Cicero	RR	1978	D	6,985	482' 10"	73' 11"	45' 09"
	Oceanex Avalon	CO	2005	D	14,747	481' 11"	85' 00"	45' 11"
IO-3	**OLDENDORFF CARRIERS GMBH & CO., LUBECK, GERMANY**							
	Elise Oldendorff	BC	1998	D	20,142	488' 10"	75' 09"	44' 03"
	FOLLOWING VESSELS UNDER CHARTER TO KENT LINE							
	Kent Pioneer	BC	1999	D	20,427	688' 10"	75' 09"	47' 07"
	(Mathilde Oldendorff '99-'05)							
	Kent Timber	BC	1999	D	20,427	688' 10"	75' 09"	47' 07"
	(Antonie Oldendorff '99-'05)							
IO-4	**OLYMPIC SHIPPING AND MANAGEMENT SA, MONTE CARLO, MONACO**							
	FOLLOWING VESSELS UNDER CHARTER TO FEDNAV LTD.							
	Calliroe Patronicola	BC	1985	D	29,640	599' 09"	75' 11"	48' 07"
	Olympic Melody	BC	1984	D	29,640	599' 09"	75' 11"	48' 07"
	Olympic Mentor	BC	1984	D	29,640	599' 09"	75' 11"	48' 07"
	*(Calliroe Patronicola '84-'84, **Patricia-R.** '84-'88)*							
	Olympic Merit	BC	1985	D	29,640	599' 09"	75' 11"	48' 07"
	Olympic Miracle	BC	1984	D	29,640	599' 09"	75' 11"	48' 07"
IO-5	**OMICRON SHIP MANAGEMENT INC., MOSCHATO, GREECE**							
	Starlight	BC	1984	D	28,354	644' 06"	75' 06"	46' 11"
	*(**Noble River** '84-'86, **Helena Oldendorff** '86-'06)*							
IO-6	**ONEGO SHIPPING & CHARTERING, RHOON, NETHERLANDS**							
	Onego Merchant	BC	2004	D	7,800	393' 08"	49' 10"	27' 09"
	Onego Trader	BC	2003	D	7,800	393' 08"	49' 10"	27' 09"
	Onego Traveller	BC	2004	D	7,800	393' 08"	49' 10"	27' 09"
IO-7	**ORION SCHIFFAHRTS, HAMBURG, GERMANY**							
	Meta	BC	1986	D	18,612	477' 04"	75' 09"	40' 08"

IP-1 PACIFIC CARRIERS LTD., SINGAPORE, SINGAPORE

Alam Sejahtera	BC	1985	D	29,640	599' 09"	75' 10"	48' 07"
(*Olympic Dignity* '85–'92)								
Alam Sempurna	BC	1984	D	28,094	584' 08"	75' 11"	48' 05"
(Saint Laurent '84–'91)								

IP-2 PARAKOU SHIPPING LTD., HONG KONG, PEOPLE'S REPUBLIC OF CHINA
   FOLLOWING VESSELS UNDER CHARTER TO CANADIAN FOREST NAVIGATION LTD.

Eider	BC	2004	D	35,200	655' 10"	77' 09"	50' 02"
Redhead	BC	2005	D	35,200	655' 10"	77' 09"	50' 02"

IP-3 POLISH STEAMSHIP CO., SZCZECIN, POLAND

Irma	BC	2000	D	34,946	655' 10"	77' 05"	50' 02"
Iryda	BC	1999	D	34,946	655' 10"	77' 05"	50' 02"
Isa	BC	1999	D	34,946	655' 10"	77' 05"	50' 02"
Isadora	BC	1999	D	34,946	655' 10"	77' 05"	50' 02"
Isolda	BC	1999	D	34,946	655' 10"	77' 05"	50' 02"
Kopalnia Halemba	BC	1990	D	11,715	471' 01"	63' 08"	36' 05"
Kopalnia Borynia	BC	1989	D	11,898	471' 07"	63' 06"	36' 04"
Nida	BC	1993	D	13,756	469' 02"	68' 08"	37' 02"
Nogat	BC	1999	D	17,064	488' 10"	75' 06"	39' 08"
Odra	BC	1992	D	13,756	469' 02"	68' 08"	37' 02"
(*Odranes* '92–'99)								
Orla	BC	1999	D	17,064	488' 10"	75' 06"	39' 08"
Pilica	BC	1999	D	17,064	488' 10"	75' 06"	39' 08"
Pomorze Zachodnie	BC	1985	D	26,696	591' 06"	75' 10"	45' 07"
(Launched as Ziemia Tarnowska)								
Rega	BC	1995	D	17,064	488' 10"	75' 06"	39' 08"
(*Fossnes* '95–'02)								
Warta	BC	1992	D	13,756	469' 02"	68' 08"	37' 02"
(*Wartanes* '92–'99)								
Ziemia Chelminska	BC	1984	D	26,696	591' 06"	75' 10"	45' 07"
Ziemia Cieszynska	BC	1993	D	26,264	591' 02"	75' 09"	45' 07"
(*Ziemia Cieszynska* '93–'93, *Lake Carling* '93–'03)								
Ziemia Gnieznienska	BC	1985	D	26,696	591' 06"	75' 10"	45' 07"
Ziemia Gornoslaska	BC	1990	D	26,264	591' 02"	75' 09"	45' 07"
(*Ziemia Gornoslaska* '90–'91, *Lake Charles* '91–'03)								
Ziemia Lodzka	BC	1992	D	26,264	591' 02"	75' 09"	45' 07"
(*Ziemia Lodzka* '92–'92, *Lake Champlain* '92–'03)								
Ziemia Suwalska	BC	1984	D	26,696	591' 06"	75' 10"	45' 07"
Ziemia Tarnowska	BC	1985	D	26,696	591' 06"	75' 10"	45' 07"
Ziemia Zamojska	BC	1984	D	26,696	591' 06"	75' 10"	45' 07"

IP-4 PRECIOUS SHIPPING LINES, BANGKOK, THAILAND

Wana Naree	BC	1980	D	26,977	566' 00"	75' 11"	48' 05"

IR-1 REEDEREI KARL SCHLUTER GMBH & CO., RENDSBURG, GERMANY
   FOLLOWING VESSEL UNDER CHARTER TO FEDNAV LTD.

Federal Mattawa	GC	2005	D	18,825	606' 11"	77' 09"	46' 03"

IR-2 RIGEL SCHIFFAHRTS GMBH, BREMEN, GERMANY

Isarstern	TK	1995	D	17,078	528' 03"	75' 06"	38' 05"
Weserstern	TK	1992	D	10,932	417' 04"	58' 01"	34' 09"

IR-3 ROHDEN BEREEDERUNG GMBH & CO., HAMBURG, GERMANY

Agena	GC	2001	D	3,380	283' 06"	42' 00"	23' 04"

IR-4 RUSSIAN FEDERATION, MOSCOW, RUSSIA

BBC Ukraine	BC	1992	D	9,594	370' 09"	62' 00"	37' 00"
(*Aurora Three* '92–'92, Makalu '92–'93, Socol 3 '93–'06)								

Fleet #.	Fleet Name / Vessel Name	Type of Vessel	Year Built	Type of Engine	Cargo Cap. or gross*	Overall Length	Breadth	Depth or Draft*
IS-1	**SCANDIA SHIPPING HELLAS INC., ATHENS, GREECE**							
	Taxideftis	BC	1984	D	29,617	590' 03"	75' 11"	47' 07"
	(Trident Mariner '84-'01)							
IS-2	**SCANSCOT SHIPPING SERVICES (DEUTSCHLAND) GMBH, HAMBURG, GERMANY**							
	Scan Arctic	RR	1998	D	7,493	415' 01"	66' 07"	37' 09"
IS-3	**SEA OBSERVER SHIPPING SERVICES SA, PIRAEUS, GREECE**							
	Krios	BC	1983	D	12,319	423' 04"	65' 07"	36' 09"
	(Fjordnes '83-'87, Star Jay '87-'87, Elpis '87-'90, Kamtin '90-'96, Falknes '96-'00, Demi Green '00-'01, Lia '01-'03)							
IS-4	**SEASTAR NAVIGATION CO. LTD., ATHENS, GREECE** *FOLLWING VESSELS UNDER CHARTER TO CANADIAN FOREST NAVIGATION LTD.*							
	Apollon	BC	1996	D	30,855	606' 11"	77' 05"	48' 11"
	(Spring Laker '96-'06)							
	Goldeneye	BC	1986	D	26,706	591' 06"	75' 09"	48' 07"
	(Sun Ocean '86-'93, Luna Verde '93-'00)							
	Milo	BC	1984	D	27,915	584' 00"	75' 10"	48' 05"
	(Silver Leader '84-'95, Alam United '95-'98, United '98-'00)							
	Orna	BC	1984	D	27,915	584' 00"	75' 10"	48' 05"
	(St. Catheriness '84-'90, Asian Erie '90-'92, Handy Laker '92-'98, Moor Laker '98-'03)							
	Toro	BC	1983	D	28,126	584' 06"	75' 07"	46' 09"
	(La Liberte '83-'87, Liberte '87-'88, Astart '88-'93, Ulloa '93-'00)							
	Woody	BC	1984	D	25,166	593' 02"	75' 09"	47' 07"
	(High Light '84-'90, Scan Trader '90-'95, Asia Trader '95-'96, NST Challenge '96-'03)							
IS-5	**SHIH WEI NAVIGATION CO. LTD., TAIPEI, TAIWAN**							
	Fodas Pescadores	BC	2001	D	11,600	387' 02"	64' 04"	36' 01"
	Royal Pescadores	BC	1997	D	18,369	486' 01"	74' 10"	40' 00"
IS-6	**SICILNAVI S.R.L., PALERMO, ITALY**							
	Vindemia	TK	1979	D	3,603	295' 11"	44' 07"	21' 04"
	(Zaccar '79-'02)							
IS-7	**SIOMAR ENTERPRISES LTD., PIRAEUS, GREECE**							
	Island Gem	BC	1984	D	28,031	584' 08"	76' 02"	48' 05"
	Island Skipper	BC	1984	D	28,031	584' 08"	76' 02"	48' 05"
IS-8	**SOETERMEER, FEKKES' CARGADOORSKANTOOR BV, ZWIJNDRECHT, NETHERLANDS**							
	Merwedelta	GC	2001	D	4,956	308' 03"	43' 02'	23' 04"
IS-9	**SOVCOMFLOT AKP, MOSCOW, RUSSIA**							
	Kapitan Vaga	BC	1988	D	9,576	372' 01"	63' 01'	37' 00"
	(Kraftca '88-'88, Kapitan Vaga '88-'95, Nathalie Green '95-'96, Kapitan Vaga '96-'96, African River '96-'97)							
IS-10	**SPAR SHIPPING AS, BERGEN, NORWAY** *FOLLOWING VESSELS UNDER CHARTER TO FEDNAV LTD.*							
	Spar Garnet	BC	1984	D	30,674	589' 11"	75' 09"	50' 10"
	(Mary Anne '84-'93, Federal Vigra '93-'97)							
	Spar Jade	BC	1984	D	30,674	589' 11"	75' 10"	50' 11"
	(Fiona Mary '84-93, Federal Aalesund '93-'97)							
	Spar Opal	BC	1984	D	28,214	585' 00"	75' 10"	48' 05"
	(Lake Shidaka '84-'91, Consensus Atlantic '91-'92, Federal Matane '92-'97, Matane '97-'97)							
	Spar Ruby	BC	1985	D	28,259	584' 08"	75' 11"	48' 05"
	(Astral Neptune '85-'92, Liberty Sky '92-'98, Manila Bellona '98-'98, Solveig '98-'00)							
IS-11	**STOLT PARCEL TANKERS INC., GREENWICH, CT, USA**							
	Stolt Aspiration	TK	1987	D	12,219	422' 11"	66' 03"	36' 01
	(Golden Angel '87-'87)							
	Stolt Kite	TK	1992	D	4,735	314' 11"	49' 06"	26' 05
	(Randi Terkol '92-'96)							

Fleet #.	Fleet Name Vessel Name	Type of Vessel	Year Built	Type of Engine	Cargo Cap. or gross*	Overall Length	Breadth	Depth or Draft*
IS-12	**STX PAN OCEAN SHIPPING CO. LTD., SEOUL, SOUTH KOREA**							
	Pan Voyager	BC	1984	D	29,433	589' 11"	78' 01"	47' 07"
IS-13	**SUNSHIP & MLB M. LAUTERJUNG., EMDEN, GERMANY**							
	FOLLOWING VESSELS UNDER CHARTER TO FEDNAV LTD.							
	Federal Manitou	BC	2004	D	27,000	606' 11"	77' 09"	46' 03"
	Federal Matane	BC	2004	D	27,000	606' 11"	77' 09"	46' 03"
	Federal Miramichi	BC	2004	D	27,000	606' 11"	77' 09"	46' 03"
IT-1	**TEO SHIPPING CORP., PIRAEUS, GREECE**							
	Antalina	BC	1984	D	28,082	584' 08"	75' 10"	48' 05"
	(Union Pioneer '84-'88, Manila Prosperity '88-'89, Consensus Sea '89-'92, Wiltrader '92-'94)							
	Sevilla Wave	BC	1986	D	26,858	600' 08"	73' 08"	46' 08"
	Vamand Wave	BC	1985	D	28,303	580' 08"	75' 09"	47' 07"
IT-2	**THALKAT SHIPPING SA, PIRAEUS, GREECE**							
	Dora	BC	1981	D	21,951	508' 06"	75' 00"	44' 07"
	(Verdant '81-'87, Luntian '87-'93, Verdin '93-'94, Oak '94-'02)							
IT-3	**THENAMARIS (SHIPS MANAGEMENT) INC., ATHENS, GREECE**							
	Seaguardian II	BC	1984	D	28,251	639' 09"	75' 10"	46' 11"
	(Seamonarch '84-'86, Sea Master II '86-'88, Sea Monarch '88-'97, Sealuck V '97-'00,							
	Seaharmony II '00-'01, Seamonarch II '01-'02)							
	Sealink	BC	1983	D	28,234	639' 09"	75' 10"	46' 11"
	(Seaglory '83-'86, Sea Star II '86-'97)							
IT-4	**THOME SHIP MANAGEMENT, SINGAPORE, SINGAPORE**							
	Mount Ace	TK	1986	D	27,350	557' 09"	75' 11"	50' 04"
	(Rita Maersk '86-'96, Magdalena '96-'97, Maersk Baltic '97-'01, Cielo del Baltico '01-'06)							
IT-5	**TRADEWIND TANKERS SL, BARCELONA, SPAIN**							
	Tradewind Union	TK	1997	D	10,600	387' 02"	63' 08"	34' 01"
	(Southern Lion '97-'03)							
IT-6	**TRITON SCHIFFAHRTS GMBH & CO., LEER, GERMANY**							
	Lebasee	BC	1997	D	3,226	266' 00"	42' 00"	23' 04"
IU-1	**UNI-TANKERS APS, MIDDELFART, DENMARK**							
	Atlantic Swan	TK	1982	D	7,286	445' 03"	62' 05"	33' 01"
	(Argentum '82-'95)							
IU-2	**UNION MARINE ENTERPRISES SA OF PANAMA, PIRAEUS, GREECE**							
	Capetan Michalis	BC	1981	D	28,600	593' 02"	75' 09"	47' 07"
	(Vasiliki '81-'85)							
IV-1	**VENUS ENTERPRISE SA, VOULA, GREECE**							
	Sea Veteran	BC	1981	D	30,900	617' 05"	76' 01"	47' 07"
	(Nosira Sharon '81-'89, Berta Dan '89-'93, Gunay-A '93-'06)							
IV-2	**VIKEN SHIPPING AS, BERGEN, NORWAY**							
	FOLLOWING VESSELS UNDER CHARTER TO FEDNAV LTD.							
	Daviken	BC	1987	D	35,532	729' 00"	75' 09"	48' 05"
	(Malinska '87-'97)							
	Federal Fuji	BC	1986	D	29,643	599' 09"	76' 00"	48' 07"
	Federal Polaris	BC	1985	D	29,643	599' 09"	76' 00"	48' 07"
	Goviken	BC	1987	D	35,532	729' 00"	75' 09"	48' 05"
	(Omisalj '87-'97)							
	Inviken	BC	1986	D	30,052	621' 05"	75' 10"	47' 11"
	(Bar '86-'97)							
	Sandviken	BC	1986	D	35,532	729' 00"	75' 09"	48' 05"
	(Petka '86-'00)							
	Utviken	BC	1987	D	30,052	621' 05"	75' 10"	47' 11"
	(Bijelo Polje '87-'92, C. Blanco '92-'95)							

Fleet #.	Fleet Name / Vessel Name	Type of Vessel	Year Built	Type of Engine	Cargo Cap. or gross*	Overall Length	Breadth	Depth or Draft*
IW-1	**W. BOCKSTIEGEL REEDEREI KG, EMDEN, GERMANY**							
	BBC Bornholm	GC	2004	D	3,482	283' 06"	42' 04"	23' 04"
	BBC California	GC	2004	D	12,837	452' 09"	68' 11"	36' 01"
	BBC Campana	GC	2003	D	12,837	452' 09"	68' 11"	36' 01"
	(Asian Cruiser '03–'03)							
	BBC Chile	GC	2001	D	7,820	353' 00"	59' 09"	33' 02"
	BBC Italy	GC	2001	D	7,820	353' 00"	59' 09"	33' 02"
	(BBC Italy '99–'01, Buccaneer '01–'03)							
	BBC Peru	GC	2001	D	7,598	351' 01"	59' 09"	33' 02"
	BBC Plata	GC	2005	D	12,837	452' 09"	68' 11"	36' 01"
	BBC Spain	CG	2001	D	7,598	351' 01"	59' 09"	33' 02"
	Nils B.	GC	1998	D	3,440	283' 06"	42' 00"	23' 04"
IW-2	**WAGENBORG SHIPPING BV, DELFZIJL, NETHERLANDS**							
	Dagna	GC	2005	D	6,000	363' 05"	45' 11"	26' 08"
	Diezeborg	GC	2000	D	8,867	437' 08"	52' 00"	32' 02"
	Drechtborg	GC	2000	D	8,865	437' 08"	52' 02"	32' 02"
	(Drechtborg '00–'00, MSC Skaw '00–'02, Drechtborg '02–'03, Normed Rotterdam '03–'05)							
	Egbert Wagenborg	GC	1998	D	9,141	441' 05"	54' 02"	32' 02"
	*(Maasborg '98–'98, **Egbert Wagenborg** '98–'02, MSC Bothnia '02–'03)*							
	Keizersborg	GC	1996	D	9,150	427' 01"	52' 01"	33' 06"
	Koningsborg	GC	1999	D	9,150	427' 01"	52' 01"	33' 06"
	Kroonborg	GC	1995	D	9,085	428' 10"	52' 02"	33' 06"
	Kwintebank	GC	2002	D	8,664	433' 10"	52' 01"	31' 08"
	Maineborg	GC	2001	D	9,141	441' 05"	54' 02"	32' 02"
	Medemborg	GC	1997	D	9,141	441' 05"	54' 02"	32' 02"
	(Arion '97–'03)							
	Michiganborg	GC	1999	D	9,141	441' 05"	54' 02"	32' 02"
	Moezelborg	GC	1999	D	9,141	441' 05"	54' 02"	32' 02"
	Nassauborg	GC	2006	D	16,615	467' 06"	72' 02"	39' 04"
	Prinsenborg	GC	2003	D	16,615	467' 06"	72' 02"	39' 04"
	Vaasaborg	GC	1999	D	8,664	433' 10"	52' 01"	31' 08"
	Vancouverborg	GC	2001	D	9,857	433' 10"	52' 01"	31' 08"
	Varnebank	GC	2000	D	8,664	433' 10"	52' 01"	31' 08"
	Vechtborg	GC	1998	D	8,664	433' 10"	52' 01"	31' 08"
	Victoriaborg	GC	2001	D	9,857	433' 10"	52' 01"	31' 08"
	(Volgaborg '01–'01)							
	Virginiaborg	GC	2001	D	9,857	433' 10"	52' 01"	31' 08"
	Vlieborg	GC	1999	D	8,664	433' 10"	52' 01"	31' 08"
	Vlistborg	GC	1999	D	8,664	433' 10"	52' 01"	31' 08"
	Volmeborg	GC	2001	D	9,857	433' 10"	52' 01"	31' 08"
	Voorneborg	GC	1999	D	8,664	433' 10"	52' 01"	31' 08"
	Westerborg	GC	1991	D	3,015	269' 00"	41' 00"	21' 08"
	(Bothniaborg '91–'04)							
	Zeus	GC	2000	D	9,150	427' 01"	52' 01"	33' 06"
IY-1	**YAHATA KISEN CO. LTD., OCHI EHIME PREFECTURE, JAPAN**							
	Lodestar Grace	TK	2002	D	14,298	439' 08"	67' 03"	38' 01"

The information in this book, current as of Feb. 15, 2007, was obtained from the United States Coast Guard, The Lake Carriers' Association, Lloyd's Register of Shipping, Transport Canada, the U.S. Army Corps of Engineers, the St. Lawrence Seaway Authority, "Seaway Ships," "Shipfax," vessel owners and operators, www.boatnerd.com and publications of the Toronto Marine Historical Society, the Marine Historical Society of Detroit and the Welland Canal Ship Society.

A barge offloads cargo from the Greek-flag *Toro*, aground in the St. Lawrence Seaway in 2006, while a McKeil tug stands by. *(Paul Beesely)*

Extra Tonnage

On Lake Erie
aboard the
tanker *Algonova*.
(Alain Gindroz)

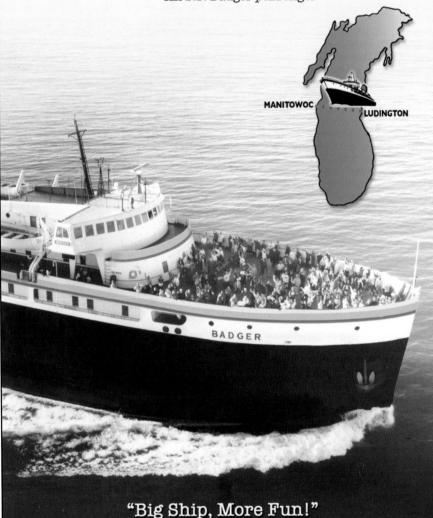

MAJOR GREAT LAKES LOADING PORTS

Iron Ore
Duluth, MN
Superior, WI
Two Harbors, MN
Marquette, MI
Escanaba, MI

Petroleum
Sarnia, ON
E. Chicago, IN

Limestone
Port Inland, MI
Cedarville, MI
Drummond
   Island, MI
Calcite, MI
Rogers City, MI
Stoneport, MI
Marblehead, OH

Coal
Superior, WI
S. Chicago, IL
Toledo, OH
Sandusky, OH
Ashtabula, OH
Conneaut, OH

Grain
Thunder Bay, ON
Duluth, MN
Milwaukee, WI
Superior, WI
Sarnia, ON
Toledo, OH
Port Stanley, ON
Owen Sound, ON

Cement
Charlevoix, MI
Alpena, MI

Salt
Goderich, ON
Windsor, ON
Cleveland, OH
Fairport, OH

MAJOR UNLOADING PORTS

The primary U.S. iron ore and limestone receiving ports are Cleveland, Chicago, Gary, Burns Harbor, Indiana Harbor, Detroit, Toledo, Ashtabula and Conneaut. Nanticoke, Hamilton and Sault Ste. Marie, Ont., are major ore-receiving ports in Canada. Coal is carried by self-unloaders to power plants in the U.S. and Canada. Most grain loaded on the lakes is destined for export via the St. Lawrence Seaway. Cement is delivered to terminals from Lake Superior to Lake Ontario. Tankers bring petroleum products to cities as diverse in size as Cleveland, Detroit, Escanaba and Muskegon. Self-unloaders carry limestone, road salt and sand to cities throughout the region.

MEANINGS OF BOAT WHISTLES

1 PROLONGED: Vessel leaving dock.

3 SHORT: Operating astern propulsion.

1 PROLONGED, SOUNDED AT INTERVALS OF NOT MORE THAN 2 MINUTES: Vessel moving in restricted visibility.

1 SHORT, 1 PROLONGED, 1 SHORT: Vessel at anchor in restricted visibility (optional). May be accompanied by the ringing of a bell on the forward part of the ship and a gong on the aft end.

3 PROLONGED and 2 SHORT: Salute (formal).

1 PROLONGED and 2 SHORT: Salute (commonly used).

3 PROLONGED and 1 SHORT: International Shipmasters' Association member salute.

1 SHORT: I intend to leave you on my port side (answered by same if agreed upon).

2 SHORT: I intend to leave you on my starboard side (answered by same if agreed upon). (Passing arrangements may be agreed upon by radio. If so, no whistle signal is required.)

5 OR MORE SHORT BLASTS SOUNDED RAPIDLY: Danger.

Some of the above signals are listed in the pilot rules. Others have been adopted through common use.

Ryerson **sounds its mighty whistles.**
(Glenn Blaskiewicz)

LOCKS & CANALS

MacArthur Lock

Named after World War II Gen. Douglas MacArthur, the MacArthur Lock is 800 feet long (243.8 meters) between inner gates, 80 feet wide (24.4 meters) and 31 feet deep (9.4 meters) over the sills. The lock was built in 1942-43 and opened to traffic on July 11, 1943. The largest vessel that can transit the MacArthur Lock is 730 feet long (222.5 meters) by 76 feet wide (23 meters).

Poe Lock

The Poe Lock is 1,200 feet long (365.8 meters), 110 feet wide (33.5 meters) and has a depth over the sills of 32 feet (9.8 meters). Named after Col. Orlando M. Poe, it was built by the United States in the years 1961-68. The lock's vessel size limit is 1,100 feet long (335.3 meters) by 105 feet wide (32 meters).

Davis Lock

Named after Col. Charles E.L.B. Davis, the Davis Lock measures 1,350 feet long (411.5 meters) between inner gates, 80 feet wide (24.4 meters) and 23 feet deep (7 meters) over the sills. Built in 1908-14, it sees limited use due to its shallow depth.

Sabin Lock

The same size as the Davis Lock, the Sabin Lock was built from 1913-19. The lock is currently inactive.

 As part of its mission of building and maintaining the country's ports and waterways, the U.S. Army Corps of Engineers operates and maintains the Soo Locks, as well as all of the Great Lakes' connecting channels.

The Soo Locks

The Soo Locks, which celebrated their 150th anniversary in 2005, operate on gravity, as do all locks in the St. Lawrence Seaway system. No pumps are used to empty or fill the lock chambers; valves are opened, and water is allowed to seek its own level. All traffic passes through the locks toll-free.

Vessels in the St. Marys River system, of which the Soo Locks are a part, are under control of the U.S. Coast Guard at Sault Ste. Marie, Mich. In the vicinity of the locks, they fall under jurisdiction of the lockmaster, who must be contacted on VHF Ch. 14 (156.700 MHz) for lock assignments.

Traffic is dispatched to the appropriate lock according to size, other vessels in the locks area and by the time the captain first calls in to the lockmaster. All vessels longer than 730 feet and/or wider than 76 feet are restricted by size to the Poe, or second, lock. A vessel is under engine and thruster control at all times, with crews ready to drop mooring lines over bollards on the lock wall to stop its movement.

As soon as the vessel is in position, engines are stopped and mooring lines made fast. If the vessel is being lowered, valves at the lower end of the lock chamber are opened to allow the water inside to flow out. If the vessel is being raised, valves at the upper end of the lock chamber are opened to allow water to enter. When the water reaches the desired level, the valves are closed, the protective boom is raised, the gates are opened, and the vessel proceeds on her way.

Vessels passing through the locks spend an average of 65 minutes from the time they enter the canal at one end until they pass the outer piers at the other end. Of this time, an average of 30 minutes is consumed in entering, raising or lowering, and leaving the lock chamber.

The first lock was built on the Canadian side of the river by the Northwest Fur Co. in 1797-98. The first ship canal on the American side, known as the State Lock, was built from 1853-55 by Charles T. Harvey. There were two tandem locks on masonry, each 35 feet (106.7 meters) long by 70 feet (21.3 meters) wide, with a lift of about 9 feet (2.7 meters). That canal was destroyed in 1888 by workers making way for newer and bigger locks.

Discussion continues about building a new lock in the space occupied by the Davis and Sabin locks. Cost of such a lock was estimated at $225 million in 1999. Economic factors make it unlikely this lock will be built anytime in the immediate future.

An upbound laker enters the MacArthur Lock at Sault Ste. Marie, Mich., at night. *(Roger LeLievre)*

Excavating the present Poe Lock, November 1964. The Poe is the only lock ever built between two pre-existing locks.

The 105-foot-wide *Edgar B. Speer* exits the Poe Lock in June 2006. *(Roger LeLievre)*

The Canadian Soo Lock

The present Canadian Lock at Sault Ste. Marie, Ont., to the north of the much larger locks on the U.S. side, has its origins in a canal constructed during the years 1887-95 through the red sandstone rock of St. Marys Island on the north side of the St. Marys Rapids.

The most westerly canal on the Seaway route, the waterway measures 7,294 feet (2,223.4 meters), or about 1.4 miles (2.2 km) long from end to end of upper and lower piers. A 900-foot (274.3 meters) lock served vessels until the collapse of a lock wall in 1987 closed the waterway. In 1998, after $10.3 million in repairs, a much smaller lock opened, built inside the old lock chamber. Operated by Parks Canada, it is used mainly by pleasure craft, tugs and tour boats.

Soo Locks facts

The St. Marys River, running 80 miles (128.7 km) from remote Isle Parisienne at its north end to the restored DeTour Reef Light at its south end, connects Lake Superior with Lake Huron. It includes two engineering marvels: the Soo Locks at Sault Ste. Marie and the West Neebish Cut, a channel dynamited out of solid rock that allows traffic to pass to the west side of Neebish Island.

The Empire State Building is 1,250 feet tall. The largest vessel using the Soo Locks is 1,014 feet long. This vessel, the *Paul R. Tregurtha*, carried 3,219,646 net tons of cargo through the locks during the 1998 season.

There are about 150 major cargo carriers engaged almost exclusively in the Great Lakes and Seaway trade. That number is augmented by a variety of saltwater vessels, or "salties," that enter the system during the shipping season.

The Great Lakes shipping season runs from late March to late December. In the spring and fall, a small fleet of icebreakers operated by the U.S. and Canadian coast guards, and commercial tugs help keep navigation channels open.

A vessel traveling from the Atlantic Ocean to Lake Superior through the St. Lawrence Seaway and the Soo Locks rises nearly 600 feet. The first lift, a total of 224 feet, is provided by the seven St. Lawrence Seaway locks that begin at Montreal. The Welland Canal, connecting Lake Erie and Lake Ontario and bypassing Niagara Falls, raises vessels an additional 326 feet. The Soo Locks complete the process with a 21-foot lift.

31,595,520 gallons of water are needed to fill the Poe Lock. To drink this much, one would have to drink 9,233 12-ounce glasses every day for 100 years. It takes about 12 minutes to fill the lock and 10 to empty.

One short blast of a vessel's whistle while in the lock means "cast off lines."

A red-and-white flag flying from a vessel's mast indicates a pilot is on board. Saltwater vessels pick up pilots at various points in their voyage.

***Manistee*, raised to the upper pool and ready to head out into Lake Superior.** *(Roger LeLievre)*

During 1953, 128 million tons of freight were moved through the locks. This mark still stands.

All traffic is passed through the U.S. and Canadian locks toll-free.

In 2005, Soo Locks handled:
- Nearly 43 million net tons of iron ore
- More than 21 million net tons of coal
- More than 4 million net tons of stone
- Almost 4 million net tons of wheat
- 647,821 net tons of salt and 518,970 net tons of cement and concrete
- Other commodities locking through include petroleum, manufactured goods and industrial by-products.

FOLLOWING THE FLEET

These prerecorded messages help track vessel arrivals and departures.

Algoma Central Marine	**(905) 708-3873**	ACM vessel movements
Boatwatcher's Hotline	**(218) 722-6489**	Superior, Duluth, Two Harbors, Taconite Harbor and Silver Bay
CSX Coal Docks/Torco Dock	**(419) 697-2304**	Toledo, OH, vessel information
DMIR Ore Dock	**(218) 628-4590**	Duluth, MN, vessel information
Eisenhower Lock	**(315) 769-2422**	Eisenhower Lock vessel traffic
Michigan Limestone docks	**(989) 734-2117**	Calcite, MI, vessel information
Michigan Limestone docks	**(906) 484-2201**	Ext. 503 – Cedarville, MI, passages
Presque Isle Corp.	**(989) 595-6611**	Stoneport, MI, vessel information
Soo Traffic	**(906) 635-3224**	Previous day – St. Marys River
Superior Midwest Energy Terminal (SMET)	**(715) 395-3559**	Superior, WI, vessel information
Thunder Bay Port Authority	**(807) 345-1256**	Thunder Bay, ON, vessel info
Great Lakes Fleet	**(800) 328-3760** ext. **4389**	GLF vessel movements
Upper Lakes Group	**(905) 688-5878**	ULG vessel movements
Vantage Point, Boatnerd World HQ	**(810) 985-9057**	St. Clair River traffic
Welland Canal tape	**(905) 688-6462**	Welland Canal traffic

With an inxpensive VHF scanner, boat watchers can tune to ship-to-ship and ship-to-shore traffic, using the following frequency guide.

Commercial vessels only	**Ch. 13 – 156.650 MHz**	Bridge-to-bridge Communications
Calling / distress only	**Ch. 16 – 156.800 MHz**	Calling / distress only
Commercial vessels only	**Ch. 06 – 156.300 MHz**	Working channel
Commercial vessels only	**Ch. 08 – 156.400 MHz**	Working channel
Supply boat at Sault Ste. Marie, MI	**Ch. 08 – 156.400 MHz**	Supply boat *Ojibway*
Detour Reef – Lake St. Clair Light	**Ch. 11 – 156.550 MHz**	Sarnia Traffic - Sect. 1
Long Point Light – Lake St. Clair Light	**Ch. 12 – 156.600 MHz**	Sarnia Traffic - Sect. 2
Montreal – mid-Lake St. Francis	**Ch. 14 – 156.700 MHz**	Seaway Beauharnois - Sect. 1
Mid-Lake St. Francis – Bradford Island	**Ch. 12 – 156.600 MHz**	Seaway Eisenhower - Sect. 2
Bradford Island – Crossover Island	**Ch. 11 – 156.550 MHz**	Seaway Iroquois - Sect.3
Crossover Island to Cape Vincent	**Ch. 13 – 156.650 MHz**	Seaway Clayton - Sect. 4 St. Lawrence River portion
Cape Vincent – mid-Lake Ontario	**Ch. 13 – 156.650 MHz**	Seaway Sodus - Sect. 4 Lake Ontario portion
Mid-Lake Ontario – Welland Canal	**Ch. 11 – 156.550 MHz**	Seaway Newcastle - Sect. 5
Welland Canal	**Ch. 14 – 156.700 MHz**	Seaway Welland - Sect. 6
Welland Canal to Long Point Light	**Ch. 11 – 156.550 MHz**	Seaway Long Point - Sect. 7
St. Marys River Traffic Service	**Ch. 12 – 156.600 MHz**	Soo Traffic, Sault Ste. Marie, MI
Lockmaster, Soo Locks	**Ch. 14 – 156.700 MHz**	Soo Lockmaster (call WUE-21)
Coast Guard traffic	**Ch. 21 – 157.050 MHz**	United States Coast Guard
Coast Guard traffic	**Ch. 22 – 157.100 MHz**	United States Coast Guard
U.S. mailboat, Detroit, MI	**Ch. 10 – 156.500 MHz**	Mailboat *J. W. Westcott II*

Great Lakes and Seaway Shipping

www.boatnerd.com

Zemia Gornoslaska in the Welland Canal. *(Alain Gindroz)*

***James Norris* passes under one of the Welland Canal's lift bridges.** *(Dan Sweeley)*

The Welland Canal

The 27-mile-long (43.7 km) Welland Canal, built to bypass Niagara Falls, overcomes a difference in water level of 326.5 feet (99.5 meters) between Lake Erie and Ontario.

The first Welland Canal opened in 1829; the present (fourth) canal opened officially on Aug. 6, 1932. Each of the seven Welland Canal locks has an average lift of 46.5 feet (14.2 meters). All locks (except Lock 8) are 859 feet (261.8 meters) long, 80 feet (24.4 meters) wide and 30 feet (9.1 meters) deep. Lock 8 measures 1,380 feet (420. 6 km) in length.

The largest vessel that may transit the canal is 740 feet (225.5 meters) long, 78 feet (23.8 meters) wide and 26 feet (7.9 meters) in draft.

Locks 1, 2 and 3 are at St. Catharines, Ont., on the Lake Ontario end of the waterway. At Lock 3, the Welland Canal Viewing Center and Museum houses an information desk (which posts a list of vessels expected at the lock), a gift shop and restaurant. At Thorold, Locks 4, 5 and 6, twinned to help speed passage of vessels, are controlled with an elaborate interlocking system for safety. These locks (positioned end to end, they resemble a short flight of stairs) have an aggregate lift of 139.5 feet (42.5 meters). Just south of Locks 4, 5 and 6 is Lock 7. Lock 8, seven miles (11.2 km) upstream at Port Colborne, completes the process, making the final adjustment to Lake Erie's level.

In 1973, a new channel was constructed to replace the section of the canal that bisected the city of Welland. The Welland bypass eliminated long delays for navigation, road and rail traffic.

The average passage time for the canal is about 12 hours, with the majority of the time spent transiting Locks 4-7. Vessels passing through the Welland Canal and St. Lawrence Seaway must carry a qualified pilot.

There are also 11 railway and highway bridges crossing the Welland Canal. The most significant are the vertical-lift bridges that provide a clearance of 126 feet (36.6 meters) for vessels passing underneath. Tunnels at Thorold, Ont., and South Welland allow vehicle traffic to pass beneath the waterway. All vessel traffic though the Welland Canal is regulated by a control center. Upbound vessels must call Seaway Welland off Port Weller, Ont., on VHF Ch. 14 (156.700 MHz), while downbound vessels are required to make contact off Port Colborne. Cameras keep vessels under constant observation, and locks (and most bridges over the canal) are controlled from the center.

NIAGARA
C A N A D A

..a canal *runs* through it.

Watch the quiet giants of the
waterway climb the mountains at
St. Catharines and Thorold

EXPLORE!

Welland Canals Centre
Lock 3, 1932 Welland Canals Pkwy
St. Catharines, ON L2R 7K6
tel: 905-984-8880
fax: 905-984-8980
www.stcatharines.ca
email: tourism@stcatharines.ca

Lock 7 Viewing Complex
50 Chapel St. S.
Thorold, ON L2V 2C6
tel: 905-680-9477
fax: 905-680-2657
www.thoroldtourism.ca
email: thoroldtourism@bellnet.ca

Kapitonas Andzejauskas **heads for the Cote St. Catherine Lock.** *(Chris Rombouts)*

The St. Lawrence Seaway

The St. Lawrence Seaway is a deep waterway extending some 2,038 miles (3,701.4 km) from the Atlantic Ocean to the head of the Great Lakes at Duluth, Minn., including Montreal harbor and the Welland Canal. More specifically, it is a system of locks and canals (U.S. and Canadian), built between 1954 and 1958 at a cost of $474 million and opened in 1959, that allow vessels to pass from Montreal to the Welland Canal at the western end of Lake Ontario. The vessel size limit within this system is 740 feet (225.6 meters) long, 78 feet (23.8 meters) wide and 26 feet (7.9 meters) draft.

Closest to the ocean is the St. Lambert Lock, which lifts ships some 15 feet (4.6 meters) from Montreal harbor to the level of the Laprairie Basin, through which the channel sweeps in a great arc 8.5 miles (13.7 km) long to the second lock. The Cote St. Catherine Lock, like the other six St. Lawrence Seaway locks, is built to the dimensions shown in the table below. The Cote St. Catherine lifts ships from the level of the Laprairie Basin 30 feet (9.1 meters) to the level of Lake St. Louis, bypassing the Lachine Rapids. Beyond it, the channel runs 7.5 miles (12.1 km) before reaching Lake St. Louis.

LOCK DIMENSIONS	
Length	766' (233.5 meters)
Width	80' (24 meters)
Depth	30' (9.1 meters)

The Lower Beauharnois Lock, bypassing the Beauharnois Power House, lifts ships 41 feet (12.5 meters) and sends them through a short canal to the Upper Beauharnois Lock, where they are lifted 41 feet (12.5 meters) to reach the Beauharnois Canal. After a 13-mile (20.9 km) trip in the canal and a 30-mile (48.3 km) passage through Lake St. Francis, vessels reach the U.S. border and the Snell Lock, which has a lift of 45 feet (13.7 meters) and empties into the 10-mile (16.1 km) Wiley-Dondero Canal.

After passing through the Wiley-Dondero, ships are raised another 38 feet (11.6 meters) by the Dwight D. Eisenhower Lock, after which they enter Lake St. Lawrence, the pool upon which nearby power-generating stations draw for their turbines located a mile to the north.

At the western end of Lake St. Lawrence, the Iroquois Lock allows ships to bypass the Iroquois Control Dam. The lift here is only about one foot (0.3 meters). Once in the waters west of Iroquois, the channel meanders through the Thousand Islands to Lake Ontario and beyond.

I want to...
ExperiencePortColborne.com

Sightsee *Marvel* *Reminisce*

MARINE MUSEUMS

Information can change without notice. Call ahead to verify location and hours.

ANTIQUE BOAT MUSEUM, 750 MARY ST., CLAYTON, NY – (315) 686-4104: A large collection of freshwater boats and engines. Open May 11-October 18, 2007.

ASHTABULA MARINE & U.S. COAST GUARD MEMORIAL MUSEUM, 1071 WALNUT BLVD., ASHTABULA, OH – (440) 964-6847: Housed in the 1898-built lighthouse keeper's residence, the museum includes models, paintings, artifacts, photos, a working scale model of a Hullett ore unloading machine and the pilothouse from the *Thomas Walters*. Open April-October.

CANAL PARK MARINE MUSEUM, ALONGSIDE THE SHIP CANAL, DULUTH, MN – (218) 727-2497: Displays, artifacts and programs. Many excellent models and other artifacts are on display, plus the former Corps of Engineers tug *Bayfield*. Open all year.

COLLINGWOOD MUSEUM, MEMORIAL PARK, 45 ST. PAUL ST., COLLINGWOOD, ON – (705) 445-4811: More than 100 years of shipbuilding, illustrated with models, photos and videos. Open all year.

DOOR COUNTY MARITIME MUSEUM & LIGHTHOUSE PRESERVATION SOCIETY INC., 120 N. MADISON AVE., STURGEON BAY, WI – (920) 743-5958: Many excellent models help portray the role shipbuilding has played in the Door Peninsula. Open all year.

DOSSIN GREAT LAKES MUSEUM, 100 THE STRAND, BELLE ISLE, DETROIT, MI – 313-833-7935: Models, interpretive displays, the smoking room from the 1912 passenger steamer *City of Detroit III,* an anchor from the *Edmund Fitzgerald* and the pilothouse from the steamer *William Clay Ford* are on display. Open weekends.

ERIE MARITIME MUSEUM, 150 E. FRONT ST., ERIE, PA – (814) 452-2744. Displays depict the Battle of Lake Erie and more. Check ahead to see if the U.S. brig *Niagara* is in port. Open all year.

(Continued on Page 138)

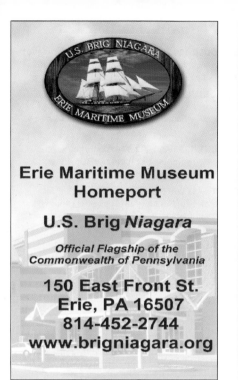
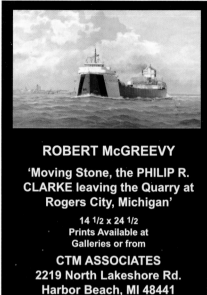

(Continued from Page 136)

FAIRPORT HARBOR MARINE MUSEUM AND LIGHTHOUSE, 129 SECOND ST., FAIRPORT, OH – (440) 354-4825: Located in the Fairport Lighthouse, displays include the pilothouse from the lake carrier *Frontenac* and the mainmast of the first *USS Michigan*. Open late May-early September.

GREAT LAKES HISTORICAL SOCIETY, 480 MAIN ST., VERMILION, OH – (800) 893-1485: Museum tells the story of the Great Lakes through ship models, paintings, exhibits and artifacts, including engines and other machinery. Pilothouse of retired laker *Canopus* and a replica of the Vermilion lighthouse are on display. Museum open all year.

GREAT LAKES SHIPWRECK MUSEUM, WHITEFISH POINT, MI – (888) 492-3747: Lighthouse and shipwreck artifacts, a shipwreck video theater, the restored lighthouse keeper's quarters and an *Edmund Fitzgerald* display that includes the ship's bell. Open May 1-October 31, 2007.

LE SAULT DE SAINTE MARIE HISTORIC SITES INC., 501 EAST WATER ST., SAULT STE. MARIE, MI – (888) 744-7867: The steamer *Valley Camp* is the centerpiece of this museum. The vessel's cargo holds house artifacts, models, aquariums, photos and other memorabilia, as well as the *Edmund Fitzgerald's* lifeboats. Tours available. Open May 15-October 15.

LOWER LAKES MARINE HISTORICAL MUSEUM, 66 ERIE ST., BUFFALO, NY – (716) 849-0914: Exhibits explore local maritime history. Open all year (Tuesday, Thursday and Saturday only).

MARINE MUSUEM OF THE GREAT LAKES, 55 ONTARIO ST., KINGSTON, ON – (613) 542-2261: The musuem's largest exhibit is the retired Canadian Coast Guard icebreaker *Alexander Henry*, which is open for tours and also as a bed and breakfast. Open February-November.

MARITIME MUSEUM OF SANDUSKY, 125 MEIGS ST., SANDUSKY, OHIO – (419) 624-0274: Exhibits explore local maritime history. Open all year.

MARQUETTE MARITIME MUSEUM, 300 LAKESHORE BLVD., MARQUETTE, MI – (906) 226-2006: Located in an 1890s waterworks building, the museum re-creates the offices of the first commercial fishing and passenger freight companies. Displays also include charts, photos, models and maritime artifacts. Open May 31-September 30.

MICHIGAN MARITIME MUSEUM, 260 DYCKMAN ROAD., SOUTH HAVEN, MI – (800) 747-3810: Exhibits dedicated to the U.S. Lifesaving Service and U.S. Coast Guard. Displays tell the story of various kinds of boats and their uses on the Great Lakes. Open all year.

OWEN SOUND MARINE & RAIL MUSEUM, 1155 FIRST AVE. WEST, OWEN SOUND, ON – (519) 371-3333: Museum depicts the history of each industry (but leans more toward the marine end) through displays, models and photos. Seasonal.

PORT COLBORNE HISTORICAL & MARINE MUSEUM, 280 KING ST., PORT COLBORNE, ON – (905) 834-7604: Wheelhouse from the steam tug *Yvonne Dupre Jr.* and a lifeboat from the steamer *Hochelaga* are among the museum's displays. Open May-December.

U.S. ARMY CORPS OF ENGINEERS MUSEUM, SOO LOCKS VISITOR CENTER, E. PORTAGE AVE., SAULT STE. MARIE, MI – (906) 632-3311: Exhibits include a working model of the Soo Locks, historic photos and a 25-minute film. Also, three observation decks adjacent to the MacArthur Lock provide an up-close view of ships locking through. No admission; open May-November. Check at the Visitor Center information desk for a list of vessels expected at the locks.

ST. CATHARINES MUSEUM, 1932 WELLAND CANALS PARKWAY ROAD – (905) 984-8880 or (800) 305-5134: Museum traces the development of the Welland Canal. Museum and adjacent gift shop open all year. Observation deck open during the navigation season. Check at the information desk for vessels expected at Lock 3. Gift shop has a wide selection of maritime books.

THUNDER BAY NATIONAL MARINE SANCTUARY & UNDERWATER PRESERVE, 500 W. FLETCHER ST., ALPENA, MI – (989) 356-8805: New research and musuem facility is the dry-land component of a collection of shipwrecks located off the northeast corner of Michigan's lower peninsula. Open all year; closed on Sundays.

WISCONSIN MARITIME MUSEUM, 75 MARITIME DRIVE, MANITOWOC, WI – (920) 684-0218 or (866) 724-2356: Displays explore the history of area shipbuilding and also honor submariners and submarines built in Manitowoc. The World War II submarine *Cobia* is adjacent to the museum and open for tours. Open all year.

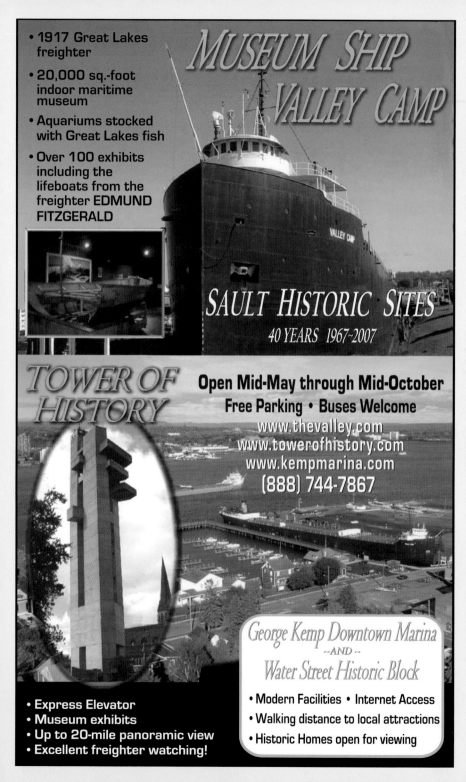

Colors of the Great Lakes and Seaway Smokestacks

A.B.M. Marine
Thunder Bay, ON

Algoma Central Corp.
St. Catharines, ON

Algoma Tankers Ltd.
Div. of Algoma Central Corp.
Dartmouth, NS

American Canadian
Caribbean Line, Inc.
Warren, RI

American Marine Construction
Benton Harbor, MI

American Steamship Co.
Williamsville, NY

Andrie, Inc.
Muskegon, MI

Apostle Islands Cruise Service
Bayfield, WI

Arnold Transit Co.
Mackinac Island, MI

Atlantic Towing Ltd.
St. John, NB

Basic Towing, Inc.
Escanaba, MI

Bay City Boat Line
Bay City, MI

Bay Shipbuilding Co.
Sturgeon Bay, WI

Beaver Island Boat Co.
Charlevoix, MI

Billington Contracting Inc.
Duluth, MN

Blue Heron Co.
Tobermory, ON

Buffalo Public Works Dept.
Buffalo, NY

Busch Marine, Inc.
Carrollton, MI

Calumet River Fleeting Inc.
Chicago, IL

Canada Steamship Lines, Inc.
Montreal, QC

Canadian Coast Guard
Ottawa, ON

Central Marine Logistics, Inc.
Griffith, IN

Chicago Fire Department
Chicago, IL

Cleveland Fire Department
Cleveland, OH

Club Canamac Cruises
Toronto, ON

Columbia Yacht Club
Chicago, IL

Croisieres AML Inc.
Quebec, QC

Dan Minor & Sons, Inc.
Port Colborne, ON

Dean Construction Co.
Belle River, ON

Detroit City Fire Department
Detroit, MI

Diamond Jack's River Tours
Detroit, MI

Dragage Verreault Inc.
Les Mechins, QC

Duc D'Orleans Cruise Boat
Corunna, ON

Durocher Marine
Cheboygan, MI

Eastern Upper Peninsula
Transit Authority
Sault Ste. Marie, MI

Edward E. Gillen Co.
Milwaukee, WI

Egan Marine Corp.
Lemont, IL

Equipments Verreault, Inc.
Les Mechins, QC

Erie Sand Navigation Co.
Erie, PA

Essroc Canada, Inc.
Upper Lakes Group, Mgr
North York, ON

Federal Terminals Ltd.
Port Cartier, QC

Ferriss Marine
Contracting Inc.
Detroit, MI

Fraser Shipyards, Inc.
Superior, WI

Gaelic Tug Boat Co.
Detroit, MI

Gallagher Marine
Construction Co.
Escanaba, MI

Gananoque Boat Line
Gananoque, ON

Gardiner Marine
Richard's Landing, ON

Geo. Gradel Co.
Toledo, OH

Geo. Gradel Co.
Toledo, OH

Goodtime Transit Boats, Inc.
Cleveland, OH

Grand Portage
Isle Royale Transportation Lines
Superior, WI

Gravel & Lake Services, Ltd.
Thunder Bay, ON

Gravel & Lake Services, Ltd.
Thunder Bay, ON

Great Lakes Fleet, Inc.
Key Lakes, Inc.– Mgr.
Duluth, MN

Great Lakes International
Towing & Salvage Ltd.
Burlington, ON

Great Lakes Maritime Academy
Northwestern Michigan College
Traverse City, MI

Great Lakes Towing Co.
Cleveland, OH

Groupe C.T.M.A.
Navigation Madeleine Inc.
Cap-Aux-Meules, QC

HMC Ship Managment
Div of Hannah Marine Corp
Lemont, IL

Hamilton Port Authority
Hamilton, ON

Hannah Marine Corp.
Lemont, IL

Heritage Cruise Lines
St. Catharines, ON

Holly Marine Towing
Chicago, IL

Hornbeck Offshore Services
Covington, LA

Illinois Marine Towing Ltd.
Lemont, IL

Inland Lakes Management,
Inc.
Alpena, MI

The Interlake Steamship Co.
Lakes Shipping Co.
Richfield, OH

Kent Line Ltd
St. John, NB

Keystone Great Lakes, Inc.
Bala Cynwyd, PA

Kindra Lake Towing Co.
Downer's Grove, IL

King Company Inc.
Holland, MI

Lafarge Canada, Inc.
Montreal, QC

Lafarge North America Inc.
Southfield, MI

Lake Michigan Carferry
Service, Inc.
Ludington, MI

Laken Shipping Corp.
Cleveland, OH

Le Groupe Ocean Inc.
Quebec, QC

Le Groupe Ocean Inc.
Quebec, QC

Lee Marine, Ltd.
Sombra, ON

Lock Tours Canada
Sault Ste. Marie, ON

Lower Lakes Towing, Ltd.
Grand River Navigation Co.
Port Dover, ON

Luedtke Engineering Co.
Frankfort, MI

M.C.M. Marine Inc.
Sault Ste Marie, MI

MacDonald Marine Ltd.
Goderich, ON

Madeline Island Ferry Line, Inc.
LaPointe, WI

Maid of the Mist
Steamboat Co., Ltd.
Niagara Falls, ON

Malcom Marine
St. Clair, MI

Manitou Island Transit
Leland, MI

Marine Tech Inc.
Duluth, MN

Mariposa Cruise Line
Toronto, ON

McAsphalt Marine
Transportation
Scarborough, ON

McKeil Marine Ltd.
Hamilton, ON

McKeil Marine Ltd.
Hamilton, ON

McKeil Marine Ltd.
Hamilton, ON

McNally Construction, Inc
Toronto, ON

Miller Boat Line, Inc.
Put-In-Bay, OH

Museum Ship
CCGC Alexander Henry
Kingston, ON

Museum Tug Edna G
Two Harbors, MN

Museum Ship
HMCS Haida
Hamilton, ON

Museum Ship
Keewatin
Douglas, MI

Museum Ships
USS Little Rock
USS The Sullivans
Buffalo, NY

Museum Ship
Meteor
Superior, WI

Museum Ship
City of Milwaukee
Manistee, MI

Museum Ship
Milwaukee Clipper
Muskegon, MI

Museum Ships
Norgoma (Sault Ste. Marie,ON)
Norisle (Manitowaning,ON)

Museum Ship
Valley Camp
Sault Ste. Marie, MI

Museum Ship
William A. Irvin
Duluth, MN

Museum Ships
Willis B. Boyer (Toledo,OH)
William G. Mather (Cleveland,OH)

Muskoka Steamship
Historical Society
Gravenhurst, ON

Nadro Marine Services
Port Dover, ON

Nautica Queen
Cruise Dining
Cleveland, OH

Norlake Transportation Co.
Port Colborne, ON

Ontario Ministry of Transportation
& Communication
Downsville, ON

Osborne Materials Co.
Grand River, OH

Owen Sound
Transportation Co. Ltd.
Owen Sound, ON

Pere Marquette Shipping Co.
Tug Undaunted
Ludington, MI

Provmar Fuels, Inc.
Div. of ULS Corporation
Toronto, ON

Purvis Marine Ltd.
Sault Ste. Marie, ON

Purvis Marine Ltd.
Sault Ste. Marie, ON

Rigel Shipping Canada, Inc.
Shediac, NB

Roen Salvage Co.
Sturgeon Bay, WI

Ryba Marine Construction Co.
Cheboygan, MI

Selvick Marine Towing Corp.
Sturgeon Bay, WI

Shamrock Chartering Co.
Grosse Pointe, MI

Shoreline Sightseeing Co.
Chicago, IL

Societe des Traversiers du Quebec
Quebec, QC

Society Quebecoise D'Exploration Miniere
Algoma Central Corp.-Mgr.
Sault Ste. Marie, ON

Soo Locks Boat Tours
Sault Ste. Marie, MI

St. Lawrence Cruise Lines, Inc.
Kingston, ON

St. Lawrence Seaway Development Corp.
Massena, NY

St. Lawrence Seaway Management Corp.
Cornwall, ON

St. Marys Cement Inc.
Toronto, ON

Ste. Claire Foundation
Cleveland, OH

TGL Holdings LLC
Plymouth, MI

Thousand Islands & Seaway Cruises
Brockville, ON

Thunder Bay Marine Services Ltd.
Thunder Bay, On

Thunder Bay Tug Services
Thunder Bay, ON

Toronto Parks & Recreation Dept.
Toronto, ON

Transport Desgagnés, Inc.
Quebec, QC

Transport Desgagnés, Inc.
Quebec, QC

Transport Igloolik, Inc.
Montreal, QC

United States Army Corps of Engineers
Great Lakes and Ohio River Division
Chicago, IL

United States Coast Guard
9th Coast Guard District
Cleveland, OH

United States Department of the Interior
Ann Arbor, MI

United States Environmental Protection Agency
Bay City, MI

United States National Park Service
Houghton, MI

University of Michigan
Center for Great Lakes & Aquatic Sciences
Ann Arbor, MI

Upper Lakes Group Inc
Toronto, ON

Upper Lakes Towing, Co.
Escanaba, MI

Vista Fleet
Duluth, MN

Voyageur Maritime Trading Inc.
Voyageur Marine Transport Ltd.
Ridgeville, ON

Wendella Boat Tours Co.
Chicago, IL

Zenith Tugboat Co.
Duluth, MN

On ships, as on buildings, stacks are used to vent exhaust smoke and provide an air draft for the boilers, if a vessel is so-equipped. Most modern vessels don't need a traditional smokestack, but they carry one for the sake of appearances.

Colors of Saltwater Fleets

Adrico Shipping Co.
Athens, Greece

Allrounder Maritime Co.
Manilia, Philippines

Amalthia Maritime Inc.
Athens, Greece

Anbros Maritime SA
Pireaus, Greece

Athena Marine Co. Ltd.
Limassol, Cyprus

Atlantska Plovidba
Dubrovnik, Croatia

Aurora Shipping, Inc.
Manila, Philippines

B&N Moorman B.V.
Ridderkerk, Netherlands

Beluga Shipping GMBH
Bremen, Germany

Blystad Tankers Inc.
Oslo, Norway

Briese Schiffahrts GMBH & Co. KG
Leer, Germany

Brovig Chemical Tankers
Farsund, Norway

Camillo Eitzen & Co. AS
Lysaker, Norway

Canadian Forest Navigation Co. Ltd.
Montreal, QC

Carisbrooke Shipping PLC
Cowes, UK

Catsambis Shipping Ltd.
Piraeus, Greece

Chartworld Shipping Corp.
Athens, Greece

Clipper Wonsild Tankers AS
Copenhagen, Denmark

Coastal Shipping Ltd.
Goose Bay, ON

Commercial Fleet of Donbass
Donetsk, Ukraine

Commercial Trading & Discount Co., Ltd.
Athens, Greece

Common Progress Compania Naviera SA
Piraeus, Greece

Crescent Marine Services
Copenhagen, Denmark

ER Denizcilik Sanayi Nakliyat ve Ticaret A.S.
Istanbul, Turkey

Eastwind Ship Management
Singapore, Singapore

Enzian Shipping AG
Berne, Switzerland

Far-Eastern Shipping Co.
Vladivostok, Russia

Fednav International Ltd.
Montreal, QC

Fisser & V. Doornum Kg GMBH
Hamburg, Germany

Flinter Groningen B.V.
Groningen, Netherlands

Fortum Oil & Gas
Fortum, Finland

Franco Compania Naviera SA
Athens, Greece

Hapag Lloyd
Hamburg, Germany

Harbor Shipping & Trading Co. S.A.
Chios, Greece

Intersee Schiffahrts-Gesellschaft MbH & Co.
Haren-Ems, Germany

Intership Navigation Co. Ltd.
Limassol, Cyprus

Isko Marine (Shipping) Co. SA
Piraeus, Greece

JSM Shipping
Jork, Germany

Jo Tankers, B.V.
Spijkenisse, Netherlands

Jumbo Shipping Co. S.A.
Rotterdam, Netherlands

Knutsen O.A.S. Shipping
Haugesund, Norway

Krey Schiffahrts GMBH & Co.
Simonswolde, Germany

Laurin Maritime, Inc
Houston, TX

Lietuvos Juro Laivininkyste (Lithuanian Shipping Co.)
Klaipeda, Lithuania

Losinjska Plovidba
Rijeka, PRC

Malaysia International Shipping Corp.
Selangor, Singapore

Marbulk Shipping Inc. CSL International Inc., Mgrs.
Beverly, MS

Murmansk Shipping Co.
Murmansk, Russia

Murmansk Shipping Co.
Murmansk, Russia

Navigation Maritime Bulgare Ltd.
Varna, Bulgaria

Novorossiysk Shipping (Novoship)
Novorossiysk, Russia

Oceanex Ltd.
Montreal, QC

Oldendorff Carriers GMBH & Co.
Luebeck, Germany

Olympic Shipping and Management S.A.
Athens, Greece

Onego Shipping & Chartering
Rhoon, Netherlands

Orion Schiffahrts
Hamburg, Germany

Polish Steamship Co.
Szczecin, Poland

Scandia Shipping Hellas, Inc.
Athens, Greece

Scanscot Shipping Services GmbH
Hamburg, Germany

Sea Observer Shipping Services
Piraeus, Greece

Seastar Navigation Co. Ltd.
Athens, Greece

Shih Wei Navigation Co. Ltd.
Taipei, Taiwan

Shipping Corp. of India Ltd.
Mumbai, India

Shunzan Kaiun Co., Ltd.
Ehime, Japan

Siomar Enterprises Ltd.
Piraeus, Greece

Spar Shipping A.S.
Bergen, Norway

Stolt Parcel Tankers
Greenwich, CT

Teo Shipping Corp.
Piraeus, Greece

Thenamaris Ships Management, Inc.
Athens, Greece

Triton Schiffahrts GMBH & Co.
Leer, Germany

Union Marine Enterprises S.A.
Piraeus, Greece

Viken Shipping AS
Bergen, Norway

W. Bockstiegel Reederei KG
Emden, Germany

Wagenborg Shipping B.V.
Delfzijl, Netherlands

Wagenborg Shipping B.V.
Delfzijl, Netherlands

House Flags of
Great Lakes / Seaway Fleets

Acheson Ventures LLC
Port Huron, MI

Algoma Central Corp.
Sault Ste. Marie, ON

American Steamship Co.
Williamsville, NY

Canada Steamship Lines, Inc.
Montreal, QC

Fednav Ltd.
Montreal, QC

Gaelic Tug Boat Co.
Detroit, MI

Great Lakes Fleet Key Lakes Inc., Mgr.
Duluth, MN

Great Lakes Maritime Academy
Traverse City, MI

Great Lakes Shipwreck Historical Society
Sault Ste Marie, MI

Great Lakes Towing Co.
Cleveland, OH

Inland Lakes Management, Inc.
Alpena, MI

Interlake Steamship Co. Lakes Shipping Co.
Richfield, OH

J.W. Westcott Co.
Detroit, MI

LaFarge Canada, Inc
Montreal, QC

Lake Michigan Carferry Service, Inc.
Ludington, MI

Lower Lakes Towing Ltd. Grand River Navigation Co.
Port Dover, ON

McAsphalt Marine Transportation Ltd.
Scarborough, ON

McKeil Marine Ltd.
Hamilton, ON

McNally Construction, Inc.
Toronto, ON

Owen Sound Transportation Co. Ltd.
Owen Sound, ON

Pere Marquette Shipping Co.
Ludington, MI

Purvis Marine Ltd.
Sault Ste. Marie, ON

Rigel Shipping Canada, Inc.
Shediac, NB

Seaway Marine Transport
St. Catharines, ON

Transport Desgagnés, Inc.
Quebec, QC

Upper Lakes Group, Inc.
Toronto, ON

Voyageur Marine Transport Ltd.
Ridgeville, ON

Wagenborg Shipping B.V.
Delfzijl, Netherlands

146

Flags of Nations in the Marine Trade

Antigua & Barbuda

Argentina

Australia

Austria

Azerbaijan

Bahamas

Bahrain

Barbados

Belgium

Bermuda

Bosnia & Herzegovinia

Brazil

Canada

Cayman Islands

Chile

China

Cote D'Ivoire

Croatia

Cyprus

Czech Republic

Denmark

Dominican Republic

Ecuador

Egypt

Estonia

Fiji

Finland

France

Germany

Ghana

Greece

Guinea

Haiti

Honduras

Hong Kong

Hungary

Iceland

India

Indonesia

Ireland

Isle of Man

Israel

Italy

Japan

Korea-South

Latvia

Liberia

Lithuania

Luxembourg

Malaysia

Malta

 Marshall Islands

 Mexico

 Monaco

 Morocco

 Myanmar

 Netherlands

 Netherlands Antilles

 New Zealand

 Nicaragua

 N. Mariana Islands

 Norway

 Pakistan

 Panama

 Peru

 Philippines

 Poland

 Portugal

 Republic of South Africa

 Romania

 Russia

 Singapore

 Solomon Islands

 Spain

 St. Kitts Nevis

 St. Vincent & The Grenadines

 Sweden

 Switzerland

 Syria

 Taiwan

 Thailand

 Trinidad & Tobago

 Tunisia

 Turkey

 Ukraine

 United Kingdom

 United States

 Vanuatu

 Venezuela

 Yugoslavia

Other Flags of Interest

 International Shipmaster's Association – Member Pennant

 Canadian Coast Guard Ensign

 Dangerous Cargo On Board

 Pilot On Board

 U.S. Coast Guard Auxiliary Ensign

U.S. Coast Guard Ensign

U.S. Army Corps of Engineers

 St. Lawrence Seaway Development Corp.

 St. Lawrence Seaway Management Corp.